# CASTRO'S
# DAUGHTER

# CASTRO'S
# DAUGHTER

*An Exile's Memoir of Cuba*

## ALINA FERNÁNDEZ

TRANSLATED BY DOLORES M. KOCH

DISCARD

ST. MARTIN'S PRESS   *New York*

CASTRO'S DAUGHTER: AN EXILE'S MEMOIR OF CUBA. Copyright © 1997 by Alina
Fernández. English translation copyright © 1998 by Dolores M. Koch. All rights
reserved. Printed in the United States of America. No part of this book may be used
or reproduced in any manner whatsoever without written permission except in the
case of brief quotations embodied in critical articles or reviews. For information
address St. Martin's Press, 175 Fifth Avenue, New York, N.Y. 10010.

Library of Congress Cataloging-in-Publication Data

Fernández Revuelta, Alina, 1956–
Castro's daughter : an exile's memoir of Cuba
/ Alina Fernández.
p.    cm.
ISBN 0-312-19308-4
1. Fernández Revuelta, Alina, 1956–   .   2. Castro, Fidel, 1927–
3. Cuba—History—1959–   4. Children of heads of state—Cuba—
Biography.   5. Illegitimate children—Cuba—Biography.   I. Title.
F1788.22.F47A3   1998
972.9106'4'092—dc21
[B]
98-22370
CIP

First published in Spain as *Alina: Memorias de la hija rebelde de Fidel Castro*
by Plaza & Janés Editores, S.A.

First U.S. Edition: November 1998

10 9 8 7 6 5 4 3 2 1

# To the Elf

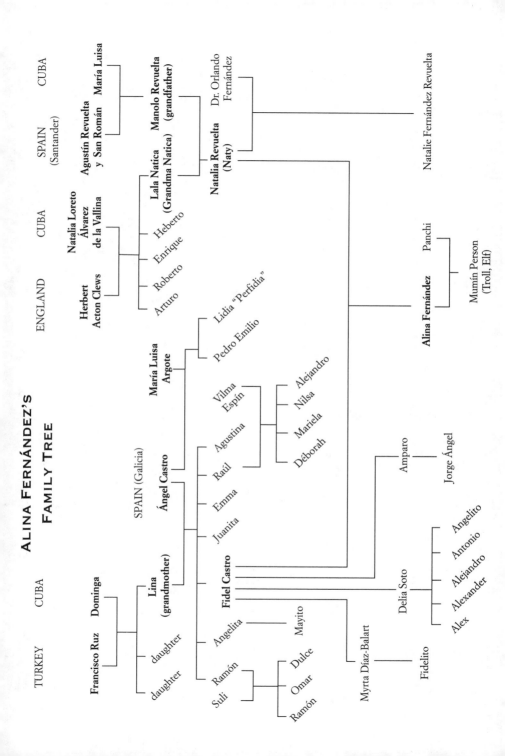

# ALINA FERNÁNDEZ'S
## FAMILY TREE

# CONTENTS

# 1

## MY GENEALOGICAL TREE

*Once upon a time* in western England, there was a young lad who lived in the town of Newcastle-under-Lyme. His name was Herbert Acton Clews.

Once upon a time in Galicia, Spain, there was a boy named Ángel Castro, who lived in a coastal town in Lugo. And once again, there was a boy in Istanbul, who had ancestral memories of a greater empire, when his family of Jewish renegades probably dropped a letter from their last name, shortening it to Ruz.

All three boys were restless with yearnings for a new life.

This was also true in the north of Spain, in the city of Santander, for a youth named Agustín Revuelta y San Román. He was a descendant of a *Caballero Cubierto ante la Reina* in the Spanish court. In some Spanish-speaking countries a *Caballero "Cubierto,"* or "covered" nobleman, was one who had the right to keep his prepuce intact. In the case of Agustín's ancestor, the term only meant that he could keep his head covered in the presence of Her Majesty.

For various reasons, these real machos all decided to venture into a faraway world. They were all adventurers who did not care much about their roots. They cared about power. Power has always been seen as good fortune, and good fortune has always meant one thing: money.

*They boarded their respective* ships at dawn. The seas offered them no resistance and peacefully allowed them the freedom of all possible destinations.

Almost in concert, with each following in the other's wake as if retracing a well-marked trail in the waters, they all arrived at the capital port of Havana. This was the location that Morgan the pirate, centuries earlier, had avoided when burying his treasure, in preference for the fleshier, more flamboyant beaches of María la Gorda, a tropical lady of joy who in the midst of her apoplectic, orgasmic panting had shown him the unique gift of a secret valley, yet to be discovered.

*Though Herbert, the English lad,* suffered from anosmia, an impaired sense of smell, he had a highly developed sense for the scent of money.

One of the Spaniards, the Galician named Ángel, arrived as a recruit of the Spanish army. He had been captured in a medieval-style levy that he had not been able to escape.

The Turk, who faced unexpected turns of events in the confusion of the colonizing wars, decided to adopt the Castilian first name of Francisco.

The other Spanish youth, the one from Santander, had brought with him a letter of recommendation. Upon arriving in Havana, he established himself in business as a haberdasher and married a local girl named María. They were soon blessed with a son, Manolo Revuelta.

The women with whom each of these men would one day start their families were already in Cuba, totally innocent of their future but waiting for the husbands destined to join them. At the beginning of the nineteenth century there were many beautiful women of mixed ancestry and social standing in Cuba: young mulattoes, the daughters of Spanish immigrants and statuesque black women; or those with proud noses and serene demeanor, whose Native American blood could be detected even centuries later; and the daughters of Chinese immigrants and mulatto women, or of French landowners and Haitian women. Over time, these racially mixed women grew lighter-skinned.

*It did not take* long for the Clews, Castro, Ruz, and Revuelta families to cross paths. Fate is promiscuous.

Only one of the men, Ángel Castro, had to return in defeat to his homeland. He was shattered by Cuba's war of independence, a heroic war that lasted three years, from 1895 to 1898, freed the slaves, and ravaged the eastern provinces. During the uprisings in the struggle for freedom, the insurgents, called *mambises,* had burned the sugarcane fields, and their women had set their homes on fire.

When the Spanish government demobilized its colonial troops in Cuba, Ángel was granted a small pension, which he promptly used to return to the Island of his dreams. He had an unmatched shrewdness and a well-devised plan to put it to work.

After buying a meager piece of land somewhere in the easternmost province, he began to create a country estate for himself in a place called Birán, gradually expanding his holdings, and thus his power. He married María Luisa Argote, with whom he had two children, Pedro Emilio and Lidia.

The British lad, Clews, had nothing to do with the Cuban War of Independence, but ended up in it purely by chance. He was a naval engineer and, during his frequent voyages, he managed to learn the value of precious woods. He already owned a sawmill before he started a business of smuggling arms to sell to the insurgent Cubans, the mambises, in their struggle against Spain. When he was denounced to the Spanish authorities, who began looking for him, he fled deep into the countryside, and by the end of the war he had attained the rank of colonel in the insurgent Cuban army.

An old daguerreotype shows him, buck naked, bathing in a river.

The prestige of having been a mambí resulted in Clews's appointment, together with a few other engineers, to build the initial section of the Malecón de La Habana, the seawall and shore drive that begins precisely at the port that Morgan the pirate had purposefully avoided. Clews's various travels took him to Artemisa, in the westernmost province of Pinar del Río, at the opposite end of the Island from Ángel's domain. There he set up an electric plant, and married Natalia Loreto Álvarez de la Vallina. They had four sons and one daughter, whom they called Natica. She was the image of perfection. Her fateful beauty came into this world with the new era.

Though Francisco Ruz may have harbored memories of past incarnations in Turkey, the one in Cuba was not favorable to him. It has been said that his lack of direction spoke for itself: giving up too easily was one of his habits. Only the winds of defeat and the divining power of snails and coconuts from his wife's *santería* finally propelled him to start moving one morning on a trek that would take them to the other end of the Island, trying to escape their dire poverty.

With his wife, Dominga, and three daughters on top of a cart pulled by two oxen, he started from a town near Artemisa. They had to trudge along for almost eight hundred miles before they reached the fateful Birán. Their youngest daughter was named Lina.

The lineage of Revuelta did not carry any patriotic prestige, in spite of the fact that it included some courtiers who could keep their heads covered in the presence of their queen. In their Spanish hometown of Santander, from pharmacist to hardware store owner, they had maintained a name of prosperous standing. But Agustín's son Manolo, a *criollo,* or Spaniard born on the Island, felt no compulsion to seek a fortune. He was the kind of man that women can't resist. He seduced them with his bedroom eyes—with that intimate look that seems to see through garments.

His handsomeness was intense but vulnerable, his personality overwhelming. He sailed through life with a guitar and the voice of a troubadour.

Actually, Manolo did not see much beyond the nebula surrounding him. He had grown fond of a popular concoction made with Cuban rum, sugar, and a sprig of spearmint, that sublime poison known as *mojito.* He never missed a chance to indulge.


*The twentieth century was* just taking its first steps when Lenin, under the spell of dear old Karl Marx and his court of celestial Engels, sat one day under a chestnut tree by the Medici fountain in the gardens of the Palace of Luxemburg in Paris, and asked himself, "What is to be done?"

Lenin had enjoyed all the pleasures brothels had to offer, and had even managed to take as booty a disease that in other times would have been considered shameful. The French government had courteously provided him with protection and assistance, and was paying him an exile's pension. "What is to be done?" he mused. The eternal murmur of the fountain waters granted him an inspiring answer. He began to write as if possessed, and was able then to rest with the clear conscience of those who know they have the power to change destinies. He returned to Russia soon after.


*After Francisco Ruz and* Dominga had traveled the length of the island in their wagon of Misfortune, they reached Birán. There were not many options open to them, except to drown themselves and their progeny in the ocean.

The only thing Dominga had left was her knowledge of magic and her three daughters. Don Ángel quickly made a choice of one of them.

He appreciated the liveliness of their youngest daughter, Lina, who was the same age as his daughter Lidia. The girl had no inhibitions. She overflowed with an exuberant, rebellious energy, quite unlike the submissive and defeated country girls whom he had gotten pregnant and who bore him many children, causing him not much sorrow but giving him little joy.

Around the same time, the British mambí, Herbert Clews, already established in the city of Havana, was trying to convince his daughter Natica—a marvel of incongruity already accustomed to stopping shows and trolley cars with her beauty wherever she went—not to marry an alcoholic inspector of public works. In his Spanish laced with vestiges of Anglo-Saxon tones, he predicted: "This is going to ruin your life."

Unflinching, Natica, one of the most celebrated and beautiful women in Havana, a muse to couturiers and the chosen target of satyrs, finally married Manolo, a penniless boozer, and left behind an endless string of broken hearts. The couple soon had a daughter, born under the sign of Sagittarius.


*Don Ángel, the authoritarian* gallego, owner of a forgotten corner of the country, who had tenderly pawed the garments off the young Lina Ruz, slowly came to adore her, and lovingly continued to give her children.

Their third child was born at dawn, under the sign of Leo. After consulting the stars, Dominga knelt, kissed the ground, and said to her daughter Lina: "This is the only one of your children destined for big things in life."

Natalia (Naty), the granddaughter of Herbert Clews, and Fidel, the grandson of Francisco Ruz, were born four months apart and at opposite ends of the island of Cuba, that lopsided alligator in the sand. They were also separated by far-reaching life forces that select and determine avatars and destinies.

Naty was properly baptized. Fidel, being born out of wedlock, could not be.

But Ángel Castro had some nobility left, hidden somewhere in his pride. He had a talk with his wife, María Luisa, and told her that the arrangement was not fair to all those children that Lina kept bearing him.

When he divorced her, María Luisa was granted only a meager pension; the powerful Spaniard kept one of his two children, Pedro Emilio.

Ángel's daughter, Lidia, became "Perfidia," developing her resentment from the moment she had to forsake the usual comforts of her farm to live in a house with her mother, the wife abandoned in favor of the mistress.

Naty grew up alone in a home strangely divided between her matriarchal mother, Natica, and her hopelessly existentialist father, Manolo. She had large green eyes and a gaze too wise for her years. She was a force of nature. At two, she managed to survive acidosis, a disease that was then killing children by the hundreds. Natica had already traveled the road to despair and back while watching her daughter fade away with unstoppable vomiting. One morning, fearing the girl was dead, she sat in the living room and burst into tears. Then she saw a black angel pass by. It was Naty, covered with the black bean mush she had spilled on herself from a pot in the kitchen. She had broken the liquid diet to which she had been restricted for days. In doing so she saved herself.

At fifteen Naty repeated her feat when she contracted brucellosis and had to spend months in feverish delirium soaking in a bathtub with ice cubes.

She survived leptospira, hepatitis, and the bite of a dog that viciously sank its fangs into her.

She turned into a beautiful adolescent and soon was the toast of Havana. She was invited to all social events because of her pealing laughter, her flexible dancer's waist, and her striking combination of blond hair, tanned complexion, and voluptuous *criolla* figure.


*Young Fidel, together with* his older siblings, spent his first days in a thatched bohío north of the Castro estate. Here his grandmother Dominga and his mother, Lina, invoked the beneficial spirits in never-ending incantations, a candle in one hand and a glass of water in the other.

Without facing any threats to his health, he was nonetheless lucky to survive his numerous attempts at flying before he was five.

His education started in a little wooden schoolhouse, several miles away from the farm. At dawn, the kids had to venture into a rough strip of land between thickets of tall guinea grass and *marabú* to get to their single classroom. Fidel's brothers had to keep him at the end of the line because while on their way he had gotten into the habit of taking three steps forward and one backward.

He also used to engage in a stare-down game of challenging the sun, until his pupils could not take the scorching and he had to give up. This used to drive him into a blind rage because he hated to lose.

When Lina went after the kids, belt in hand, to punish them for some mischief, all the children disappeared in order to avoid the strapping—all but Fidel, who lowered his pants and, displaying his behind, said to her: "Hit me, Mamma." This didn't fail to disarm her.

He experienced his first humiliations when seeing his half brother, Pedro Emilio, riding very proudly on horseback next to his father, while he and his siblings had to stay in the shadows like a shameful blemish.

It was quite a relief for him when Lina took María Luisa's place and the children could quit the rural schoolhouse to go as the Castro clan to the best schools in Santiago de Cuba, capital of Oriente province. But it was even better when he was sent to Havana, and all of that was left behind as part of an unredeemable and secret past.

*Good luck seemed to* follow Naty with a vengeance. If she grabbed a tennis racket, she would win the match. If she jumped into a swimming pool, she came out of the club with a medal around her neck. If she looked at a man, it did not take long for him to kneel down before her.

It didn't take long, either, before another sudden illness brought her down. Thanks to a ruptured, gangrenous appendix, she met Dr. Orlando Fernández, who, fascinated by the exquisite perfection of her pearly innards, asked for her hand in marriage.

She accepted and they had a daughter named Natalie.

Tired of so much unshared good luck, Naty turned her attention to the needy and to the victims of a republic that, like all the others, was corrupt. With a profound anti-Imperialist conviction, she joined the Liga de Mujeres Martianas (League of Women Followers of José Martí), who tried to keep the precepts of that incurably romantic Cuban poet-patriot alive. She discovered a voice that deserved to be heard in Eduardo Chibás, leader of the Cuban Orthodox Party. Whatever the cause, that is where her sympathies lay. Chibás had accused a cabinet minister of stealing from the public funds. In August of 1951, during one of his weekly radio programs, he confessed his inability to offer proof of his accusation, and shot himself. Naty raced to the radio station and dipped her hands in the blood of the man who did not want to live with his honor tainted as originator of unfounded rumors.

Around the same time that Dr. Orlando Fernández fell for Naty's endearing beauty, Fidel had dazzled a very beautiful young girl named Myrta, whose last name, Díaz-Balart, had family links to the political aristocracy of the Island. One of her uncles was minister of the interior.

The couple married and had a son, Fidelito.

Without finishing law school and having no other skills, Fidel attempted all sorts of business enterprises, from raising a large number of chickens on the roof of the building where he lived, to managing a street-corner *fritanga* (fritter) stand in La Habana Vieja (Old Havana). Both enterprises met with failure.

He then decided to use his shrewdness in the field of politics. He succeeded in getting rid of his rivals, and in a gradual rise, helped by convenient "accidental" events, he attained the status of student-activist leader at the University of Havana. He even became an Orthodox Party candidate for the House of Representatives, sponsored by Chibás's own brother. Fidel stood tall and was gifted with a roguish charm.

Paralleling the coincidences of two other women in the past, Myrta and Naty bore their first children almost at the same time.

Even though there were some suspicions that Fidel somehow had been connected with Chibás's suicide, since he later became the head of the Orthodox Party, such rumors never reached Naty. Or if they did, her everlasting confidence in human integrity was in no way diminished.

*Fidel received a key* inside a linen envelope that emanated a mysterious perfume, Lanvin's Arpeggio, no less. It was the front-door key to an apartment in the affluent Vedado district, and with it came the offer of that space and of wholehearted allegiance to the continuity of the Orthodox cause. The note was signed by Naty Revuelta. She had that same key copied three times and sent also, without making any distinctions, to two other high-ranking men in Chibás's political party.

Naty used to overlook, or maybe not take into account, the fact that her face, her slender waist, and her high-society status made men's hearts beat faster. Perhaps she did not think of herself at all.

Soon after receiving his key, Fidel dressed in his best starched guayabera, the crease of his pants freshly pressed. He appeared at Naty's door wearing Grandma Dominga's pathfinder amulet under his clothes.

After he passed the careful scrutiny of the clairvoyant maid and the inquisitorial mother, the owner of the key was sent for.

When Naty entered the parlor, the *coup de foudre* left both of them deaf and blind.

They connected immediately, and the rest of the world ceased to exist. For her, it was the first adult attempt at breaking her restraints; and for him the action represented trespassing in a forbidden temple. Naty invited him to her social club, the Vedado Tennis Club, and he invited her to a student demonstration on the grand staircase of the University of Havana.

He, of course, did not go to her club, since exclusive social clubs did not tend to agree with his ideas about a just society. He would have felt as much out of place as coal-black Cucaracha, his former assistant at the fritanga stand.

But Naty had nothing to fear from a student protest demonstration; after all, she looked as fresh and pretty as any of them, and besides, she wore nicer clothes.

In the midst of the crowd of young people shouting out of control and protesting a firing-squad execution that had occurred more than half a century earlier, and thanks to that magic that sometimes appears to be a coincidence, they felt an instant attraction for each other. In the midst of all the turmoil, his hand grabbed hers tight and he led her to an improvised platform where he delivered the first and the best of his public speeches. As Fidel spoke, he was interrupted by police officers who had grown excited by the increasing number of backed-up motorists blaring their horns in protest.

Naty returned home very late that night, but no explanations were required because Orlando was, as usual, on duty at the hospital and their daughter, Natalie, was peacefully asleep under the careful eye of one of the maids. She was able to bask in this blinding new light until the dawn of the new day. The only one to notice the spark of determination that had displaced her customary docile manner was Chucha, the cook, but she didn't say a word.

For Myrta that night, like many a night lately, was full of anxiety. Her husband had gotten into the habit of coming home very late, and he was the one who gave Fidelito his medicines. And that particular night, the baby's state of health had become critical. He had been born sickly and underweight, and a siege of vomiting and diarrhea was making him quickly slip away from her. The pediatrician and Fidel met downstairs. The doctor had discovered that the poisoning was caused by an overdose of vitamins that, according to Fidel, was supposed to help the baby reach his normal weight faster.

The following day, the doctor broke his Hippocratic oath of silence and voiced his complaints to Myrta's family. No one, however, was able to break through the barrier of pride and terror she had built to shield herself from her husband's irrationalities. Neither her uncles nor her brothers could convince her that she was living in a dangerous situation.

After the death of the extraordinary Chibás, Fidel, the elected leader of a political party of ideas, decided to take action instead. A clandestine organization divided into many parts or cells was created, and with it, a kind of hierarchy that inevitably led to stratification. He chose the city of Santiago de Cuba for his first raid because he was more familiar with it than with Havana. Under the pretext of some weekend practice maneuvers, he summoned all the cell leaders, who were totally unaware of their destination, to an assault on Batista's largest military post in the provinces.[1]

Naty knew all about the attack because it was practically conceived in her home. She had contributed to it by selling all her jewels and providing the money to buy the needed weapons. She was in charge of the distribution of political pamphlets in the streets of Havana at the precise time of the assault, five in the morning.

By then, Naty had lost her notion of right and wrong. Bewitched as she was, rather than just in love, she was quite capable of entering into the most byzantine schemes on behalf of Fidel. She was ready to follow him wherever he would take her. She wrote a letter to Orlando, her husband, confessing her improper love, and life became a little hell for everyone in her family. She was totally oblivious to that.

In Santiago, Fidel as usual overlooked the human factor, letting his troops think they were engaged in a routine military exercise. Practically none of the more than seventy men were taking the attack seriously. Those coming from Havana got lost in the winding streets of

Santiago. The plan of operations they had been given was so ill-conceived that the rebels attacked the government barracks when half the soldiers were returning from the town carnival festivities. Fidel's men were trapped in a crossfire. The whole operation resulted in such confusion and bloodshed that it was never determined who were the real heroes and who were just unwitting victims. Since retreat had not even been considered, they were caught in a mousetrap.

Due to that much-talked-about disaster, Fidel acquired instant fame. For some obscure reason—perhaps it was the intervention of Lina's saints and Dominga's *santería* offerings, since both women had been continually sacrificing goats and chickens from the moment they found out about Fidel's plan—many of his men died or suffered torture, while Fidel had not even a scratch.

He was, after all, married to a niece of the minister of the interior. He received a lenient sentence, to be served in the panopticon on the Isle of Pines.

Naty also suffered a stratification of her own; but during the two years Fidel spent in jail, she reached out to him in many different ways until she dominated the prisoner's time and space. She would lead him step by step into her own brand of freedom, highlighting the events of every day, describing every moment for him, the kind of light, the smells, the people in each place. Everything she told him was bathed in a romantic and abstract idealism about justice, man, and society.

She showered him with personal attention, books, and goodies to eat.

Naty wrote Lina a letter appealing to her mother's heart. She also wrote to Raúl, Fidel's younger brother, who returned the attention in tender missives addressed to "my little sister." And she even took care of providing for Myrta and Fidelito.

She became the Princess of the Rebels. She was omniscient.

And Fidel returned her passion. He read all the books she sent him and distilled their essence in critical analyses of astonishing, high-minded spirituality. His minuscule handwriting, scarcely legible, even made use of the margins, and after finishing, he imagined the yet unknown intimate connection with Naty, and drifted into self-gratification.

\* \* \*

*They wrote to each* other at a relaxed pace, in a conversational tone that could continue indefinitely. It would be easy to imagine them alone as sole survivors on an island, one indoctrinating while the other one listened. And the island could even suddenly let go of its moorings and set forth on an unpredictable journey, with the two of them lying on the grass, wrapped in the mystic fragrance of *his* words.

While Fidel was busy telling Naty what wonderful use he was making of her ream of paper, he was also writing to Myrta, his wife, and sometimes, his imagination running dry, he duplicated the manuscripts. One day the jail censor, tired of having to decipher the two letters with a magnifying glass, mixed them up, perhaps on purpose, perhaps not, and mailed to each the letter addressed to the other. So Myrta found out that Fidel had a mistress—or, at least, that there was another woman he loved. She felt hurt and made it known.

Naty, on the other hand, forwarded the letter to Myrta unopened.

The prisoner received his parole and his divorce at the same time.

However, Naty remained married to Orlando the doctor, who did not find her platonic, ideological infatuation reason enough for a divorce.

After months of heavy correspondence, during which their love got more and more inflamed, Fidel had no other open doors and no open arms but Naty's. He sought and found refuge in the embrace of this warm and devoted woman, in spite of her circumstances. He promised that green-eyed beauty who had sneaked into his soul all the wonders of the world or, at least, those on the patch of land where they were standing.

They were meeting secretly at an apartment rented in someone else's name. One afternoon, at a time when he did not expect it, they conceived a child, Alina.

A few months later during Fidel's involuntary exile in Mexico, when he found out about Naty's pregnancy (for which she sweetly held him responsible), he had his doubts. He asked her to join him in New York right away, without taking into account that pregnancy is not like an air balloon that can release its ballast and immediately take flight.

When Naty did not show up in New York, he was disappointed. But how could he mistrust her and her self-sacrificing zeal? What else could she have done, being condemned to absolute prenatal rest?

It was not easy to resign herself to inaction. The fetus was struggling with all its might against its confinement and mucous oppression. No fetus, disregarding the fact that it is ill-equipped to peer into its future, can easily overcome gravity. With big, soft pillows and by keeping as immobile as possible, Naty managed to overpower it. After a bloody earthquake of contractions, overwhelming and horrifying, that left both mother and daughter exhausted, Alina entered the world at her proper time and stage of development. The date was March 19, 1956.

*Limbo does not exist,* and besides, a soul is never at rest, not even for a second. Nothing matches a soul's determination. Don't tell me it is capricious. This girl was purposefully on the threshold of receiving the gift of a life with a turbulent fate.

*During her months of* forced inactivity, Naty devoted herself day after day to writing to Fidel, sending him countless letters stuffed with press clippings from every Cuban newspaper.

Could there be any doubt of her good faith? Fidel needed another proof, and he sent Lidia "Perfidia," his half sister, now conveniently dedicated to the Rebel cause, to check for birthmarks on the newborn baby girl. With her rather mannish appearance and broad nose, Lidia did not look like any of the regular visitors and well-wishers, but Naty treated her like a messenger from heaven.

"What did you name the child?" Perfidia asked.

"Alina, 'a Lina' [to Lina] for her grandmother."

"May I see her? Fidel asked me to take a good look at her."

"Of course, of course. Tata Mercedes, bring the baby!"

Lidia Perfidia pushed up the sleeve of the fine linen garment to uncover the baby's left arm.

"Well, at least she has the beauty spots triangle." She then turned the baby facedown to inspect the backs of her legs below the knees. "And here is the other birthmark. This baby girl is definitely a Castro," she pronounced.

Because of her loneliness and position of weakness, Naty felt grateful rather than offended.

"Fidel sent some gifts."

For the mother, a set of large hoop earrings and a bracelet of embossed Mexican silver. For the baby girl, a pair of platinum-stud pearl earrings with the tiniest of diamonds.

As if having received approval from Mount Olympus, Naty was now able to relax after her ordeal.

By the time Fidel's pleasure-yacht invasion landed on the Island and he was given up for dead, presumed killed in battle or executed, Naty had already turned his mother, Lina, into her best ally.

Lina traveled to Havana to see her new grandchild. She pressed Naty's hand, and said: "Don't be afraid, my dear. Last night, riding on a white horse, St. James the Apostle came to me in a dream and told me that my son is alive. So don't worry anymore. I'll make sure that when I die, there will be something for my granddaughter. A while ago I pawned some diamonds with the farm treasurer in Birán. They must still be there. They will be hers."

Naty recovered from her childbed fever just as she had from all her other catastrophic illnesses.

To offer Fidel some comfort during his sojourn as a rebel in the mountains of the Sierra Maestra, Naty kept sending him, seemingly in competition with *Life* magazine, all sorts of good things to eat. On occasion the messenger was her own mother, Natica. In spite of her distaste for these "long-haired, bearded riffraff," she supported her daughter's efforts to have Fidel give his name to the baby, even though Naty's husband, Orlando Fernández, who knew all about the whole affair, had chivalrously lent the child his own family name. Natica risked her life to deliver money and mounds of chocolates to the foot of the mountains. The poor woman had always embraced her fatalism with resignation.

Fidel was very fond of the French delicacies from La Casa Potín, the most famous confectionary in Havana, of everything chocolate, and of literature. In return Naty received a few empty guns shells as souvenirs. She had to retreat into her own world in order to be able to stand the ugly rumors about her shameful pregnancy, her worries about the future, and the pain and sadness for her family and others that her love affair was causing. She wielded her love as a shield, in the same way that Charlemagne had brandished the Christian sword without waiting for a gesture of approval from the Supreme Pontiff.

As for Fidel, almost three years later on his overwhelmingly triumphal march into Havana—a victory that turned upside down any notions he might have had about human nature—he met with the immutability of a situation that he had long considered resolved.

The child lost her symbolic dimension and became a nuisance instead, a source of guilt, seemingly closing the door that had opened for him such a wonderland of miracles.

*Being the way I* am, a wandering soul, it would be natural for you to ask me why I lingered so long in Havana. Ladies and gentlemen, the truth is that Havana was a place where one could spend a whole lifetime.

You were never far from the sea, and the sea was everywhere, with its corrosive, salty spray, always forcing the city to renew itself with fresh paint and new wood.

There was always sun and spray in the air. Havana was a magic city. She would cast a spell on you with all her smells, her moods, her concerns. Nowhere in the world have I seen a more feminine city.

In the oldest district—stonework burnished by time and smoke—the half-moons of stained glass that crown the enormous windows, and the wrought-iron gratings that curve out in exuberant arcs (called *guardavecinos* or "neighbor-savers") between the balconies, completely overpower the old Castilian manly austerity.

From that section of Old Havana, heart of the city, from its red tile roofs, precious woods, and shaded colonnades, the narrow, cobbled streets took you, as if in a siesta dream, to the pastel colors of the newer houses, which seemed to embrace you with their columns. Columns that existed only as pretexts for the ample verandas.

In the verandas, the tropical air shed its torrid edge before sneaking deep into the interiors of the houses, and many Cubans chose to stay out there from dusk till night, playing dominoes. There were porches for friendly gatherings and for enjoying the breeze, street corners where you could buy fresh oysters. There were smells of all the fruits of the world. And outdoor cafes. There was an air of austere dissipation. Any young mulatto woman could seem to be stepping out of a famous novel from another century. From a park bench in the Paseo del Prado you could see history parade before your eyes.

Havana was a cosmopolitan city. It had gaiety and nightlife. Even the nouveau-riche neighborhoods had the elegance of good taste. There was comfort, space, and sunlight.

But after Fidel's march into Havana,[2] the city began a regression into the past, like those women who, in the splendor of their beauty, foresee its eventual ruin and begin accommodating their future wrinkles.

It is understandable that many people were swept away by the excitement of the moment: some of the politicians even had to flick the ashes of their Havana cigars away from their laps. But it hurt the soul to see war tanks parading along the Malecón Drive. Worst of all were the people. Between one day and the next, Cubans exchanged their effortless laughter for a destructive frenzy, and began to be dragged into hysteria by this man. In less than two days, no hotels had been saved from some destruction, and no fences protecting private property, no glass panels, no cars. Even parking meters were destroyed. These were all, as Fidel used to shout, haranguing the masses, "symbols of tyranny."


*Believe me, a revolution* is a revolution. I do not know what this wandering soul will tell you next. I am now biting my nails at the prospect of my commitment.

$$\smallsmile \quad 2 \quad \smallsmile$$

## ALINA

*I was baptized Alina* María José, as if Alina alone would not be enough.

There was no public announcement of my birth.

Nor was there any special premonitory sign.

Not one of the Three Wise Men poked his greasy head into my manger.

But that dawn I felt the stars cry through all the windows in heaven, and it made my heart shrink.

I took refuge in a dream of denial, without yearnings or tears.

I was a mild baby, not a screaming nightmare.

Since then, each time I open one eye, someone spits in it, because I evoke extreme reactions in people.

*But, let's get back* to the cradle song.

Pampered with eau de Portugal and wrapped in fancy cloth diapers, I searched for a nipple, but there was none in sight. I attempted to call attention to myself by coughing. Because of my coughing I poisoned night-years in the life of my nanny, Tata Mercedes, my cinnamon and vanilla statue, who used to console me in a wistful blue rocking chair, for having been born.

Tata did not know how to tell stories, and she did not like grown-ups. But she was too tall to be an elf.

She raised me, enlivening with tenderness the biological inertness of milk from bottles.

My mother was a sprite. You must know some. Sprites are very distant and mysterious. When they disappear, the miracles leave with them. They are capricious.

My sprite decided to fall in love with the wrong person. To those living in the fifties within Cuban society, that was unforgivable and unredeemable.

Sprites prefer very old stones and tall, pointy people. They like to inhabit their own ruins.

I compensated for my mother's absences by tearing at the lacy inserts of my linen gowns and sucking wildly at my pacifier. When she came close to me she was more essence than presence. She looked at me with emerald eyes that filled her face with the intensity of a high fever. I coughed sweetly for her.

My father was "Orlando Doctor Doctor." He wore a white gown like Tata, but without the little pleats. He was a magician and builder of hearts. *Cardioblogist,* I used to say. His forehead bulged a little, like a dolphin's.

He would bend down to embrace me when he came home from work at sundown, and the sun rays filtering through the glass door created a brilliant halo around him.

His doctor's office was downstairs, on the first floor of our large house. That is where he patched up people's hearts.

Because of him I fell in love with the goddess of Medicine, and it was from him that I learned, through his fluoroscopic lamps, about the pulsating magic of life in the fragile latticework of the rib cage, the secrets of Our Maker.

My sister, Natalie, was my father's favorite. Her life seemed strange to me. She cried when she was asleep, and wasn't even happy on Sundays. Sunday was the day we sat to have lunch under a crystal chandelier that, when lit, shed a thousand Baccarat tears.

The only thing that made Natalie happy was going with Daddy to the hospital in the evening, when he was on duty. "And you cannot go because they don't allow children or dogs," she said to me.

Chucha was our cook. She was black and shiny like patent leather. Her hair was all tied in little knots, wrapped in pieces of hairnet. She explained her hair to me by saying that it was not hair, but "the kinky mat of Congolese women." She had little moles all over her. She would rock me in the wistful blue rocking chair, enveloping me with her opulent perspiration and its mesmerizing, bittersweet charm, redolent of angel cake, syrup, and onions. Chucha did like to tell stories. *Patakines,* she called them, mixing the Holy Child of Atocha with Little Red Riding Hood, and Elegguá, the child *oricha* of Afro-Cubans. She regaled me with those patakines, which were followed by the trail of gunpowder that her contagious laughter seemed to explode.

"Elegguá was clearing the path in the woods for Little Red Riding Hood. Her grandma is Yansá in her death robe, and Ogún the Warrior is the one who kills the wolf."

I used to cling to a black-and-white raw-silk dress, crying out "Lala! Lala!," and nobody understood why.

It was the dress Grandma Natica, the Grandmother Sprite of the garden, wore when she wanted to relieve the infinite thirst of her flowers.

She came every day, as surely as the moon, gave a few instructions, had lunch, and then rested, remaining half asleep, until her interior clock would make her jump out of her rocking chair. In that white uniform scattered with black flowers, she would go to her garden, where she invented grafts, or planted seeds and seedlings even out of season. Then they all grew and grew in a mad fury, because Lala has a green thumb, people said.

She liked people a lot; but me, not much.

*Grandmother Sprite Natica, it* seems, had made a big mistake one afternoon, years before my time, when she let a man into the house.

Her doorbell rang at about five o'clock, and Chucha had taken a peek through the keyhole.

"Don't make me open the door, Señora Natica! Don't you open it, either! It is the Devil himself!"

Grandmother Sprite Natica didn't know how to read auras, and didn't like to receive orders from servants, either. She walked to the entrance door and let in a man dressed sharply in a perfectly starched and perfectly white guayabera. The only thing she didn't like was his weak and, at the same time, almost double chin. It was a double chin that seemed to indicate he was vulnerable to the manipulations of people more perverse than he. She firmly believed that Christ had let his beard grow to hide a second chin much like that one.

"I am looking for Naty Revuelta. Is this her home?"

"And who are you? Young people have no manners these days. Don't you have a name?"

Years later, she would say the same thing to my friends.

*Everything. Everything belonged to* me. The two Sprites and their absences, the greyhounds in the garden, the large family mansion, the stairs that were almost too difficult for my clumsiness, the gallery of rooms and terraces, the garden in bloom, Tata, and Chucha. They were all mine.

I didn't have much to worry about, although my house's atmosphere often bothered me like an uncomfortable diaper. People's eyes used to become narrow and daggerlike, and they would shout at the most beautiful Sprite, who would vanish, not allowing herself to be caught easily. She was involved in "Revolutionary" stuff, people were saying.

Everything in my world went wrong one morning that I remember too well.

I was sitting quietly, wearing my Foreign Legion cap and chewing on a rubber dog bone—that is why my teeth didn't hurt—when the cartoon I was watching on television disappeared. Shouts of "Viva Cuba libre!" (Long live free Cuba!) thundered through the living room. The television screen filled up with hairy people hanging like bunches of monkeys from some frightening vehicles that cracked the street pavement as they went by. Sherman tanks they called them. The hairy people were called rebels.

The rebels carried sticks in their hands and were wearing burnt-green uniforms with rosaries made of seeds around their necks, like the ones Chucha used to take out of her drawer when she got into that thing of spitting firewater on a cigar and then smoking it from the wrong end while praying to her saint.

Women beautiful like flowers were throwing more flowers at these rebels.

It was January of 1959 and this was the Triumph of the Revolution. The triumphal festivities went on for days until the most important monkey arrived and stopped there to talk. He talked a lot. Until he was totally hoarse.

Uncle Scrooge, his nephews, and Mickey Mouse vanished from the television screen forever. We have had bearded, hairy men on television in Cuba for almost forty years now. Try to imagine that.

That year we did not have any Christmas because the Sprite, in civic protest against the old regime, had forbidden any kind of celebration. We did not celebrate the gift-giving of the Three Wise Men, either. There were only those hairy men everywhere. They were even in our own home one night.

It was the Sprite, and not Tata this time, who got me out of my crib and took me to the living room, with its everlasting wicker furniture that today still bears all the visitors' rear ends.

The Sprite put me on the floor in the midst of a cloud of cigar smoke, and there, his head lost in a bluish stinking cloud, was the top hairy man, the most pointy monkey. He bent down the way Daddy Orlando used to do to be at my height, and inspected me.

"She looks like a curly little lamb. Come here, little lamb," he said, and handed me a box. Inside the box was a baby doll, dressed just like him, beard and all, with little stars in red-and-black triangles on its small shoulders, a military cap, and boots.

I did not want to give the man a kiss: his face was too hairy. I had never seen anything like it at such close range.

The very pointy monkey was "Fidel Viva Fidel," which was what all those women beautiful like flowers called him, and the crowds of people called him, as he passed by in those ugly tank things. It was the first time that I had received a present that was no good. I grabbed the doll, and started pulling out its beard to make it look like a baby again.

Someone shouted, "Shame on you!" It could have been him, but it was Tata, who wiped my face with a cloth dipped in eau de Portugal to exorcise the stench of hot tobacco that had been slobbered over me. She then rocked me to sleep to restore the peace of my soul. It was also Tata who said: "A fetish! A fetish of himself, that's what he thought of as a present for a little girl!"

The following morning, she told Chucha the whole story, and Chucha agreed.

"I warned Señora Natica years ago not to let him in, that he was the Devil himself."

Around then, people on television began screaming: "Paredón! Paredón!" ("To the [execution] Wall!") They were furious now. A blindfolded man was standing in front of a wall with his hands tied; and his white shirt got covered with red spots. He fell down very slowly, killed by those same long sticks the hairy men had brought with them when they arrived in Havana. The ones that made a rat-a-tat sound. It was an execution, someone said. It was sad.

Two men—a snooty one they called Che and a little Chinese guy they called Raúl, who looked like one of the street vendors selling produce or petticoats at the corner—were the ones ordering these executions. Though they were both short, Raúl was the brother of the most pointy one.

*Around this time, Orlando* Doctor Doctor began to fade. So much so, that I only remember his smile, as if it were the only thing he left with me before disappearing, just like the Cheshire cat did with his mistress Alice, in Wonderland.

Orlando Doctor Doctor's temple of the goddess of Medicine was condemned because the hairy men quickly "intervened." That is what they called taking possession of things. Doctors could no longer bring hearts home and fix them. That was considered "private enterprise," and was forbidden. The same thing happened with selling tulle petticoats in the street. It became forbidden. One morning I saw the street vendor being carted away by the new policemen right in front of my home. I could never go with Tata again to the stalls in the covered colonnades in La Habana Vieja to buy colored chickens or fresh fruits, or ice cream, or flavored ice cubes, because they all were considered to be private enterprises. That was when Daddy Orlando's hand really began to tremble. He had no hearts left, not even that of the Sprite.

Natalie's eyes grew bigger and bigger because her mommy was breaking Daddy Orlando's heart.

The last time I saw him he gave me a key.

"Here, Chipi-Chipi. This is the key to the room with the lamps, the one where Lady Medicine sleeps. Take good care of it, and I hope one day you can open it again."

Fidel enjoyed being in our house. He always came in the small hours, preceded by the sound of Jeeps braking and boots thumping. Sometimes he was alone; sometimes he came with Sad Beard or with Red Beard.

Tata used to pretend not to hear when the doorbell rang, and grumbled every time she had to take me back and forth from my crib to the living room.

For Chucha and for Grandma Sprite Natica, and for Tata, Fidel was really bad. In fact, he alone had won the great battle with the tyrant, Batista, who was a demon as bad as they come. Fidel was just like St. George killing the Dragon.


*Batista's face was full* of pockmarks, and his wife had to keep having babies all the time to avoid turning into a giant.

"Now that Batista has fled, the henchmen are gone. The bad men are not going to come at night again to search our house," Natalie used to say.

I thought the henchmen were fine. They liked my Foreign Legion hat, and if I asked them not to speak too loud, they didn't. They did not burn holes in the furniture slipcovers, and they did not leave in our living room an unbearable cloud of smoke and little heaps of ashes.

These new visitors, it seemed to me, were bothering everybody more than the old ones, because the new ones came in almost every night, way past midnight. I heard in the kitchen that henchmen are very much alike; and about thirty years later, it was my turn to await in dread the visit of a different kind of secret police.

*    *    *

*The only one happily* levitating around at this time was the Sprite. She had suddenly become talkative, and she has stayed that way.

A feverish, merciless need for activity had taken hold of her, and even though words like "emulation" and "vanguard" were not yet being used in slogans, she seemed to have a premonition of their importance in the immediate future: she began applying them to her daily life.

She and Fidel, the bearded man, saw each other away from the house, it seemed, because when she came home, her face all aglow with a smile coming from within and her eyes lost in mystery, she seemed to be blind and deaf to the obvious discontent oozing from her family and her household.

Grandma Lala's epicanthic folds weakened and fell while she cried her British eyes out, lamenting how her brother Bebo had to suffer when he was deprived of his position as Cuban consul and as "Jamaica's best-dressed man of the year." He had been condemned to perpetual exile, forever forbidden to return to Cuba.

"Naty, I beg of you, speak to that man! You know how Bebo granted asylum in Jamaica to many, many rebels, and how many medicines he sent to the Sierra Maestra!"

"That's enough, Mom! I have never asked Fidel for anything, and never will!"

"He had no qualms, however, about emptying your jewel box and your bank account, to buy the damned weapons for that bloody attack on the Moncada barracks!"

One day Lala told her friend Piedad about it.

"Oh, Piedad! He has no class and he's a bastard! Naty is not enough for him. He has been sleeping around with a lot of other society girls. The hussies! The other evening, when I told him to have a little more respect for my daughter, do you know what he said? That I shouldn't worry about it, that he had kept his boots on. How crude can he be! I suppose he doesn't take his pants off either, right?"

And I thought, Oh, God! I hope he doesn't hurt his little worm with the zipper!

I wanted to comfort her, but Lala Natica was giving me such cross looks, as if I were turning uglier and uglier, and I didn't know why.

"Lala, why are you upset? Uncle Bebo was not executed on television, like the uncle of the Mora sisters and . . ."

She then became really angry. It was surely then that she got the idea of giving me those injections when my elf's buttocks became bony.


*I became totally confused.* Mobs of people seemed to show the same enthusiasm for destroying capitalist symbols in the streets as for getting into a sudden frenzy and yelling "To the Wall! To the Wall!" The big wall of death. Around our house everybody was either angry or sad except the Sprite, who was always elegant, visionary, sparkling. She seemed to overflow like a horn of plenty.

"Mommy, Mommy, who are 'the meek'?"

"They are the poor, dear. Those who have to work very hard to live, and have a very hard life."

"But you work for Essostandardoil and have a pretty house and a new car. This revolution, did Fidel do it for you, too?"

"And for you, too, love."

"Tata is really poor. And so is Chucha! Did Fidel come so they could be rich?"

"Not rich, but so that they could have a better and fairer life."

I immediately darted into the kitchen, where the radio was no longer on because soap operas were gone, too.

"Tata! Chucha! The hairy man is going to give each of you a big house! Just wait and see! He came so that you won't be poor anymore."

They both looked at me with infinite patience.

"Who is putting those thoughts into this girl's head?"


*"Who is putting those* thoughts into this girl's head?" Fidel asked the Sprite a few days later, when I begged him very politely to put Tata and Chucha at the top of the list of the people who were going to be not rich, but not poor anymore.

On some late evenings that man, Fidel, would come only to play. They would take me out of my crib, and since I then stayed up late, I was relieved somewhat from the torture of coughing.

When we played on the floor and the cloud of tobacco smoke lifted, he had a manly smell, a clean smell without the help of cologne. It felt good.

When he didn't come to our house, he sent Tita Tits for me. She was a friend of the Sprite, a beautiful Asian girl who worked at INRA, the Institute for Agrarian Reform, I believe. When Tita did not come, it was Llanes, the chief of the Comandante's Personal Guard, who came.

But I preferred Tita Tits, because not only did she have that pair of fresh melons hidden under her blouse, but also she took me in a red Buick to that INRA, and she would lift me up onto those melons so that I could reach and press button number 7 for her. At the INRA door there was always a soldier without a smile. I could no longer take my Legionnaire's cap because someone had hidden it from me.

It was at INRA that I met the snooty Che, with his little bulges here and there on his monkey forehead, and a wheeze coming from his chest.

"Did you know," he said with his strong Argentinean accent, "that I have a little girl just like you?" He showed me a photo with a little Chinese girl. He called her Hildita. Her mother, who was next to her in the picture, looked like a big frog.

"Come back to pick up Chichi in an hour," Fidel said to Tita.

They did not talk to me much then. It seemed that Che was a doctor, because he was worried about some pill he was supposed to sweeten so the farmers could swallow the cooperatives.

"Just look at what happened in the Soviet Union. . . ."

And they used to carry on like that.

An hour is a long time, but not as long as my only visit with Fidel out in the open air, when he let me ride first on a tractor and later on a little horse.

In the colonial Quinta de los Molinos (Country Manor of the Windmills), a lot of people were sweeping the floor, and I asked Fidel, "Why are all these people sweeping at the same time?"

"They are doing voluntary work."

"And what is that?"

"That is work people do without pay. They do it because they want to."

"Are you, too, going to sweep the patio?"

What he did instead was sweep people out of his way.

"Who is this really pretty girl, Comandante?"

"She's a relative. Look, Tita is coming to pick you up. . . ."

I liked Fidel a lot, but I found the meek very annoying. The truth is that if he didn't come, I didn't miss him, because he was always on television, speaking nonstop to a bunch of meek people.

Most often he was telling them that the Revolution had been fought for them, and since they shouted "Viva! Viva!" he would go on and on, without being able to stop. I began to get confused between what was true and what I saw on the screen.

One day I asked him:

"Fidel, why do you talk so much?"

"So that people will stop shouting and applauding for a while."


*The dinner table at* home was never again good for anything. I think the same thing happened all over the country. Everybody was extremely busy. People were either at the Plaza de la Revolución shouting "Viva! Viva!" at Fidel for hours and hours, or doing voluntary work or something like that. There was no time left for bourgeois traditions like dinner. All that was fun or delicious was a bourgeois tradition.

That is how I lost my rank at the dinner table, where I had been in command in my high chair for elves. Nothing was following its normal course, except Lala Natica's appearance at lunchtime. She came and sat there, dry as a prune, and would not open her mouth, which was now just like a straight line, unless it was to say:

"Don't disturb me, I'm going to take my siesta."

In those days she had not turned wicked yet, giving me vitamin injections.

That came later, when for me, and for all the other children as well, there were no more pasta stars or alphabet letters to put into the soup. Without those bits of pasta, nobody could swallow that deadly concoction.

My first big change, a very personal one, came when I started to divide all my time between the backyard and the kitchen. Our life in the rest of the big house had fallen apart.

There was a nice warmth in the kitchen, tempered by Chucha's smell.

I even lost my fear of greyhounds. Together with Tata I put my hands into the laundry sink out in the patio and tried to make the clothes really clean. We were playing four hands with the recurrent music of the water, and there was no need for talking.

When the sun was about to fall from the sky, I used to run to the main entrance door to see if Daddy Orlando would ever come back, but he never did. This made me cry, but not too much.

The air got to be difficult to breathe in the big house, and then it happened: the Sprite turned "proletarian."

That little word began to be heard everywhere, especially after all the speeches at the Plaza de la Revolución, when the people started to celebrate by holding hands to sing the "Internationale." They swayed from side to side as if in a marathon for drunkards. Just like Grandfather Manolo used to look when he got home sloshed to the gills on mojitos, until a sudden heart attack did him in.

The Sprite announced one morning that she was no longer going to wear her pergolalike skirts or her pearls. She donned the blue-green uniform of the militias, with a Spanish beret like that of the *bodeguero,* the grocery-store owner. Having decided that our big house was no good for us, she gave it to the Revolution, with everything in it.

My first thought was that Fidel had finally given us a bigger castle to live in, but the opposite was true. With not much more than the clothes we had on and a bundle of kitchen pots and pans to make life possible, we moved to an apartment in Miramar, on First Avenue and Sixteenth Street. Right by the sea.

Lala Natica's protests at such idiocy still reverberate like an eternal echo in the atmosphere that surrounds this family of matriarchs.

Poor Lala was able to rescue the crystal chandeliers, with their thousands of teardrops, but they were useless in our new place because the ceiling was too low.

I think I felt very desolate. I was three years old, and still abusing my pacifiers.

I began to wake up with my eyelids stuck shut, tighter than oyster valves. I suffered from dry stomach cramps, and I coughed and coughed as if possessed.

The sea became a consolation for me, and so was my first girlfriend and next-door neighbor, who did not love me as much as I loved her. I was always eager to sleep over at her home because her mother told us stories in bed and there were always eggs, from some relatives who owned a chicken farm. She had a brother even more obnoxious than Natalie, who had become unbearable. It was impossible even to sleep with her. She screamed, "Daddy! Daddy!" and cried, without even waking up.

*I don't know if* Castro's Revolution—or Guevara's, or Pérez's, or whatever you want to call it—was responsible for this in any way, but since it had started, many things began to appear and disappear (not only the ones that usually do) like rabbits in a magician's hat.

"The electric power has been cut off!"

"There is no water!"

"The ration books are here!"

The same thing was happening with people: "José is gone," or "María received her exit permit."

Meat, eggs, sugar, and butter were also gone or had received their exit permit. You had to go with your ration book to the bodega or you would not get "what you had been allotted." That wasn't much, it seems, because even though Tata spent hours waiting in line, our meals suddenly were of only one color. For weeks I had to eat something green called "spinach puree without milk." When the spinach was gone, the food became brown and it was called "lentils without salt." Not even Popeye would have eaten that, so I didn't either.

The "meek" people managed better than we did because they carried around a mysterious bag called the black market bag. You could find everything in it: fruit in light syrup, and chocolate, for instance. It even seemed that the Wise Men had hidden some of their gifts there too.

The only person who would not touch that bag was the Sprite. "Not appropriate for a revolutionary," she used to say.

"Look, dear, I brought you some crackers I got as a snack at INRA while doing my voluntary work."

"Could I have them with a little butter?"

"Ask Tata, but I think the butter hasn't come this month."

People no longer said "Let's buy this and that," because things were disappearing on their own. They "have not come yet," or they "haven't come for months." Nobody here could say, "Let's buy some eggs and have an omelet today," because eggs only came once a month, and sometimes not at all. It was the same with tomatoes and potatoes.

Nor was anyone able to say "Let's go to the drugstore for some rubbing alcohol," because it had never been around since it left, when I was a tiny gnome, not yet an elf. The same went for sanitary napkins and tampons. . . . But what am I talking about?

When food was yellow—we called it cornmeal mush—it was bad, but *gofio,* or toasted corn flour, was the worst.

"That," Tata said, "is only fit for pigs."

For the Sprite, however, mush or gofio was the same as ambrosia.

The occupation of a cook, like Chucha, became obsolete and disappeared. So I also lost her and her crazy world of black gods, and Christian virgin queens, and wicked children engendered by good and evil.

Gone was Chucha's explosive laughter. In order to hear it and see Chucha, Tata and I had to go through the calvary of the infrequent, jam-packed buses on Sundays to get to her little room in Old Havana. She lived with her dear, blind mother, who was as wrinkly as a little raisin.

Chucha seldom came to visit us, and when she did, there was always the same business of spitting firewater in the corners, smoking cigars from the wrong end, and swishing the air with a bunch of sprigs. She called it a *despojo,* "to shoo away all the evil spirits from this house."

I begged her to stay, because without her there was no fun at our dinner table. But she always said no.

"I am not like Nitza Villapol, that shameless whitey who keeps doing her television show every week just like before, but now with recipes for corn mush or boiled lentils. How dare she call it 'Italian polenta' when it's only boiled cornmeal without any garlic or salt! I don't know how to cook without food, child. And I wouldn't want to, either, for people who have forgotten how to enjoy life. Perhaps Señora Natica misses me, but Señora Naty, she forgot how to eat long ago."

There was not much truth in her words, because on weekends the Sprite used to gobble up the cornmeal mush, with or without an egg on top, and Lala Natica would eat it every day. To be eating boiled lentils without salt, but brought in by a maid, in silver bowls and hand-painted fine china, while my grandmother taught me how to serve myself *à la russe* or *à la française*—was the most bizarre thing in the world. I would rather have died than invite home any of my friends.

*I couldn't eat that* insipid slop, but it didn't matter much, since we elves are never hungry anyway.

My poor nutrition was blamed on the heartless bearded man. Tata and Lala had put some pressure on the Sprite. But it was Fidel who first brought this up.

"What is wrong with this child? Look how pale she is! And thin as a rail. I'll call Vallejo to see her."

"I don't think she needs to see Dr. Vallejo."

Vallejo was his personal druid.

"There must be something wrong with her. She is sick."

"I don't think so."

"Ah, no? Well, then, tell me, for goodness' sake. What is it?"

"The trouble is she is not eating."

"Not eating? Why on earth doesn't she eat?"

"Because . . . It's that . . . I . . ."

"Because there is no food!" interrupted Tata like a fury, without allowing the Sprite to continue her roundabout discussion for even one more second. "I don't know what world you are living in, but one must be deaf and blind not to know that half the people in this country are hungry!"

Both Tata and the Sprite drove Fidel's adrenaline into a frenzy. That was bad for him. He already had ten million people shouting at him and applauding him all the time. I think that at that moment he decided to stop worrying about things like that.

"What do you mean there's no food in this house?"

The Sprite was visibly ashamed.

"Well, this month the ration book only gave us lentils. We didn't get any milk, or . . ."

The following day a happy young soldier brought a milk can from the Comandante's own little farm.



*Life went on like* this, until I suffered my first transcendental tragedy: I was taken to a wretched school where I did nothing but pee and vomit on myself all the time. It was called the Margot Párraga School, and I had to wear a white uniform with lots of difficult-to-tie knots and bows and two-tone saddle shoes that made me weep with anger.

The social life did not agree with me. I became self-destructive and one morning, shamed by peer pressure, I threw my pacifier out my bathroom window.

"No more pacifiers!" I declared.

In a cataclysmic gesture, I gave up the best oral satisfaction of my childhood.

My tender and brand-new willpower could barely stand the eight hours of education torture. When I got out of the school bus, all wet, smelly, and totally desperate, I started sniffing around like a dog on the lawn below the window of my misfortune.

No pacifier.

The Sprite told me, "You yourself decided to throw it away. When you make a decision, you have to stick to it. No matter what!"

For the Sprite, there was no difference between ideology and stubbornness.

I decided then to be indecisive for the rest of my life, and what's more, I became compulsively so.


*Martin Fox was a* very rich man and not meek at all. He owned the four buildings facing the little beach where I lived. He was good because he built a natural swimming pool in the rock for us children, and added some swings. He had a pet lion, and a monkey that he kept tied to the wall around his property.

That year the Three Wise men were very good to us at Christmastime. Even though the pine tree had been exchanged for a fake palm, it seems that the Magi never get disoriented, and underneath the palm tree there were a lot of pretty presents for both Natalie and me.

Things after that weren't going so badly, until one night I was awakened by some shots and a lot of shouting: "Assassin! Assassin!"

The following evening when Fidel came, he didn't come to play with me, but instead to scream, in a paroxysm of anger, at the Sprite.

"So Llanes makes an attempt on my life, and you still open the door for him and let him come into this house!"

"What do you mean? I haven't opened the door for anybody!"

"I don't believe you! He escaped from jail and came here directly! There is no excuse for what you have done!"

"That is not true at all!" The Sprite had to defend herself. "A few gunshots and a lot of screaming next door woke me up. From what you say, maybe it was Llanes. But I must tell you something else: If he comes here and knocks at my door, just as he has done a thousand times, of course I am going to open it for him. That is how you always wanted it, and if he comes and knocks, how am I to know that he is now a fugitive?"

"There is no excuse at all for opening the door to someone who has tried to kill me, whether he is a fugitive or not."

Llanes was the chief of Fidel's Personal Guard, and his right hand. Suddenly he was being accused of trying to kill his Comandante.

The Comandante was higher on his horse than usual, red in the face, and menacing. He left possessed by the same fury he had brought with him, and did not show up again for a long, long time.

The Sprite was desolate.

"Oh, my God!" she lamented one day, opening her arms wide. That was the last time I heard her talk to God.

God did not answer her. I thought He had also left the country, together with all the poor priests that Fidel himself had put on boats and sent away to exile. Lala Natica complained that it was hard for her to say her prayers at home. All the churches had been closed after the meek people began carving lots of very bad words on the church doors, as well as some ugly drawings of a pair of little balls, a fat baseball bat in the middle, and something else that looked like a fruit sliced open.

The truth was that the Comandante made everything disappear. Llanes, who was kind and used to bring me the things I wanted, was gone. The young soldier with the milk can was gone, and even my sister, Natalie, was now gone.

One morning, she was not in her bed.

"Where is my sister?"

"Orlando came for her in the middle of the night. They didn't want to wake you up."

"And Daddy didn't even give me a kiss? But where did they go?"

"They left the country."

Oh, my God! I couldn't bear even to imagine it! The shock almost killed me. Fidel kept repeating over and over on the radio and television: "Those who leave the country are nothing but lowly worms." Everybody, everybody who left the country, I was convinced, would turn into a worm right on the plane. I was completely sure of that, whether they were kids or old people. My Doctor Daddy and Natalie turning into something so repulsive!

Tata had to give me a massage to alleviate my terror attack, and to make me stop sobbing. It was Tata who explained it to me.

"That is another one of those lies, m'child. Like the one about how much better off the poor will be."

How awful! I thought. Since Fidel stopped coming, it's as if he left us with a little trail of bad things happening, one after the other. The Sprite then got sick with hepatitis, and the way she was staring with her yellow and olive-green eyes, I was afraid she was going to die on me. Lala Natica became Grandma Nightmare. She would chase after me, even in my dreams, with hundreds of blunt hypodermic needles. She sterilized the instruments of my torture by boiling them in a sinister pot. Then, brandishing a needle, she would throw me across her lap and nail me with a whole shot of vitamin $B_{12.}$

The Three Wise Men also lost their way. Everything turned into "one basic toy" and "two nonbasic toys" that were exhibited in the bare hardware store windows, among a few hammers, wires, and toilet floats.

Toys were for children under eleven, and the coupons for them came in the Industrial Ration Books. The basic toy was all right. It could be a doll, a pair of roller skates, or a Chinese bicycle, but the store ran out of them very quickly, and then they could only be taken out of the black market bag. The Sprite would have none of it. The nonbasic toys were always the same little plastic dolls: a pink girl, a blue boy and nobody wanted them. For some children, the Three Wise Men kept bringing gifts, but their parents had to be friends of Fidel or work with him. People called them *dirigentes,* and they were all cabinet ministers. Tata used to say that these friends of Fidel were "the new bourgeoisie." They didn't know how to speak well and wore the ugliest clothes, and their wives went around with their hair in rollers and had red toenails, which showed because they wore thongs.

Tita Tits came to say good-bye one day. She also became a worm, so there was nobody left to take me to see Fidel at INRA. I urgently needed to see him and convince him to come back to our house, because things had been terrible since he left.

He never stopped appearing on television, so I stole from Chucha the firewater she used for her witchcraft.

"With permission of all my dead ancestors, Serafina Martín, Cundo Canán, Lisardo Aguado, Elegguá Laroye, aguro tente onu, ibbá ebba ien tonú, aguapiticó, ti akó chairó . . ."

I knew her litany by heart. I got a mouthful of firewater and spat it over the television set.

My witchcraft worked. When Fidel returned, he fixed things in a big way, and we all moved back to a real house again.

*      *      *

*Our new house was* in Miramar. It had pink walls around a front garden with an African palm full of thorns from top to bottom, and some bushes with fragrant flowers and the most beautiful worms in the world. The worms had black bodies with yellow stripes and a red head.

There was an upstairs and a downstairs, and the only thing I didn't like was the beige-and-black tile floor. The situation at home was getting worse. When I learned to count I became more compulsive: if I didn't cover twenty-four squares in eight steps, heaven forbid!, some really terrible thing would happen; perhaps my mother would die. And if I didn't walk on forty squares four times . . . would my Tata die?

I had a large bedroom, and a bathroom all to myself.

The joy I felt the moment I entered that bathroom was truly electrifying. The water gave me an electric shock, and I had to keep jumping while washing my hands. Taking a bath was a special pleasure, because when I got my washcloths soapy and scrubbed my whole body, the washcloths would, by themselves, change color to green, violet, or blue. I had to soak them and leave them to dry until they got white again. Only Tata saw this, and she made me swear not to tell anybody because, she said, magic was a black-people thing.

The real magic, though, was in the garden. It was an enormous garden where any elf could imagine a forest with its enchanted population of goblins, gnomes, trolls, and a bevy of fairies surrounded by royal poincianas, jarcarandas, and banana trees, plus croton and giant aquatic taros that sweetened my grandma gardener's bitterness. She had started wearing her raw-silk dress again, casting her spell on the soil. In less than a year she had turned it into a magical place.

To become less proletarian was good for the Sprite. She had been having a rough time, because a rumor was going around that during his negative and sudden exit, the Comandante had decided not to set boot in our house again. The Sprite, poor woman, could not even find a job. It was as if she had turned into one of those untouchables from India, or a "sacred cow," as she used to say, which is also from India, I think.

Our new home was in a "frozen zone," which was the name given to the neighborhoods where the wealthy people had lived. The person in charge of our zone was called La China and she was mean. She forced out of their good homes the few owners who had not left the country. She emptied the houses of everything and assigned them to political leaders. People were saying that Fidel himself had given her that job.

Our home address was 3704 Twenty-second Street, between 37 and 41, and the telephone number was 2-5906. We had a kitchen, a laundry sink, a pantry, two garages with a room for the family chauffeur, and a maid's room, which saw a parade of different women, *"compañeras"* employed to help Tata take care of that unmanageable mammoth of a house.

Across the street was the Parque de los Ahorcados or Park of the Hanged. It was full of grandfather trees, which had long, airy beards and were all crooked, twisted, and knotty from arthritis.

Once in a while, people who had been executed appeared hanging from those trees, I was told, but after we moved to the neighborhood, they began to be called suicides.

I reached my fourth birthday without any mishaps, and I was taken to a public school that had opened in that section of Miramar "to become a *pionera,*" said the Sprite, who was still very proletarian, though not so meek.

Then the humiliating feeling that I was different from other children began to acquire the color of tragedy. Mainly because my classmates were the ones who lived in the tenement next to our back garden wall, or in little dollhouses bordering another neighborhood called Marianao, which was not "frozen."

I pleaded with the Sprite to please not take me to school in the Mercedes-Benz anymore, because nobody else was driven to school, except another "cutesy" called Ivette, and another kid, whom they also called cutesy though his name was Masetti. I am sure the others called me cutesy too. The other mothers were washerwomen or housewives—heaven knows what that meant—and none of them wore earrings, or gold watches, and they didn't have a nose like my mother's, let alone green eyes or . . .

Tata began to take me to school then, and that was even worse. She refused to stop wearing her starched white linen uniform, all nice with little pleats.

"I don't have any other clothes, m'child," she told me.

And that was true, because I had looked into her closet.

"Mommy, please, give Tata some new clothes. Pretty please."

"Look, Alina, do you see what I am wearing? This was a long skirt ten years ago. Juana altered it and made it into a dress. I don't have many clothes left either."

True! The thing was that my mother could go around in patched-up clothes without stockings, and still look like a queen.

The worst thing was that I did look good all dressed up in the fine linen and silk organdy dresses handed down to me from my sister the worm. Tata would deftly starch them and then press and press them treacherously until they made me look like a floating, frothy meringue. I would go to school events and to birthday parties in the tenements all dressed up, bourgeois style.

For costume parties, I don't even want to remember. Anyway, I had inherited a costume especially made for my sister long ago, designed by the best theater designer in the country. It was all heavy green satin, with paillettes of black sequins, matching dancing slippers, and a tight headdress with antennae. It was a grasshopper costume. Even when I was not attempting to be different, I looked absolutely ridiculous.

That thing of being different did not improve. It caused me more humiliation when I was given the nickname "Lefty." I was writing my numbers and letters backward, and the teaching comrade could not read my homework unless she put it in front of a mirror.

I got cured of that habit, but the nickname stuck.


*When Fidel started coming* to our house again, so did the Three Wise Men, who were really fake. The food started coming too, which was very real. Though he no longer came practically every night the way he had before the argument with the Sprite and his needless accusations, one could feel his presence like a warm mantle protecting our home.

Grandma Lala even lost her hypodermic needle.

The young soldier came back with his milk can, and he also brought rancid butter, a box of abominable coconut yogurt, meat, corn, and taro roots "from the Comandante's little farm." Between one round of applause and the next, Fidel had found some time to grow a few things.

Even *turrones de Navidad,* those wonderful Christmas sweets from Spain, were brought by the young soldier on orders from the new chief of Fidel's Personal Guard, José Abrantes, a loving, dark, and handsome hunk of a man. He immediately became Uncle Pepe, and he liked to let me slide down his knees.

My gastronomic curiosity was over by then. This usually happens to gnomes on their way to becoming elves.

The generous gift-giving of the Magi and the abundance of food also brought me some heartaches. I could not invite my classmates to visit me at home. Even though their parents might know where the black market bag was hidden, the *turrón,* the butter, and the yogurt had not gotten there yet, so an Omertà code of silence for these and many other things was established at home. I couldn't mention my record player, because the school would then be constantly asking to use it, nor could I ride the new Chinese bicycle that the Three Wise Men had left with Uncle Pepe Abrantes for me. It had to remain hidden in the garage.

I really was not comfortable at home, and I preferred to emigrate to Ivette's house. Her mother was as beautiful as the Sprite, but she was a homemaker and was always there.

So I moved my headquarters over there and was able to enjoy family weekends with a father, a mother, grandparents, a dog, and even an older sister. We all used to go to Santa María del Mar, that blessed beach less than twenty minutes from Havana. On the way, we stopped at the home of Ivette's godfather, changed into our bathing suits, and then jumped into the water and did not come out until we were all wrinkled.

Some Sundays Fidel also went there to swim. That part of the beach was frozen too, though this now sounds funny.

We always knew when he was there because first, his sullen-faced henchmen would search all the houses nearby, and a little later one of them would come to take me to his empty house. There were no other children. And no pictures on the walls. Only tough men. I even felt sorry for the Comandante and started to be affectionate with him, which he enjoyed for a little while before sending me back.

Ivette's mother was greatly relieved when I returned.

"Thank God, nothing happened to you!" she sighed, always afraid that someone might make an attempt on Fidel's life while I was with him.

*It was around then* that the thing about the Atomic Bomb started. Fidel was extremely busy with Nikita Khrushchev, an old man who looked like a white seal. He was always trying to kiss Fidel on the mouth. And there was Kennedy Frog Eyes Monroe, the master of Imperialism.

The shouting would get started as usual, but instead of "Viva! Viva!" or "To the Wall! To the Wall!" people began shouting "Down with Imperialism!"

That whole incident became known as the October crisis [Russian missile crisis], and it seems that the one with the frog eyes was obsessed with dropping bombs on the Island. The Sprite fixed up one of our garages as a shelter because, as she said, "the attack can come at any moment." We were all excited.

The most fun was when the meek people got dressed in militia uniforms and had to march with wooden rifles in hand, singing military marches, and do night watches. If anyone had real weapons, the police took them away.

People seemed terribly eager for that bomb to fall on them.

*Let them come! Let them come!*
*And we'll teach them how to run!*
*Fi-del! Fi-del!*
*What's your secret, Fidel?*
*Whichever way they turn,*
*You give the Yankees hell.*[3]

But Fidel seemed sad to me. I don't know. He wouldn't come to our house or go to the beach, and suddenly he appeared on television in a costume with a hairy hat and was always getting kissed by Nikita the Seal.

He was in the Soviet Union, with the weirdest people. They all spoke gibberish, and all the men liked kissing one another.

It was after this that Russians began showing up in Havana. Their hair was very blond, they liked gold teeth, and they smelled so bad that there are no words to describe it. They looked at Cubans blankly, as if we were transparent. They introduced Russian canned meat and bottles of vodka into the black market, and from that same black market, they got the gold for their teeth. At least they brought with them some new animated cartoons, like the grandmother Baba Yaga, and Old Jotavich, who would pull a hair from his beard and perform miracles. The Russians liked to flock together going to and from their clubs, and their children did not attend public school with us.

A wondrous thing happened one afternoon. Fidel came to our house in the daytime. It was as if he didn't have to hide his visits anymore.

He said he was coming straight from the airport.

"I brought two suitcases for the girl, all full of things."

He also brought very dirty nails, so I went ahead and manicured them for him, and I buttoned his shirt, too. But those suitcases with things he promised never made it home. Fidel doesn't like to say he's sorry, so he blamed Celia Sánchez, his chief of staff and personal witchcraft counsel. She had already been blamed for a few other ugly things too, like the day that the Sprite took me to the bunker on Eleventh Street to see Fidel, who was sick. Celia issued an order not to let us in, and we had to wait outside on the street, totally humiliated.

"The trouble is that Celia got confused and distributed the gifts meant for you among the children of the Personal Guards. This is all I was able to recover."

He gave me a baby doll, two panties, a pair of two-tone shoes made in Czechoslovakia, but he also gave me a bear. His name was Baikal and Grandma Lala didn't want him in her garden, so I had to go visit him in El Laguito, another one of those "frozen zones." No kid ever believed I had a real, live bear.

\*       \*       \*

*Shortly before the guys* with gold teeth came, another plague reached Havana. Most people in this plague had no teeth at all. They were the Makarenko and Ana Betancourt girls.[4]

These poor girls, mostly from the countryside, came to live in the most affluent neighborhoods, in houses vacated by people who had left the country.

They had to march in platoons all the time and sing their slogans, "Homeland or Death" or "Fidel this" and "Fidel that."

They were issued brown uniforms and big black school shoes like the ones we children wore, which were very hard. Many of them left their shoes around the corner. They would rather go barefoot, just as before.

The "repossessed" houses were then called *albergues* or hostels. Also converted into hostels were the FOCSA building and the magnificent Hotel Nacional.

That's how the city's landscape, and its smells and its noises changed.

Broken toilets began to adorn gardens on Fifth Avenue and all around Miramar, along with the bidets those young women pulled out because they had no idea what they were for and found them to be just a hindrance in their bathrooms. They were using the bathtubs to wash their clothes.

Washing machines also ended up on the front lawns, and electric stoves and freezers, with their opened doors like insect-eating plants, their gaping mouths corroded by the ocean spray. Backyards were used to build wood fires for cooking and narrow little houses that were latrines. "That is what the country girls use for peeing and doing everything, because they never had electricity or running water," the Sprite explained.

The truth is, by then no one had much of either. At any given moment we could find ourselves without water, or the lights would go out. They both took time coming back. The Sprite was perfectly happy with this.

"They are here to get an education. The peasants have been oppressed for hundreds of years."

"Oh, I see."

I was moved. Moved and repulsed. To walk around the gardens of the Hotel Nacional had become dangerous because these girls used to throw things out their windows, including rags stained with menstrual blood. That made Tata, my nanny, furious.

It was Fidel who gave me the best explanation, one evening when I asked him why he was allowing Havana to become so ugly.

"When they go back to the countryside, they are going to be the best defenders of the Revolution."

The trouble was that many of them didn't go back: they stayed as teachers.

It seemed that the Revolution still needed more defenders in the countryside, because more and more people were being brought to Havana. Since they had no place to go, people in general were asked to open their homes to them. The boy we got, Panchito, had transparent ears and the saddest eyes I had ever seen. He was fourteen.

He told me he was from the mountains called Sierra del Escambray, in Las Villas province. He was the oldest of five children. His father had been an *alzado,* a farmer who was fighting against Fidel from the beginning. At first I didn't believe him, because in Cuba there is only one important sierra, the Sierra Maestra, plus no one had ever rebelled against Fidel. Quite the opposite.

But Panchito described the caves where the alzados were hiding and where he brought them food, hidden under his shirt and hat. He told me how his uncle had been caught and killed. Then he and his family were being relocated in a jail-like town. Because his documents had been lost, he was taken to a couple who claimed to be his parents. They saved him from going to jail, and sent him to Havana under the new educational plan.

Would I, please, appeal to Fidel for him? He had to get his mother and sisters out of that jail-town where they were being beaten. He himself had seen how the soldiers had smashed his younger sister Evangelina's lips when they took her prisoner.

I asked Fidel to get Panchito's family out of that jail place, and I don't know what happened, because one morning Panchito was nowhere to be found.

This was not the only thing I asked Fidel then.

People had to be sharp and persistent to be able to find out where Fidel was. They would wait for him around the Hilton Hotel because they knew he liked the twenty-fourth floor, but he would escape from them through the underground garage. They watched for him on Eleventh Street, but an armed detail blocked all access from the four corners. It wasn't long before they started standing guard by my house way past midnight when he visited, and they were still there in the morning.

People waited until I came out to the garden to play and, one by one, in rigorous order they would come to me.

"Little girl, please, give this letter to Fidel."

"And this one."

"And this one."

I delivered a couple of missives, which he pocketed. Then he began to leave them on the side table next to the recliner he had installed in the Sprite's sitting room. She finally told me to stop annoying him, that the poor man could not solve all problems, being so busy as he was.

Of course I already knew that he was busy and that he kept everybody else busy with the "Socialist Emulation," the "voluntary" work, and the large gatherings at the Plaza de la Revolución, but it began to seem to me that he was mean. My heart ached for these poor people, and even though I kept selling them lemonade because I needed money for school snacks, and they were always thirsty after standing there for so long, I began to hide their woes around my bedroom, under the mattress, between the freshly laundered sheets, and in every dark and forgotten closet corner.

Their letters spoke of fathers, sons, and brothers who had been shot by Raúl Castro or by Che. Of people dispossessed of everything they had: a drugstore, a hardware store, a couple of houses. Of wives who could not get the exit permits that would allow them to join their husbands in exile, and of children and parents who were waiting in exile for the arrival of sick relatives still on the Island. One tragedy after another.

When Tata tucked me in and made me kiss my day good night, and the Sprite surrendered to her constant weariness, I would take out those last gasps of hope and read them until I collapsed under the weight of other people's miseries.

That is what I used to read from the time I learned how. I also read the memoirs of the Count of Romanones, two or three old books left by my sister, and the weekly *Pionero,* which was a rag. And I have kept reading compulsively my entire life, always searching for something good that would make people feel better, all to no avail.

*Celia Sánchez, La Venenosa* (the poisonous one) exerted an irreverent power over the Sprite. Widely known as Fidel's chief of staff and for having "fought alongside him in the Sierra," she was less well known as official witchcraft counsel in charge of the Comandante's personal clothes as well as his occult paraphernalia. She was a witch with style of sorts.

Celia kept her dark, unruly hair tight in a ponytail, to one side of her egregious head. A few inches of her lacy slip were always showing under her dress. For the finishing touch to her skinny legs, she wore a pair of bobby sox with stiletto heels. Her esthetic flair showed up in some public images, such as that of the female transit police corps, nicknamed *las cotorritas,* the little parrots, thanks to their uniforms, which combined in poor taste all sorts of strident colors of her choosing.

Many people owed their meteoric rise or seismic fall to her. She would oust anyone who stole from her a piece of the Comandante. The Sprite and I were an inconvenient pair. So when we received the ukase to leave for Paris, I wasn't surprised by the Sprite's comment.

"This is Celia's doing."

The Sprite felt sentenced without the right to appeal.

Fidel then explained her mission. He generously gave her five hundred dollars for clothes and other necessary installation expenses, gave me a kiss, said good-bye, and vanished into the night. Naty was left sitting and with an expression of utter disbelief that was quite unforgettable. As her undercover job, along with that of first secretary to the Cuban embassy, she was to perform an exhaustive investigation of all secrets of the French chemical industry. She knew as much about chemistry as I did about trigonometry. For the Sprite, though, life was all a matter of ideology.

"Mommy, do the French talk like we do?" I asked.

"Well, no. They speak another language," she answered, making noises in her throat as if she had bronchitis.

Lilia, my comrade educator, gave me private lessons accelerating my third-grade studies, and Grandma Lala took me to Juana the dressmaker.

It was exhausting.

"Wait, not that way! Can't you see how the fabric wrinkles and doesn't fall naturally as it should?"

Poor Juana looked at my grandmother, terrified. She shook her head, her thick lips full of pins and needles that my grandmother commandeered along the hems and tucks, the way a brigadier general deploys his men.

The Sprite and I said good-bye to several of Fidel's sisters whom she was friends with: Agustina, who had grand pianos in her home because her husband was a concert pianist, but no furniture—she was very poor; Angelita, who lived on an enormous farm in Capdevilla with her son, Mayito; and Juanita, who became a worm around that time.

I spent a whole farewell afternoon with my poet uncle, Pedro Emilio, who always liked having me visit on Sundays to help him finish his poems.

It wrenched my heart saying good-bye to my Tata, and then to my dearest friends, Ivette and Tota la Gorda.

I boarded the plane with my fatalism in full bloom but with resignation. Even though I was on my way to the place where storks come from, with babies hanging from their beaks, and where once upon a time princes and kings lived in enormous castles and oppressed their people so much that the guillotine had to be invented for them.

On our plane, the Sprite was not the only one on her way to steal secrets. A baker's dozen of bronze-skinned youths were also on board, with the Parisian mission of extracting the secrets of fermentation in the making of yogurt and cheese, something Fidel urgently needed.

Everybody had a mission except me. I was only seeking to satisfy the yearnings of my secret inner karma. This did not take long.

"Anything I can bring you? A soda?" It was a cute young flight attendant, but I was feeling sicker by the minute.

"No, thank you. I have a lump here on my neck, and it hurts a lot."

"Wow! That has to be the mumps! I can't get close to you!"

The young man was wasting his talent as a diagnostician by serving sandwiches in the air, because he was dead right. The next day I was in bed in Madrid, my face deformed, and running a fever fit for a horse. It was the first time in my life that I had been sick without Tata. Standing there in front of my bed, the Sprite didn't know what to do.

The worst was yet to come. To take my temperature, the nurse wanted to stick the thermometer in my behind! My God, how could they be such pigs! Who could have thought of such a thing?

Each person then must carry his or her own, I suppose, for it's one thing to share it if you put it under your arm, but to take it from one behind to the other? And the thermometer wasn't all; I think they did the same thing with aspirins!

Thank goodness the Sprite was incapable of touching me so intimately. Anyway, I was glad Tata wasn't around, because she wouldn't have listened to my objections. So I hid the arsenal of suppositories under my pillow and enjoyed my monumental, mumpsy face.


*The city of Paris* was pretty, but that cumbersome, rusty junk structure in the middle of it spoiled everything. This could not be said in the presence of any French citizen, because the French are not patient people. People say it was by eating a lot of snails that the French succeeded in imposing their menus and their ineffable manners on the whole world.

We stayed at the Hotel des Acacias, on the Rue des Acacias. We had no shower in our room, and no bidet at all, so for personal cleanliness the Sprite bought us a contraption for intestinal enemas that dispensed water when hung from the wall.

She also had to buy me some clothes. She wanted me to look elegant without spending much, so she decided everything had to combine with everything else. Shades of brown, green, blue, and dark gray might blend very well, but they look dead, sad, burnt. And there they were again, a pair of two-tone shoes!

After choosing my clothes, she chose a *hábitat* on Avenue Foch, near the embassy. She rented it from a marchioness who was obviously into body hygiene, because the bathroom was the largest room in the house.

Once installed in Paris, the Sprite chose a hobby for me, because she said that the mind must be kept busy.

"And what is a hobby?"

"A hobby is something we do in our free time. You should collect stamps. It's very interesting. Begin by collecting those with flowers and flags."

How horrible! Let's not forget her complaining that Lala Natica had always insisted on choosing her shoes and handbags until she got married.

Next, she said she had chosen a school for me.

"The name is Pension Clair Matin, and it's about fifteen miles from Paris. I'll take you there tomorrow."

I didn't dare ask her how I was going to travel back and forth so far every day.

By train, of course! Really fast. And that's how we got to Saint-Germain-en-Laye on a Sunday before sunset. The Sprite was carrying a little wicker suitcase, the size of a large handbag.

The pension faced a large, gray wall with a sign that read "Danger."

"What does that mean?"

"It means, Don't get close."

My aura turned grayer than the wall, and I felt the impending doom on my back.

The two owners of the pension—one a chubby, white-haired woman with a ruddy complexion, and the other a woman hard and dry like a woody grapevine shoot—were already waiting for the Sprite.

She handed my small suitcase to a girl with a sullen expression, who said something to me in those gargling sounds everybody made around here.

"I'm not going to sleep here, am I? Tell me, Mommy. Mommy, please!"

"Go with Michelle, dear. There is nothing else we can do."

Of course there was. She could not tell me that there were no schools closer to that bathroom where we lived!

The only thing I managed to get from her was the promise to come for me the following Saturday so that I could spend the weekend with her.

Michelle dragged me to a room with three beds. I was still throwing a tantrum, and her patience was running short. She made my head turn with the first slap on my face in my entire life.

I cried until my soul ran dry.

When the Sprite returned the following weekend, I had already made my round-trip between good and evil, and had forgiven her.


*A good routine can* lift the burden of sorrow. I attended classes at a public school every day, which was miles away. Since there were no classes on Thursday, *Vive la France!,* that was the day set for the weekly bath with Tamara in the big tub, which we left really dirty after use, with a thick gray mix of caked soap and dirt. I had to go along with this because if they ever caught me taking a bath without permission, they made my bottom red hot.

I wrote to the Sprite each and every day, tears smudging the ink of my pleas. Her replies came to me in envelopes with stamps of flowers and flags for my collection. In her heart there was no room for anything but the chemical industry.

One day De Gaulle came to town and the children went to welcome him and throw him flowers. As he went by shaking hands, I held his left hand. I felt like a hero. Back at the pension, I proudly told my story, but they made fun of me.

"A Communist shaking hands with De Gaulle?"

This didn't bother me. He had touched my left hand.

Being made fun of and having to defend Communism and poor Fidel from all the jokes also became a routine for me.

The jokes were puns on his name, and they made fun of his evergreen uniform.

People would stop the Sprite on the street to ask her if I was Charlie Chaplin's daughter. I resembled Geraldine, they said. It seems that Chaplin had had children with some beautiful American women. The Sprite answered that my father was a far more important clown than Chaplin. This only served to confuse me, since I never saw Daddy Orlando dressed as a clown.

At the pension I was forced to eat artichokes and rhubarb preserves, even though they made me throw up. It didn't matter how battered my spirit, my identity, and my confidence were, because I lived only for my weekends with the Sprite, who was busy breaking hearts in Paris. She had a whole collection of beaux of all ages and nationalities after her all the time. That made me take advantage of her Italian suitor, Egidio, an industrialist from Milan who sent her dozens of roses and gave me crisp one-hundred-franc big bills in silk purses, provided I put the Sprite on the phone, or opened the door for him when she pretended not to be home. I even pressured her a little bit into allowing him to love her, but she did not want to.

"Whenever he takes me by the waist, his hand trembles so, my stomach turns."

Thanks to Egidio's generosity, I accumulated a few good things to bring back with me, like a giant plastic swimming pool for the garden and a tent canopy with white and blue stripes to take to the beach at Santa María del Mar on weekends. Also a chemistry set with test tubes, compounds, and burner, and a biology set with slides, a slide holder, and a microscope.

The end of the year was wonderful. Lala Natica appeared one day at the pension and the Sprite took all of us in her Mercedes-Benz, which had crossed the ocean in a ship and was sporting a brand-new diplomatic license plate, all the way to Normandy. Her mission there was to convince André Voisin, a scientist who had invented an intensive method for raising sheep, to go to Cuba at Fidel's invitation and try his method with Cuban cows.

The Sprite suddenly cut our vacation short.

There were two reasons: another bombing threat on the Island, and a vicious rumor. It was being said that she was going to ask France for political asylum, together with her mother and daughter. Her integrity could not allow this, particularly at a time when Cuban diplomats abroad, like Guillermo Cabrera Infante in London, were asking for asylum. She could not tolerate being compared, even in thought, with the traitors. Since she could not return to Cuba without completing her chemical espionage mission, what better way to shut those damned people up—and force them to stuff their words right down their own throats—than to send her mother and daughter back to Cuba.

My nightmare was suddenly over, and I began to have faith in miracles again.

*What a blessing to* be able to embrace again my Tata *chérie*! And to recover her sweet habit of putting my shoes on while I was still in bed in order to bring me out of the pleasures of sleep slowly.

Fidel came to pick up his presents the first night we got back. We had brought two cut-crystal pistols filled with whiskey, some papers, and a second suitcase full of cheese, because the first one the Sprite had sent ended up in the garden of the historian Le Riverend and was blasted open by secret agents. Poor man, he had sent for them when the suitcase started to bulge and stink. I imagined a whole battalion of Gallic worms deployed on the grass. They must have quickly opened their parasols when the Island's torrid sun caught them by surprise.

I showed Fidel how to play French jacks, which consist of knucklebones and no ball. We played on the floor. I then took out my microscope and test tubes, with all the equipment that would launch me in my medical career. He wanted to know where I had gotten the money for it. He loved the story of how the Italian industrialist had to pay dearly for his passion for the Sprite.

"But you're going to study industrial chemistry. Remember that!"

I did not like that idea at all, but I would rather have died than annoy him. I even thought that he had sent us to France as some kind of punishment for all those letters, my stories about that awful woman, La China, who used to drag people out of their homes, and my complaints about children in jail.

Not again! I had to be sweet to him, like the Sprite, or like the courtesans to the kings of France, all smiles and no mention ever of any affairs of state. When he was in the mood for some affection, he sat comfortably on the sofa and demanded his manicure.

Since he did not like his *café con leche* in a cup, I brought it to him in a tall, fat glass. Then he unbuttoned his uniform and relaxed, peacefully puffing at his cigar.

I liked to sit on his lap. The Sprite's friends didn't like me to do that. It made them feel uncomfortable, but not him.

We spent some good times together late at night during the five months the Sprite was completing her French mission. I loved to be able to stay awake and wait for him, but Lala Natica hated these midnight visits. Fidel is a nocturnal being.

"That man doesn't have one single good habit!"


*Trouble began when I* returned to school—me, so well bred, so know-it-all, raising my hand to ask for permission, while the teacher wondered if I had some kind of epilepsy or what. The other children asked me all the time whether I had a cold, because I still had traces of French stuck in my throat.

That lasted for weeks. Less time than it took me to realize that I was now even more different than before I left. A little bit of me was going to stay behind forever, thousands of miles across the sea, as if over there in France an annoying second-rate spirit had gotten into me. The songs of Jacques Brel and of Brassens, or the fables of La Fontaine, kept popping into my head when I was supposed to be chanting in chorus the Pioneer slogans.

I was now in the fifth grade, having skipped the fourth. I did not understand anything, not even Cuban history and geography, which were easy. Everything had been rewritten, changed. The new official version of history, by Le Riverend, did a somersault, starting from the times when the Taíno and Guanatebey Indians were being impaled and burned by the savages of Christianization, and rolling directly up to the times of Fidel's Revolutionary accomplishments and the bad influence of Imperialism. Cuban history had a new beginning. It started with the Rebel attack on the Moncada barracks.

But how could I take that historian seriously? He had ordered the execution by firing squad of a suitcase full of cheese.

We now had to memorize all the places on the map where Fidel and his Rebel Army had been, and we learned that Núñez Jiménez alone seemed to have discovered the origin of our island: a mound of bird droppings and bits of garbage that the tides and the Gulf Stream had accumulated here in this navel, in this key location between continents.

Fidel kept speaking on television as usual, but now he only talked about "artificial insemination." It was a very strange thing.

The Sprite had convinced André Voisin to come to Cuba. The poor old man, received and celebrated by our Leader, was so impressed when he arrived that his heart stopped instantly. His widow, who by government invitation travels every year to visit him at the Cementerio de Colón, says that her husband died of joy.

Fidel has the strange power to impact those around him. When he embarked on a project to produce a new breed of cattle, he intended to use this power. He wanted to create a national cow. The Canadian Holstein crossbred with the zebu from India, he said, had more meat and tolerated the climate better. Fidel spoke about genetics for hours, keeping the masses in awe of the genius who had now created breeds F1, F2, and F3—the "F" stood for "Fidel"—and these new cattle were the future source of meat for our people. One could quietly be watching the Russian cartoons of Old Jotavich on television when suddenly there was a cow on the screen being "inseminated by Cuban technicians who received their diplomas in the Soviet Union." They would lift her tail and stick a whole gloved arm into her ass, all the way to the shoulder. The beast let out a horrendous moo, and they pulled the bloody arm out of her.

And I was complaining about French thermometers.

That and not much more is what my friends were learning. That and not much more is what we could share. I could not lend my friends my Barbie dolls. They were so capitalist that I was embarrassed. I could not lend them the many Tintin and Club des Cinq books I had brought. They were in another language.

It's bad for a child not to be like the others. Thank God I had other resources. I set up a *laboratoire* in the *chauffeur*'s room on top of the *garage*. That was my refuge. There, with my physiology book I could find sirenomelus, simpus dipus, pygopagus, cephalothoracopagus, and other abnormal fetuses, along with the first recorded medical case of a man with milk in his breasts, and many more with breasts but no milk. This disease, I learned, was called gynecomastia.

*It took five months* after I came back for the Sprite to return from France with the satisfaction of having carried out her mission. Almost a master of industrial chemistry. She had taken care while in Paris of the well-being of the bronze-skinned cheesemakers, and even of Pello el Afrocán's orchestra, so that they would not be looked down on as a Communist musical trifle. She had dug André Voisin out of the depths of Normandy for Fidel's pleasure and the contentment of Cuban cows, who were enjoying uninterrupted orgies of hay thanks to Voisin's theory of "intensive breeding." I still don't understand why Fidel didn't come back home as soon as the Sprite arrived. There was no firewater left to make witchcraft invocations. I had to burn the only three hairs from his beard that I had saved, to see if they worked miracles like those of Old Jotavich, but it was of no use. More than eight months went by before he came home to pick up the garlands of the Sprite's defeat. Of all the fancy Italian cheeses, coming from even farther away than France, that had filled the third and last suitcase she imported to the Island to inspire those apprentice cheesemakers she had helped in Paris, there was nothing left. Not even the smell.

That night when Fidel came, I left them alone, because she certainly had not one, but a thousand commentaries for each late night she had stayed up waiting for his visit. She was anguished because she had no job. There was not a soul in the country who dared to hire her without a word from Fidel.

The following day she had two pieces of news:

"Fidel has named me chief of documentation and information at the Centro Nacional de Investigaciones Científicas. And I am going to straighten out my life," she told Tata.

She was now in charge of the library of CNIC.

But it seems that it is easier to straighten out your life if you have a husband. Soon after that she got one. He was very good-looking, but he seemed to disappear into the woodwork. Like a good male chameleon, he took on the color of the furniture in the living room, which is where I remember him because one afternoon I saw him there eating a slice of fresh watermelon, and the red of the melon made him visible.

They were divorced in a year. She could now devote her time to her job.

The Sprite used to go from one meeting to the next. She was obsessed with an obscure conspiracy directed by Celia Sánchez against her being elected to membership in the Communist Party. To talk to the Sprite, I had to go visit her at work.

The first thing I saw, as I came into her office, was a pregnant black woman, her secretary, feet up, sleeping on a sofa. My mother was going from her own desk to her secretary's, alternately sitting at each to do the work of both, and with a finger to her lips, asking for silence to respect the woman's sleep.

I liked the genetics laboratory at CNIC, better known as the Circus, "because where else can you find a hunchback, a one-legged man, and a dwarf?" as the scientific staff used to say jokingly about itself.

There was a large tank full of abnormal fetuses all sealed with wax in wide-mouth jars. They let me pick whichever ones I wanted and take them with me to the room above the garage, where I subjected them to tests of my invention. They were my homunculi, my succubi, and my incubi.

Che's best friend, Dr. Granados, made me his assistant. He was working on an experiment to raise fatter rabbits. Having anesthetized them, he tied them to the operating table and, with an electrode, destroyed the center of satiety in their cerebellum.

That method proved to be too expensive, he was told, and most of the rabbits, instead of getting fat until they looked like dogs, stayed asleep forever. It was very lucky, I thought, that Che's doctor friend had been assigned to work on rabbits and not people.

*One morning, an invitation* from the Provincial School of Ballet reached my class.

When I was accepted, the best part of my life began.

We studied languages and music and, on weekends, attended performances of the Ballet Alicia Alonso.

We didn't have to march or learn slogans, and the school uniform was not Mao style, but a black skirt with a white blouse.

I grew tall and skinny; my head was covered with very tight, tiny braids. I learned to turn the tips of my feet out so that I could walk like Charlie Chaplin. I also became very silly, which is what happens to all children who are inspired to follow a particular vocation early in life.

At the Provincial School of Ballet, I was in wonderland. Tata came at noon with lunch, adamant about not letting me eat cold food prepared in the morning. She did this even though she had to suffer the torture of the overcrowded city buses.

Near the school was the Coppelia ice cream parlor. It was another of Celia Sánchez's ideas. You had to stand in line for hours because it was the only one in the country. People came from far away in the provinces to try the ice cream, but it was worth it. With fifty-four flavors, there was even an avocado ice cream, and a tomato ice cream. Amazing.

Around this same time my heart turned poet, and since reality is unforeseeable, I was not the only one to be surprised. The Sprite almost fell over backward. The neologisms I had brought from France were to blame, and all the sad loneliness that I carried deep in my soul.

I wanted my mother and me to share something nice and I gave her my opera prima.

"I did this for you, Mom."

She was impressed. So much so that she showed the poem to her friends the psychedelic painters, the same ones who had desecrated with well-intentioned abstract pointillism almost all of the walls and much of the furniture in our house. They treated the Sprite as their Maecenas. They exerted their influence and had my poem published in the weekly *Pionero,* the rag that came out on Sundays.

One Sunday my friend Tota la Gorda woke me up with a surge of unconditional love, stomping up the stairs to my room with the same timeless fury of troglodytes on the attack.

"Alina! Alina! My truest bluest friend, wake up! You are in the *Pionero,* photo and all! Oh, my precious skinny one!" (How I would love to hear those words now, at this point of my advanced age!)

And she jumped on top of me.

I felt a tingling sensation running from my toes all the way up to my belly and then up to my head, totally overwhelming me. I exploded, laughing and crying at the same time. Even though this might seem like the description of an orgasm, it was really a paroxysm of anguish.

Joy and sadness meet somewhere, and my natural reserve almost killed me the morning the Sprite sprang this surprise on me. It made me feel that all my trusting, intimate affection had been betrayed, desecrated.

The photograph that I saw in the newspaper that morning had been taken by Alberto Korda during one of those wretched afternoons for which Fidel had sent invitations out to hear him at close range as he addressed the country. How tired and stupid I looked!

But that was not the worst. The worst was my biographical note. "Alina speaks French and plays with her dolls. . . ." The perfect idiot! I thought. And very petite bourgeoise besides.

A cold determination overpowered me. I'm never going back to school, and I'm just going to tell the Sprite, and that's that. I ran downstairs.

"Tata! Tata! Look what my mother has done to me! Look!"

Tata glanced at the newspaper.

"Well, and so what?"

My tragedy did not touch her unflappable notions about life.

The Sprite came home late in the afternoon in a gingham dress with tiny red and white checks, pockets highlighting her breasts, and circular skirt with a white belt. Pure fifties paraphernalia. She looked like a fashion model.

She got out of her Mercedes, and there I was, in total harmony with Guarapo, our dog, whose barking in anticipation always coincided with my own happy premonition that she was coming home at last.

The sneak! She had been keeping the news of that article from me for about a month. I escorted her in strict formality to her sitting room, put some background music on, and sat her in Fidel's recliner, where she normally only sat when she wanted to get into esoteric communication with him.

"I have to talk to you," I said. Oh, forbidden words! The poor soul, the last thing she needed was to come home and have to sit down and listen to me, *my sweetie pie, my child, but I am so tired . . .*

"Why? Why did you do this terrible thing to me? How come you never told me?"

"Oh, Alina, you're right. I should have told you before, my baby, but I didn't want to be the one to tell you."

"Oh, no? And it had to be Tota la Gorda? Who else knew?"

"How could I know? A lot of people, I guess."

"Great! So you told the whole world but me!"

"Try to understand me, Alina. I was hoping Fidel would tell you. He hasn't come to our house for so long. . . . I thought he was about to show up."

Great! Even the Comandante knew about my poetic peccadillo! At this rate, I was on my way to get the prize for poetry from Casa de las Américas.

"I will *never* forgive you for this."

"Don't do this to your mommy, please. I won't get up from this chair, and you won't move either until I've told you everything."


*This is what the* Sprite told me:

"You still remember our house at Fifteenth Street and Fourth, don't you? We had lots of things. We were well off, with nothing to worry about. Natalie was growing up, healthy and beautiful. I was working at Esso Standard Oil. I could have stayed home and spent my time playing bridge and tennis and sipping cocktails, like most of my friends, who didn't know how to do anything else, nor did they care to. But you know me. I can't stand not feeling useful. In school, you've heard about Batista, the army sergeant who was moving up until he forced himself in as president against the will of the Cuban people. Well, even before he assumed power, bodies were appearing in the streets.

"With his control of the military, he put an end to civil rights. Strikes even ended in bloodshed.

"One morning, there was a dead boy lying in front of our house. Batista's henchmen had assassinated him. But first, they had torn him apart.

"I think that opened my eyes, because I began to see more clearly that most people lived without dreams, and thousands of children grew up without any hope of getting out of poverty.

"We were hearing a lot about Eduardo Chibás by then. He was a man of honor who wanted to do something for Cuba and had a wonderful slogan: 'Integrity against Money.' He claimed that people in government should not get rich by abusing others or stealing from the people. Chibás founded the Orthodox Party and would have been a good president. He warned us against Batista's growing powers.

"Eddie Chibás's had a radio program. One evening he publicly accused a cabinet minister of stealing money from the people, and promised to offer proof. He couldn't do it, so, out of a sense of honor, he committed suicide. That was in August, 1951. I listened to his program the night he shot himself.

"That night I couldn't sleep. The next morning at dawn, I dressed in black and went to the radio station. There was blood everywhere. It was the blood of Chibás's integrity. I touched it. I looked at my bloody hands and knew that unless I found a way to fight injustice, I would feel guilty all my life.

"I had to get to my office at Esso. On the way I stopped at a locksmith's and had three copies of my house key made. They were for the three most promising leaders of the Orthodox Party. One of the copies was for their candidate for the House, a young man who replaced Chibás in his radio program. It was Fidel. I didn't know any of them, but I wanted to make sure they knew my home was at their disposal, and that I was willing to help them and their families.

"Fidel thanked me for the gesture. Not in person, of course. He also gave me the radio band and time that I could listen to him. I remember trying the whole dial for a long time and not finding him. On the tenth of March, 1952, Batista staged a coup d'état and made himself president of Cuba. He was a usurper and an assassin, and the Cuban people felt the duty to fight him. I joined a clandestine organization of women, Mujeres Martianas, but we could do very little.

"Fidel was busy establishing himself as Chibás's successor in the Orthodox Party. That same year we were introduced. There was a public protest on the twenty-seventh of November, the anniversary of the execution [in 1871] of eight medical students accused of desecrating the tomb of a Spanish military officer, and in commemoration of another officer, Federico Capdevilla, who broke his sword when he found out about this atrocity. At this protest, the police tried to stop our actions by cutting the power. I was there with the Mujeres Martianas, and had no idea that Fidel was going to take part in this demonstration as well. He was standing on the grand staircase of the University of Havana when I first met him.

"We laughed a lot at this first meeting, and he repeated his thanks for my gesture with the key. He was full of vital energy, and I found him very attractive.

"I next heard about him in March of 1953. I remember, because around that time I had lost my second pregnancy. It was going to be a boy. Or maybe it was you, who wanted to be born earlier. Only a woman can ever understand this kind of sadness. You can't understand it yet. I was very sad and depressed.

"Fidel then let me know, very humbly, that he was interested in visiting our house. I told him that Orlando would be back from work after five.

"It didn't take him long to show up. He was like a visionary, saying that we had to use violence to get Batista out of power because that was how he had grabbed power, and that we needed an innovative revolutionary movement. He didn't understand the passivity of our traditional leaders, who did not represent the Cuban fighting spirit, nor that of our forbears the mambises. I invited him for dinner.

"Chucha prepared her first menu for us: pineapple-glazed ham broiled in butter and brown sugar, mashed potatoes, and mixed vegetables.

"Fidel left that night after dinner with all the money that we had at home, and Orlando considered the chapter closed. Not me. I felt my horizon had expanded. I had found a way to fight for my convictions."

"But, Mommy, why are you telling me all this story? What does all of this have to do with my poem?"

"What poem?"

"The poem that was for you alone, and you let it be printed in that damn *Pionero*!"

"Oh, honey, it seems we are talking about different things!"

Well, of course! That happens when one has fixed ideas.

"But let me finish my story. And then I'll give you all the explanations you want.

"Fidel started to visit our house more and more frequently. Those were dangerous times. Some of the young people with him didn't even make it through that conspiratorial stage alive. I hosted them and didn't meddle, but then they began to consult me. The Movimiento 26 de Julio was created right before my eyes. And so I began to accompany them during negotiations and contacts. Then one day Fidel asked me to choose the music to be broadcast by the Cadena Oriental de Radio on the day the Rebels were going to attack the Moncada barracks. He wanted music that would arouse people. He wanted revolutionary music, because there could be loss of life. I spent whole afternoons at the listening booth in Radiocentro. I recorded some Beethoven, Prokofiev, Mahler, Kodály, Dvořák, Berlioz, and the national anthem, besides the 'Himno Invasor' from the War of Independence, and the 'Ultimo Aldabonazo' (Last knock on the door) from Chibás's last radio program.

I asked one of the boys one afternoon to teach me how to fold the flag. The flag I had was the same one with the black band that was on my terrace when Chibás died.

" 'Hey, why don't you give it to us? We'll fly it in Santiago on the day of our action. We'll take it with us and it will be as if you were there.'

"I had a mezzanine built in our house at Fifteenth Street and Fourth, that's where all the weapons for the assault were hidden.

"Fidel called me one last time to ask for the recorded music and to hand me a manifesto that I was to distribute among political personalities and press reporters at the same time the attack on the Moncada was taking place.

" 'People should know the reasons for our struggle,' he told me, and then asked me not to distribute the manifestos before five-fifteen A.M. on Sunday, July 26, 1953. He wanted to have the two actions synchronized.

"Nobody, Alina, not even the attackers, knew that the raid was going to be an assault on one of the tyrant's main army posts. Fidel had told them it was a weekend military exercise. The only ones who knew were his brother Raúl, who was going to attack an army post in Bayamo at the same time; Fidel's personal assistant, José Luis Tasende, who died in the attack; and myself.

"That morning I woke up Orlando to tell him I was running an errand for the Movement and would be back in three hours. I went to distribute the leaflets.

"Then, at the home of the editor-in-chief of *Prensa Libre,* I learned the assault had failed.

"I was suddenly desperate. I ran to our parish church in the Vedado and went to confession with Father Hidalgo and took Communion. I prayed for the dead.

"Orlando met me later at the Biltmore Country Club, as we had agreed. We decided to stay there for the afternoon.

"You can't imagine my anguish during the days that followed. My helplessness, my fear. We knew that the survivors were seeking refuge in the mountains of Oriente, in the Sierra Maestra. But what was going to happen to me?

"Many of the men had visited me at home. I had pawned my jewels to pay for the necessary weapons. Surely somebody must have taken note of all this.

"You would never guess it, just to look at her, but Lala Natica became my greatest concern. To help me, she had been storing arms and documents. For days she traveled all the way to Santiago on an uncomfortable, rickety train. She said she felt the need to know whether her daughter had to go into exile because of the alarming rumors she had heard. It took her four days to get there. And you don't have to believe this, but she had lost all her hair. In spite of that, I refused to go anywhere without Fidel's instructions.

"Orlando and I started going to the movies just to see the newsreels. We did see a few scenes from the events in Santiago, like a soldier bending over a suitcase and taking out and waving a flag with a black band: it was my flag. It wasn't until years later that I found out that another soldier had sold two books that belonged to me, which had my full name and even my home address. It was his cruel selection of a buyer that saved my life, because the buyer was, of all people, Abel Santamaría's mother. Her son, Fidel's second in command at the Moncada assault, had his eyes gouged out before he was killed by government henchmen. My books and my flag were then kept out of the investigation and I was not directly implicated in the attack. I was really lucky.

"The boys who had not been killed were captured in a few days and taken to court. You have studied *History Will Absolve Me* in school. It was Fidel's brilliant self-defense in that trial.

"Fidel was sentenced to prison, and I didn't hear from him until November, four months later. He was serving his sentence in the Presidio Modelo on the Isle of Pines. I sent him the same menu he had been served at dinner with us, pineapple-glazed ham. It was a way of saying that there was still a place set for him in our home.

"I had another idea, perhaps because I knew how Lina, Fidel's mother, must have felt. I wrote her a short, anonymous letter. It began 'To Lina' [*A Lina*], and that's where your name comes from: A-lina. Wait, I'll show it to you."

She got up and floated to her room. She came back with a miniature safe, and took out three little packets of envelopes tied with ribbons of different colors.

"These are miscellaneous letters. These are from Raúl. And these,
from Fidel."

Fidel's were tied with a pale orange ribbon, and that afternoon I
learned that love was the same orange color that fades at the break of
dawn.

Sitting there, entranced with this story of heroic Sprites, I would
have stopped time. I finally understood why my mother seemed to go
through life in a daze. It had to be terribly difficult for her to keep all
those details from such a long time ago, even before I was born.

Then she read:

I am taking the liberty of writing these lines because I know you
must be going through anguished and terrible times, and I think
that perhaps a few words of encouragement that you did not expect could help you find peace in your soul, and more pride for
your son Fidel. I don't know how you feel about him at this moment, but I am sure that, as you have always done, you are contin-
uing to give him the moral and emotional support that only a
mother can offer in such trying circumstances. Though I never met
you or your husband, or Myrta or your other sons, I am thinking
about all of you.

"At the beginning of November, I received a letter from Fidel himself.
It was censored. Did you know that all letters from prisoners are read
before being mailed? I have it here. Look, it's this one.

Dear Naty:
Affectionate greetings from my prison cell. I love you and I am always thinking of you. Though you haven't written in a long time.

I am keeping, and will always keep, the tender letter you wrote
to my mother.

If you have had to suffer on my account for any reason, please
know that I would gladly offer my life for your honor and your
well-being. What people think should not matter to us; the only

thing that counts is what we know in our conscience. There are things in life that endure despite our daily miseries. And there are everlasting things, such as the image I have of you, so indelible that it will accompany me to my grave.

Yours always,
Fidel

"That is how we began a beautiful exchange of letters, Alina. They were like doves, invincible carriers of peace and joy from one to the other. Look at this other one:

Dear Naty,
I am answering your last letter right away, though I know it will not be in the mail until Monday. The best way is to tell you whatever I feel, without much thinking or organizing, spontaneously, under the fresh impression of your bright thoughts and the charm, always new, of your words. Today I feel like writing to you freely, and being unable to do so depresses me greatly. These lines are prisoners and yearn to be free, just like the one who is writing them. Perhaps I am feeling this limitation more strongly than usual, because today is like one of those days when, feeling frustrated, anxious, or sad, I would go to your house, where my feet would unconsciously take me. Because there I could always find joy, relaxation, and inner peace.

In the warm welcome I invariably received at your home . . . in the presence of a spirit full of life and of noble feelings, I turned into joy and encouragement precisely those hours that, instants before, were being spent on fighting hopelessness, so often brought about by the darker side of human nature. . . .

Naty, what a formidable school this prison is! It is here that I am forging my vision of the world and can complete the task of giving my life purpose. I don't know whether it will be brief or long, barren or productive. But I do feel my commitment to sacrifice and struggle growing stronger. I despise an existence that depends solely on the miserable trifles of one's own comfort and greed. I don't abjure my fate, however, nor do my comrades, each of whom has sacrificed the small world of his personal life to the great world of ideas. The day will come when these anguished times will be remembered with joy: tomorrow, when dark clouds dissolve, the sun will come out, the dead will rise to their places of honor, and a flutter of wings will be heard all over the Cuban skies. Have you noticed how I am getting to the end of my paper, and every paragraph and every line from your so very interesting letter is still unanswered? I promise you this time that in order now to answer you quickly, I'll leave that for my next. . . . I don't want my letters to become a headache for you, which is what it seems to me is happening, judging by the circumstances of time and place in which you write to me.

The censor who checks our correspondence is a polite, kind, and knowledgeable young man. This is the fair and honest concept I have of him.

Will this get to you by Christmas Eve? If you are truly loyal, you will not completely forget me, and at dinnertime you will have a glass of wine in my name, and I will be with you. He who loves does not forget.

Fidel

"I became his eyes and ears for the world outside. I tried to give him a taste of all the flavors of life: a few grains of sand from the beach; a kaleidoscope, to give some color to that gray shadow that a jail cell must be. He would sometimes glue a wing of some lost butterfly to his letter. I tried to fill his time. I would provoke him to reflect and open up, just as a teacher does with a good student, or a mother with a son suffering from a long illness. I gave him questions to ponder. I kept sending him carefully selected readings and would challenge him to write his comments. This will give you an idea of how he answered me."

You ask me if Rolland could have been equally great had he been born in the seventeenth century. Do you think I would have written letters like this had I not met you? . . . Human thought is irremediably conditioned by its circumstances. For a political genius, I daresay thought depends exclusively on circumstance. During the time of Catherine the Great, Lenin would have been, at best, a diligent defender of the Russian bourgeoisie; if José Martí had lived during the English occupation of Havana, he would have defended Spain's national flag together with his father; Napoleon, Mirabeau, Danton, Robespierre: what else would they have been in the time of Charlemagne but humble servers of the glebe or anonymous dwellers in some remote feudal castle? Julius Caesar's crossing of the Rubicon could never have taken place during the early years of the Republic, before the intense class struggle that shook Rome reached a critical point and the great plebeian party developed, a situation that required, and therefore made possible, its access to power. . . . On this issue, it has always interested me how it came about that the revolutionary French had such a large Roman influence, until reading for you one day about the history of French literature, I found out that Amyot, the French writer of the sixteenth century, had translated from the Latin *Parallel Lives* and *Moralia,* by Plutarch, whose celebration of the great men and the great stages of Greece and Rome served as reference point two centuries later for the protagonists of the Great Revolution. But what becomes evident to the political genius is not so clear to the artistic genius. I am referring to Victor Hugo. The concept of eternity is intrinsic in the poet and in the artist. And it is eternity which lends these geniuses their irreducible greatness. The concept of timelessness found in art is alien to the concept of progress. It might have, and it has, certain duties with respect to progress; but it does not depend on it. It does not depend on any of the possibilities of perfectibility in the future, or on any linguistic development, or on the death or birth of any language. Containing within itself what is immeasurable and innumerable, this timelessness cannot be dominated by any other argument and it is equally pure, equally complete, equally sidereal, equally divine whether in the midst of full-blown savagery or of advanced civilization. It is beauty, variable according to the nature of the creative genius, but always equal to itself: supreme!

Rolland could have been born half a century earlier and be as brilliant as Balzac or Victor Hugo; or a half century before that, and have emulated the character of a Voltaire, but he would have been the exponent of ideas different from those of this century, in the same way that I would say other things if I were writing to another woman. . . .

Oh, my God . . . What a long story this was turning out to be. In all truth, I didn't need so much lyric torture to capture what was being suggested to my imagination, namely that they had been very good friends. But at this point there was no stopping Naty. Out of boredom and drowsiness, I began to nod off, and since that evening, it has been impossible for me to ever read the letters the Comandante sent Naty from jail, which are many. Besides, after all this superlative poetic virtuosity, how could I go back to whining about my miserable little poem?

Since then it's been very difficult for me to write poetry at all, or to accept the idea that one must produce perfumed shit for people even when that isn't always possible.

I was looking at the bunch of Fidel's letters, which she was so eager to show me, when she reached over and took out the "miscellaneous" one instead. The best poetry, it seems, still lay ahead. This time the creation was hers.

Dear Fidel:
I am writing you under the wonderful and sweet impression left with me by your last four letters. How I wish it were possible to free my time and my mind from so much interference and to answer each one of them as you deserve! In every sense I feel very small beside the monumental frame that holds your way of thinking, your ideas, your affection, the breadth of your knowledge. Especially because I find even more monumental the flattering and generous way in which you want to share them, and manage to, with the greatest of ease. You lead me by the hand through History (with a capital H, as in Human Being and Humanity), Philosophy, Literature; you give me a wonderful treasure trove of feelings, of principles; and constantly open new, unexplored, and unexpected horizons for me. And then you pretend, after all this, that I am the one behind your ideas and your actions like an enduring, hidden conscience. No, Fidel, all that richness is in you, and you do not owe it to anyone. You were born with it, and it will die with you. Your desire and ability to share it, that is another story. But I would be totally insincere if I didn't tell you how happy the way

you are makes me, and it would make me very proud if you never changed.

Yours always,

Naty

Had she finished? No. No way. The Sprite needed to add a few more details. She had provided for his wife, Myrta, and his son, Fidelito, so that they had everything they needed while he was in jail. And then what a shock it was when the good censor and very honorable gentleman, Miguel Rives, being so utterly bored in his job on the Isle of Pines, famous for its parrots (now extinct) and its grapefruit (with their citric character, more enduring), got tired of the acidity, of chattering birds and of jailbirds and devised a way of having some fun by switching Fidel's censored letters so that Myrta received the one destined for the Sprite, and vice versa.

As a result, an offended Myrta phoned the Sprite to reclaim the piece of epistolary communication that was rightfully hers. It was forwarded to her unopened in the next mail; but the nature of the feelings manifested in the letter that the wife had already received and read provoked in her such deep sadness that she passed it around for her friends to read.

Since the Sprite's good name was at issue, the semantic flow and the sending of books and miscellaneous packages to Fidel had to stop right then and there. She also sat down to write Daddy Orlando a letter, because things can be better expressed in writing. She told him that, though there was nothing yet between her and Fidel, she had fallen helplessly in love with him.

She went on to tell me that Fidel was given amnesty after that. His first move after his release had been to go see her at her office. He had been allowed to stay in Havana for only a brief period of time before leaving for exile in Mexico. He took her to a Vedado apartment, which Aunt Lidia Perfidia had rented, but since it wasn't proper for them to be alone in it, Perfidia had also rented the one next door. There they met whenever possible during May and June.

And that was when and where I was conceived.

For seven months I persistently tried to get out ahead of time. Naty had to have absolute rest, she said. To occupy herself, she would look for press clippings to send to him, and made all sorts of animals out of Japanese paper. Origami, I think they are called. She told me that this had been the best time of her life.

"A few days after you were born I sent Fidel, who was in Mexico already, a photo and a little ribbon from your first clothes. I was told he felt happy and sentimental, and that was when he sent you those earrings that you lost in Paris, and some silver things for me with a note telling me how happy he was. I went back to work, and Fidel's messages became less frequent, while rumors increased about his romance with someone by the name of Isabel."

The thought of this betrayal made her eyes turn a desolate green, as vivid as the moment she was reliving in her memory.

"I could not just leave, go with you to Mexico, and abandon Natalie. Nor was Fidel in a position to be with a woman and a newborn baby. He was about ready to board that beat-up yacht in which he attempted to invade the Island. I had no word from him until February 1957! By then he was already in the Sierra Maestra. He sent me as a souvenir two .75-caliber shells."

When the Sprite finished her fairy tale, I had to pick up my lower jaw, which had dropped, and the upper one too, because they had both become disjointed at once. How was I going to punish her for hiding things from me when, with her magic wand, she had made me into a princess? I bet nobody else has received such a gift on her tenth birthday!

"Mommy, Mommy, call him. Tell him to come here right away. I have so many things I want to tell him!"

I had a ton of things to tell him. I wanted him to find a solution to all the shortages: of clothes and things like that; of meat, so it could be distributed again through the ration books. I also wanted to ask him to give our Christmas back. And to come live with us. I wanted to let him know how much we really needed him.

"I cannot reach him, Alina."

"Then we'll have someone tell him that I am very sick and that I am dying, or something."

"I can't. I have already sent him many messages, and it's no use. He's not coming. But look, you could indeed write to him. And, at the same time, send him your poem. I'll try to see that he gets it."

So she, the Sprite, transcended her sidereal space to turn into a mother. I didn't feel at all the ominous weight of her lack of understanding that I would come to feel later. She now looked like a tired child, sitting there with shoulders bent under the weight of her confession and of her own life story, dragging her wounded morale and trying to stand tall.

I immediately started on my letter-writing career. The confrontations began the following day.

"Ivette, Fidel is my father."

"I knew it, but my mommy made me promise I wouldn't tell."

Ah, how it hurts when your friends hide things from you.

"Grandma, Mommy told me that Fidel is my father."

"Oh, yes? So what else is new?"

"Tata, my Tata. Fidel is my—"

"So your mother finally let it out? She couldn't keep the dammed secret to herself? She has done enough harm, and now she is bothering you with it."

So I had no father, but wow!, my two mothers made such a fuss! I'll never forget how angry Tata was, and all the things she said to my mother.

She even said she was going to resign and leave us!

Fidel didn't answer my letter with the poem. I sent him another with a green satin slipper, which was already too small for me, from my grasshopper costume. Korda, the photographer, came to report he was very touched by my poem. But from Fidel, not even a little thank you note. I kept writing him letters from a sweet and well-behaved child, from a girl who was a Vanguard student[5] at school, a brave but sad girl. Letters resembling those of a secret, spurned lover, heavily protected with paper clips.

But I could not distract him from his cows and get him to come back to my mother.

# 3

# EL COMANDANTE

*The only sign of* the Comandante came months later, in the person of Pedro Trigo. Pedro "Intrigue" was a hero of the Moncada assault, and the manager of the national airlines, Cubana de Aviación. He was full of invisible seams. It was as if he had been emptied out and refilled with wicked sawdust.

I had to call this emissary of my father "Uncle."

One night I was quickly dressed in my Sunday best and my only pair of shoes. I seemed to be aspiring to become a Chinese empress because for the last three years my feet had been squeezed into the same pair of shoes. I had not been able to get the right size through the ration book.

Pedro Intrigue was exultant. Mommy's gaze was lost in an old dream, her smile painted on by a pre-Raphaelite artist.

"Fidel is sending for you so that you can go and see him play basketball."

Big deal!

It was past ten o'clock at night. I had not been able to watch *The Adventures of Blackbeard* that day on television because Fidel had been making a speech until nine-thirty. He had not answered my thousand and one letters, and had paid no attention to my mom's messages either. And I didn't like basketball. But Tata had gone home already and there was no one around who could help me defend myself, so I got into the Alfa Romeo with Pedro Trigo.

When we arrived in Ciudad Deportiva, Uncle Pedro guided me through the fascinating labyrinth of dressing rooms and then sat me in the first row of the presidential box. You could count the number of spectators on one hand, but crouching and hidden behind the grandstands there were plenty of "securers," policemen dressed in State Security costumes.

The scheduled match was between the Political Bureau team and the Cuban National basketball team.

Suddenly the court was lit up. A collection of ebony statues, of Bantu gods, black, gleaming, and perfect in their shorts and tank tops, advanced to greet the nonexistent public. They grouped on a bench. I was just getting excited when another spectacle, totally different, started. Trotting single file, some whitish, flabby guys, headed by Fidel, made their appearance on the court, running and making the ground shake with the grace of Soviet circus bears.

The one good part was that, instead of shorts, they were wearing long pants in imitation of their Comandante. The bad part was they wore no tank tops.

They trotted around for a while to warm up, their every flaccidity jiggling and dangling.

The one who fascinated me the most was the tallest guy, taller than Fidel, because he had a pair of large breasts, long and aggressive, complete with two enormous, dark nipples.

"Uncle Pedro, who is that man with the white wavy hair and the large, pointy nose?"

"That is Llanusa, the minister of education. He is in charge of all the Cuban schools."

"Uncle Pedro, may we leave now?"

"No way! The Comandante has not even made a basket yet!" Then he winked at me.

To this day I have never seen a stranger match. The National players, instead of stealing the ball from the Jelly Shimmy team, put it in their hands. When it was Fidel's turn to dribble and then try to score, the black players opened a path, like the Red Sea for Moses. If he scored, they would applaud him and scream "Viva!" Anything to break the monotony.

Bloated from drinking too much soda, I waited for the whole thing to end; it was probably past one in the morning when Pedro dragged me off in a rush and sat me on an infirmary gurney. Fidel came in after a little while and behaved as if I were part of the furniture. After three hours of watching that spectacle, with my feet clamped into that pair of torture molds, and having to hold my pee, I was incensed.

He was not the same as when he used to come to our home to visit us in the middle of the night, and I was no longer confused by the unexpected joy of being allowed to stay up late. I wasn't about to ask him for an explanation of his two-year absence; adults lie a lot, anyway.

"How are you?"

"Fine."

"And how's your mother?"

"Fine."

"Tell her I have already talked to Yabur about your name situation, but it's going to take some time because we must change the law."

Bipartisan silence. I knew nothing about this procedure.

"Your mom has a problem. She is much too good. Don't be that good to any man."

The Comandante had just finished giving me this piece of advice when I decided I had to pour out my diagnosis.

"Llanusa, the minister of education . . ."

"Yes, what about him?"

"He suffers from gynecomastia."

"Suffers from what?"

"Gynecomastia. Enlargement of the breasts in men."

"What?"

"His tits are too big for a man. He has to see a doctor!"


*Mommy did not like* me to bring my colored homunculi down from my laboratory, and since my poetry continued to be constipated, I looked around for another productive, fun thing to do that she might like. I grabbed a little board and some paintbrushes. I painted a woman for her with a psychedelic baton, long black hair, and arms reaching up to an orange sun.

"How pretty, Alina. How is it that you can paint so well? It's beautiful. I am going to hang it here in the living room. Why did you show the woman from behind?"

What a silly question!

"Don't you see that in the painting the sun is behind her? How is she going to be able to touch the sun if I paint her from the front?"

The next day, first thing in the morning, we were sitting in Dr. Elsa Praderes's office.

"Elsa, here is Alina. She is painting women from behind. Look!" said Mom, and pulled the little board from an envelope to show the doctor.

I explained again the principles of perspective as perceived by a ten-year-old, or by anybody else for that matter. There was no need for this, it was self-explanatory. The little painting was psychedelic but not abstract.

"Naty, you see that this is only a woman seen from the back."

"Elsa, I know my daughter, and I know what I am saying. Take care of her, please."

And she went back to work, her conscience cleared.

Elsa took care of me. She had me take vocational and aptitude tests, and summoned my mother to give her the results.

"This girl has no problems for now. But if you want to do something for her, you will have to take her out of the country because socially, she will always have problems of maladjustment here in Cuba."

"Do you know what you are saying? Me, leave? Not even feet first! After I spent that year in Paris, I swore that I would never leave Cuba again. I felt like I was missing everything, that the process of the Revolution was just going on without me."

Ave Maria! When was my torment going to end? I couldn't ever write, I couldn't ever paint, and now as a crowning touch, I was labeled with that ailment called maladjustment.

"Then what you need is to help her be whatever she wants to be. I did some vocational tests and . . ."

"Elsa, she is going to study chemistry. That's what her father wants. I am going to put her in another school this year. She is wasting her time in ballet school."

Oh, Lord, have mercy on me!

"Mommy, but why? How could you take me out of ballet school? I am the second in my class. . . ." My voice suddenly sounded raspy, as if I had swallowed some rosin.

"There are several reasons. You have too much brains to earn your living just kicking your legs. You'll also be closer to my office."

To console me for these great misfortunes and all I had to give up, she promised me a whole week with her alone, all to myself. We were going to take a trip through the interior of the country.

*The trip through the* interior of the country consisted of an exhausting trek leading to—can't you guess?—the farm in Birán where Fidel was born.

When we got there we were not allowed in. Admission was only by government invitation. And it had to be approved by Celia Sánchez.

As a second choice, Mommy decided to spend a few days with Uncle Ramón, the Comandante's oldest brother, who is just like him, only a peasant version.

He and his wife, Suli, exchanged looks of hatred for each other while their three children wandered about with the look typical of children growing up without love. Uncle Ramón welcomed us by singing an old popular song, accompanying himself on the guitar.

> *No matter how high is the sky,*
> *Or how deep the ocean blue,*
> *There's no barrier the whole world through*
> *That my deep love will not break for you.*[6]

Mother and I were the ones breaking the sound barrier on our way back to Havana, with two pigs and three turkeys in the backseat of our car clamoring their bewilderment in stentorian tones until they reached their destination twenty-four hours later.

I couldn't wait to get to Havana so I could pump Uncle Pedro Emilio, my fiercest and most tender confidant, for the shameful truth lurking behind the evident lack of love in that family.

What he told me, on one of those Sunday afternoons dressed up in poetry, was this: "We had to marry Ramón to Suli in a hurry because at thirteen he had fallen in love with a Haitian woman, for whose ardent steatopygia, combined with her invincible voodoo spells, your grandmother Dominga's witchcraft and exorcisms were no match. Her 'made-in-Cuba' Congolese witchcraft had no effect on Papa Legbá and Baron Samedi. Ramón used to escape every night of his life to run after his black lover. He would come back the following day, pale and shrunken ('de-semenated,' as Dominga used to say), murmuring words in her patois, words so sweet that there was no need to understand them to know that they were the names of the perverted fruity smells of his chocolate paramour."

Ramón was living at the other end of the Island. He was being punished by Fidel and was condemned to watch over a truck depot, because he had never wanted to help his rebel brother in the Sierra. When the Revolution triumphed, though, he got an olive-green uniform for himself.

"I'm not blaming him," Pedro Emilio continued, "because everybody knows I did the same thing. After the triumph of the Revolution, I added the rank of captain to my uniform. Anyway, my dear, I was running for mayor under the old regime and, far worse, I am a rhyme maker, something that my half brother considers a sure trait of weak, good-for-nothing types. At some point, he will forgive Ramón, but he will continue to despise me all his life.

"It's possible that the spell cast by the offended Haitian woman was intended for the woman who took her place, because Suli has attempted suicide again and again. When she did not have any poison left, she tried butchering her veins. Two of their sons left home raving mad, and even Ramón escaped one day."

Later I found out that by the time they moved to a house in Miramar, Ramón was already in charge of all the cattle classified as F1, F2, and F3, conceived thanks to his brother's genetic contributions. Then Suli hanged herself from the stairway banister. No one was there to rescue her.

*   *   *

*My hormones started kicking* mainly because of the pigs and turkeys that Ramón made us take in our Mercedes to his sister Angelita.

I was amazed at how grown-up my cousin Mayito was! I went crazy over his pair of floating ears, his long and elegant body, his hazel eyes, and his shaven head. Fidel wanted to make him into a rocketry expert, and even though he looked more like a figure in a painting by El Greco than a soldier, he was studying at the Belén Military Academy.

He was a health nut and had self-prescribed cures based on tannic iodine, cod liver oil, and vitamin compounds that burned your throat and churned your stomach.

He used pyrotechnics to clean his military boots. First he would spread on a black tarlike substance and then set fire to it. I attended the ritual of cleaning his boots and helped by handing him the swabs, the rags, and the brushes, like a nurse handing instruments to a surgeon.

He was a lonely, tender being, and he had kept, hidden in his bedroom, the altar that Grandmother Lina had bequeathed to her eldest daughter. Together we used to ingest his infernal health formulas, and afterward he took me for a ride in one of the cars his mother allowed him to drive. We had no friends, and not many places to go.

It was before Mayito's altar with all its Catholic saints and their Yoruba cousins, aligned in rows and columns according to their hierarchy and exerting their syncretist solidarity, that my cousin embraced me and attempted to introduce his tongue, hard like a dart, into my mouth for the first time. Another, even harder dart kept growing under his pants. My knees weakened, and a pink tickle shot up below my navel, wetting my panties.

An atavistic terror got hold of me, because the only thing I knew about sex was that since Ivette and I had started being hirsute between our legs, we were no longer allowed to bathe together.

When I told Tata about the incident, I got a sonorous slap on my face, the only one I ever had the honor of getting from her.

"So young and getting the hots? I hope I live long enough to watch over your 'private room'!"

I was eleven and he was eighteen. He became my recurrent image of love.

* * *

*Ciudad Escolar Libertad is* such an enormous school that identities are lost the first day.

*Hut, two, three, four,*

*Hut, two.*

We marched and marched through interminable avenues.

A girl who seemed to be stuck to a nose approached me on my first day.

"My name is Roxana Yabur. And yours?"

"Alina Fernández."

"My father is the minister of justice."

She was the daughter of the man in charge of straightening out my lineage.

"Oh, really? Well, my father is Fidel Castro, and over a year ago he asked your father to make a law so that my last name could be changed."

"Fidel Castro? The real one?"

"No, silly. The fake one! My name is Fernández because my mother was married to Daddy Orlando, but there is a law that says no man can legally recognize a child 'not his own' from an adulterous relationship, so he told Yabur to change the Civil Code for him and to make a Revolutionary one, so my name would be as it should be, and not Fernández, as it is now."

Roxana did not say peep, but by the next day, the whole class knew and by the next week, the whole school. It was as if the news that Fidel had a daughter could spread only by geometric progression. Kids came from every far corner of the immense school, no matter how many miles they had to walk, and they would stick their heads into my classroom to take a peek at me.

"Hey, take a look! They say she's Fidel's daughter!"

"That's a lie! The Horse's daughter taking the bus, and without a chauffeur or bodyguards? Don't give me that shit!"

"Hey, girl, come here! Is it true you're Fidel's daughter?"

"Yes . . ."

"Then why don't you ask the Horse for a pair of shoes? Those are going to run after you the day you throw them away!"

"Hey, listen, if it's true Fidel's your father, why don't you tell him to distribute some food, eh?"

"Is your mother married to Fidel?"

"Why don't you have his last name?"

"What happened was that her mother fucked the Horse but wasn't married to him!"

More than once I went home in desolation.

"Grandma, what does 'fuck' mean?"

"What kind of language is that? This year you'll see how my geraniums thrive. They say a pregnant woman has to pee on them. I am sure I don't have to go out of this house to find one. The way maids are today! There are no morals!"

Lala Natica has always made weird associations of ideas.

"Mommy, what is the meaning of the word 'fuck'? You know, at school . . ." I had to speak to her in a very low voice because her secretary was again starting to dream about the one who would become her third "godson." She was still sleeping on the office couch.

"You tell me about it later, love. I'm leaving right now for a Party meeting."

"Tata, what is 'to fuck'?"

Tata stared at me with her silent lucidity. But I found out.

"Tota, do you know what is 'to fuck'?"

"Gee, you must be a retard! It's the most wonderful thing! At least, that's what Mom tells Dad when instead of sleeping, they start putting that thing in and out. That's how babies are made, silly!"

Every day I got up and went to my calvary, but luckily novelties always wear themselves out, or else we get used to them.

Yabur's daughter, Roxana, became my best friend. We used to study together in her father's mansion, the one with a tennis court, a privilege her father enjoyed because of his political rank as minister. Iccon, her Lebanese grandmother, was my belly dancing teacher. She gave us lessons in Arabic diction while loosening up our hip armatures by means of magic tricks that, according to her, would be useful to us in future stages of our lives.

\* \* \*

*Che Guevara was killed* in Bolivia that year. An orchestrated outpouring of sadness put the whole Island in militant mourning, repeated in compulsory and solemn vigils in the Plaza de la Revolución, funeral odes, and requiems for martyrdom.

Korda the photographer hung his photo of the Heroic Guerrilla Warrior on every wall in the universe, and the Comandante abandoned his ruminating on the struggle for better bovine genetics to direct one of the most masterful publicity campaigns of this century.

He announced that Che's death mask and his cut-off hands, which had reached Havana in a cooler, were going to be preserved, mummified, and exhibited at the Museo de la Revolución. I thought it was an awful idea, so I swallowed my pride and wrote him my letter number one thousand and two, asking him to put away the death mask and bury the hands.

The national obsession with a new breed of cattle suddenly vanished from our television screens, to be replaced by another obsession showing much more perspective and futuristic potential, the creation of the New Man.

Cuba was to be the petri dish for this kernel of universal progress, and our schools would be the frontline laboratories.

The success Fidel achieved with the death of Che restored his gift of gab and gave him the energy to spend hours orating outdoors under the sun, in the rain, or in the evening dew, at the Plaza de la Revolución. He insisted that we Cuban students had to fulfill the Apostle José Martí's dream, which in time had come to coincide with Che's.

The people cheered.

The new schools needed a Five-Year Plan, Fidel insisted, for this to become a reality, and with everybody pulling together and doing voluntary work, the dreams shared by the Apostle and the Guerrilla Warrior would sooner become a reality all over our homeland. The students were going to live and work in these schools and thus learn firsthand the sacrifices required of farmers and of all the poor on earth.

The people cheered and chanted: "Viva! Viva! / Fi-del, Fi-del, / What's your secret, Fidel? / Whichever way they turn, / You give the Yankees hell!"

People on the rest of the planet were adjusting to the Age of Aquarius, letting their hair grow, widening the bottoms of their pants into bell shapes, turning their skirts into miniskirts, singing with the Beatles, hanging Che's portrait on the wall, and making an unprecedented effort to love one another, while we in Cuba were marching to martial rhythms. Any use of English was forbidden. Boys' school uniform pants were being ripped at school or in the street if they did not pass the litmus test—a Ping-Pong ball had to be able to slide all the way down the legs—and boys' heads were being shaved if they dared let their hair grow. They were much less hairy than the original hairy ones at the triumph of the Revolution. A second offense of any kind would send them to serve time in the forced-labor camps of the UMAP (Military Units to Aid Production), together with the homosexuals, the artists, and the priests. When they came out of one of these camps, they were no longer the same people.

One morning our English teacher, Ananda, interrupted her class to ask us to write down our shoe and pant sizes on a list.

A week later, we were each handed a pair of work boots like the ones sugarcane cutters wore in the field, a change of clothes all in Mao gray, and a hat.

Everything was "one size *feets* all" because no stylistic distinctions could be made for so many students in the process of becoming the New Men.

We were sent home with our new clothes and a list of instructions. We had to report to school extra early for our journey to the Escuela al Campo, or Special Country School.

Provided with blankets, bedsheets, wooden flip-flops for shoes, and metal buckets for our personal hygiene, all stuffed in luggage made mostly of wood and reinforced with metal and padlocks—in ample evidence of the people's ingenuity, since there was no luggage to be bought—we were deposited by our loving parents at the threshold of this new experiment. I still remember with affection the metal jug that Mom had engraved for me, with my name emblazoned to eclipse all others. Nobody dared steal it.

Packed into prehistoric school buses, we mutants, en route to becoming a Vanguard species, were sent to bring to fruition the fertile oneiric musings of our beloved Apostle Martí and our Apostle the Guerrilla Warrior.

The boys were going to cut sugarcane. As for the girls . . . we had no idea. Neither parents nor children knew our precise destination.

Two entire generations were in suspense.

Sometimes, while others dream, I have nightmares. I was retracing memories of Apocalypses in other lives when I was rudely awakened by the eloquence of the travelers' secular shouts: "We are here! This is it!"

Facing us was a crude barracks built of the woody part of palm fronds and thatched with the softer leaves. To the right there were a few outhouses just like those the Makarenko girls had built in the gardens of the Miramar mansions. A barbed-wire fence with an iron gate encircled the senile grayness of the whole thing.

We had to line up in alphabetical order and then march into that dreadful place to occupy our "beds." These were simple pallets, less than two feet apart, consisting of crude burlap nailed to wooden logs.

When I realized that inside that shed more than a thousand people, in ten rows of fifty pallets each, would snore and stink together for two and a half months, I almost fainted.

"At least poor Martí is dead."

"What was that?" inquired the secretary of the Communist Youth.

"Martí is dead so that we could dream of this marvelous . . ."

Whenever I was forced to take a trip against my will, I quickly got sick with that something called maladjustment. There was a hole in the ground for doing number one and number two, and in the flooded bathroom we had to attach two pieces of wood to our feet with rubber strips cut from bicycle tires, and walk in those if we wanted to avoid stepping into the fetid slush generated by the excretions of a thousand people. As soon as I saw all this, my usual little cough started. It soon became a wheezing, sibilant noise coupled with a raging fever.

To make matters even worse, some perverted force of nature was on the loose, fondling the girls' tits when they got up to pee in the middle of the night. In fear of the Great Dyke, we emptied our bursting bladders in any dark corner. Oh, the effluvia of puberty!

*   *   *

*At the crack of* dawn, before the roosters started crowing, kerosene lamps were lit and in less than ten minutes we were outside in formation.

Frozen breath clouded around our mouths the moment we began shouting our slogans.

I thought of my mom, instead of the Virgin Mary, and every night I prayed to her for a miracle appearance. At that time she still had the inclination, and the vehicle, to make the eighteen-hour weekend drive to the site of my misfortune, but since the rest of the meek Cubans were only pedestrians without means of transportation, she said to me:

"I'd better not come to see you on the first Sunday, so your classmates won't feel bad on account of our privilege."

That was fair. Because, for some unknown reason, privilege seemed to show more on me.

I waited impatiently for her visit, filling and loading all the boxes of tomatoes that were necessary to win the competitions we were forced to be in. My heart was always pumping dangerously out of control, and air reached my lungs only in random bursts.

One Sunday a miracle happened and my Hollywood star stepped out of the Mercedes, wearing the uniform of the militias.

When I saw that Tata was not with her, my spirit crumbled. There would be no one to get me out of that promiscuous hell.

"Mommy, please, I beg of you! For God's sake! For Fidel's sake! For Lenin's! Get me out of here!" I pleaded, wheezing. I sounded like a Bulgarian baker.

"No, hon. You know very well that you have to stay here with your classmates. Try to make me happy being a Vanguard student. Look, Tata sent you a little frozen steak she's been saving for you since the last time there was meat. And I brought you two whole loaves of sliced, toasted bread and a parboiled can of mushy condensed milk so that it lasts you more than a week. And a package of toasted corn flour."

I was busy turning her visit into a long pleading session.

"If you keep whining, I'm leaving right now!" she exclaimed.

She left me in that state of desperation and abandonment that only children are capable of experiencing.


*I completely devoted myself* to being a Vanguard student the following week because I have an ironclad, unconditional loyalty. I had already mixed up my sleep time and my wake-up time, and I felt totally lost in the timelessness of my miserable situation. Devilish skin blisters began covering my neck and face.

I was taken to a doctor at the Policlínico. The very young man attending me pretended not to hear my erudite medical opinion.

"Look, I have a collapsed section in the vortex of my right lung, and I also have a cardiac arrhythmia, along with tachycardia and dyspnea."

He sent me to Havana, on a trip classified as urgent, for fear that my facial blisters would spread to the other students.

Even the sun itself was about to cry in the noon skies because of the extreme heat by the time the teacher-guide deposited me into Tata's arms, with a wild-beating heart and a wilting desire to live.

Right away I sought an emotional encounter with my white porcelain toilet, the civilized immaculate conception for number one and number two.

"Tata, there's blood in my urine!"

"Let me see, m'child, it can't be! Could it be that time of the month?"

But no, it wasn't that time yet, according to the piece of paper in her own handwriting that I had discovered in a desk drawer, which read: "On November 11, 1965, Alina became a young lady."

"Tata, I think I'm going to die."

Tata called my mother with the news at the special phone number reserved only for emergencies, but Mom did not come until late afternoon because she does not believe in death. She had survived gastroenteritis, brucellosis, a perforated and gangrenous appendix, acute hepatitis, mononucleosis picked up when she donated blood for the meek, and even a bite in her palate from a dog suspected of being rabid.

A psychiatrist on duty that night, at the same hospital where they repaired Aunt Suli's butchered veins, diagnosed me as "nervous" and put me in a belladonna coma.

When I opened my eyes I knew I was dead. Feeling outrageously tired, I saw above my head Old Jotavich himself, floating on a white cloud. I was about to pull out all of his white beard to make him perform the miracle of bringing me down from Limbo and into my home, when a mom, overcome by anguish, almost succeeded in disconnecting all my pipelines by picking me up from the bed and whisking me into her arms as if she were an outlaw.

In reality Jotavich was Vallejo, Fidel's physician, with his captain-from-the-Sierra uniform hidden under his gown. I was alive at the Hospital Nacional, in a room of his special wing for foreigners.

"Her right lung is collapsed, no bigger than a small fist. Her liver is enlarged, her transaminase is sky-high, her spleen is enormous, and her kidneys are half rotten. I'm giving her eighty million units of penicillin intravenously. But don't worry, Naty. While there's life, there's always hope."

The idea of being so ugly inside troubled me considerably because, as Lala Natica says, "one must be elegant, even when about to die." I went to sleep peacefully, in the certainty that I had not been born to go anywhere before my time in such a rotten state. I woke up a week later.

"You were very sick, Alina. You were unconscious for over a week."

"And Fidel didn't come to see me?"

"No."

"Why?"

"I don't know. Why don't you ask Vallejo?"

I have always done what I am told.

"Dr. Vallejo, why didn't Fidel come to see me?"

"Because he doesn't know you're sick."

"How come he doesn't know?"

"He doesn't know because I didn't want to worry him, and I haven't told him."

"But now you can tell him that I *was* sick."

"Now I cannot tell him at all. He would kill me for not having told him before."

Unflappable, he left the room.

*The rest of the* students returned from the Escuela al Campo without major mishaps, except for Mario, a boy in my class, who had lost a leg. There was also the loss of a few digital phalanges, spread among a few hands.

Mario's leg was lost on his way to cutting sugarcane, under an overturned cart. The fingers had fallen victim to sharp machetes wielded by inexperienced hands.

All the girls survived whole. We all went back to our enormous school, our classes and our marches at the Ciudad Escolar Libertad.

"Is there a grammar school section anywhere?"

"Mommy, there is everything. There is even an army airport."

"Then your cousin Deborah must also be a student there. Why don't you look for her? I hear she's in the third grade."

Deborah was the oldest daughter of Vilma and Raúl Castro.

To find her was easy because a couple of guards were on duty in obvious "secrecy" outside her classroom. I got by this hyperprotective barrier by briefly explaining my family relationship and my controversial ancestry.

Deborah was a good angel, a porcelain doll with delicate skin and ash-blond hair that has continued being her greatest luxury later in life. Our affection for each other was instant. Through her I discovered the warmth of family life, and a certain liberation from my daily after-school trip home on the overcrowded 22 bus. She, her military escort, and her chauffeurs were nice enough to bring me home every afternoon after that.

Therefore, instead of my vesperal hanging out with classmates, as soon as school was out I went in search of my little cousin.

Her family lived on the seventh floor of a building between the Cementerio de Colón and the Chinese Cemetery, because it was easier for Personal Security to watch over the dead. You had to wait in the middle of the street until the guard on duty saw you, got permission from the illustrious dwellers, and then took you up to their apartment in an elevator that worked by means of a code.

Raúl was affectionate, and smiled often. He had a movie theater built on the first floor, and even the guards' children could sometimes come to the Sunday matinees before lunch.

"Mom, I asked Uncle Raúl to invite you to come to lunch with me."

"Oh, yes? And what did he say?"

"That all the places at the table were already taken. But it was not true."

"Don't you worry about me. I know that Raúl loves me. I am going to show you the letters he wrote me." And she returned with her miniature safe. "Look at this one. It begins 'Naty, my dearest sister . . .' "

She went on with her romantic babble about something written fifteen years before.

I didn't know it at the time, but poor Raúl didn't dare do anything—move to another house, get a divorce, or even see people—unless his brother Fidel gave his approval first.

It was while waiting for the elevator to visit my uncle Raúl that I met my brother Fidelito for the first time. His hair was wavy and matted like straw, the kind of hair some mixed-blood *criollos* have. It was as if some big mulatto had sideswiped one of his grandmothers. He was tall and beautiful, with a pair of romantic eyes. Just to look at him made my blood rush suddenly to the place where premonitions lie dormant.

"You are my brother!" And I hung from his neck.

The poor thing turned cross-eyed at my unexpected outburst.

He finally accepted the evidence when we were introduced by our aunt and uncle, who left us alone to talk.

*"Then you should know* that we have another brother."

"Another brother? How's that?"

"Easy. His mother, Amparo, met Fidel on a trip to Oriente province that lasted three days."

Fidel did not know that he had left her pregnant until much later.

"And how old is he?"

"He's my age."

A trip to Oriente that lasted three days! They weren't in much of a hurry, were they?

"What's his name?"

"Jorge Ángel. Jorge Ángel Castro. I'm . . . leaving for the Soviet Union next week and I don't have any time to introduce you, so I'm going to give you his telephone number and you—"

"To the Soviet Union? What are you going to do there?"

"I'm going to study nuclear physics. The Old Man wants me to."

*Mamma mia!* That had to be worse than chemistry.

"Are you going by yourself?"

"No, no. I have three friends going with me."

"And why aren't you taking your brother?"

"He's staying—he's studying chemistry." Fidelito smiled at me with a kind of half-smile that ran to the left side of his mouth and made me feel uneasy, sort of inferior. He said good-bye right after that. "Don't forget to call Jorge. When I come back on vacation, we'll get together, the three of us. Till then you and I can write to each other and get acquainted."

That afternoon I returned home with a sweet dove fluttering inside of me.

"Tata, Tata, I met my brother Fidelito."

"Oh, did you? And what does he look like?"

"He's tall, beautiful, and eighteen years old."

"Did you ask him if he knew about you?"

"Yes, he did."

"And then, since he is already a man, why hasn't he come here before to get to know you?"

"I don't know."

"Be careful, m'child. You don't need a brother who doesn't love you."

The following week Tata died.

To live through Tata's death I cried and cried, oblivious to everything else. It was a tragedy that had me in a sickly trance for months. I didn't comb my hair, take a bath, or even eat, because I did not know how to do any of those things without her.

Even now, as I write this, my eyes fill with tears. "There are life blows so overwhelming . . . I don't know! Blows that seem to come from God's hatred; as if they summoned an undertow of past sufferings, to occupy a deep well in our soul . . . I don't know!"[7]

Tata Mercedes was the compass rose of my life.

*Hilda Gadea, Che's widow,* made a joint discovery with my mom in those days: their respective daughters were very lonely and both in need of a friend.

One afternoon I met in our sitting room a very cute Chinese girl who was with a lady that looked like an Inca totem pole, something like Venerable Mother Frog.

The Chinese girl was Hildita Guevara. She was not Chinese at all, but a beautiful South American Indian. She had lots of black and satiny hair, substantial but well-shaped legs; and a pair of prize-winning boobs.

We looked at each other with hatred, and with even more hatred at the mothers who had thus entrapped us.

"Why don't you two go upstairs to your room and play? Alina, show Hildita your Barbie doll collection."

I almost had a heart attack. Barbies! Now Hildita was going to think that, instead of locking myself up in the library to puff on grandfather Manolo's pipe, I was the type that would go upstairs and secretly play with dolls.

We went up to my room, where there were still traces of my (now also blocked but once blooming) pictorial phase, on the walls and on the furniture, along with improvisations from psychedelic and pointillist artists.

"Wanna smoke?" I asked.

"Awright!"

I took out a box of cigars, *aromas,* from my night table, and handed her the matches.

"Shit, these are *suaves!*"

Hildita smoked black tobacco.

We immediately became inseparable.

It was a cathartic and sad friendship at first. We used to fall asleep holding hands, our eyes moist with the abandonment we suffered from our heroic fathers: hers, dead without having had the opportunity of being forgiven for his neglect, and mine, so alive, but more absent than if he were dead.

Hilda Gadea's counterpart to Celia Sánchez was Aleida March, Che's Second Widow, who monopolized all the honors and privileges for her four children with Che.

Adolescence is a missing link in the healthy process of growing up. When we reach that stage, we leave at its door the ballast of our existential anguish and join the living.

Hilda Gadea finally granted attention and respect to a handsome young man and married him. Hildita and I wanted to know how the Old Venerables fucked, and to shake off our innocence once and for all. One afternoon when the couple retired "to have a siesta," we began, very slowly, to open the bedroom shutters to prevent the brightening daylight from giving us away, we thought.

I was banished from Hildita's house without appeal and never returned, but we continued to be friends somehow.


*I was already a* national legend at Ciudad Escolar Libertad when I sneaked into its Swimming School. I became one of twenty girls preparing to form the first aquatic ballet team in the country. If I was short on art, in the sport of swimming I was not.

Mothers with nubile daughters began to take action. The school gave them an excellent opportunity to leave their offspring in the hands of the Socialist state.

The school was a culinary paradise. And it was full of tanned youths. In any revolution, athletes are part of the propaganda machine and always receive privileged treatment. In Cuba it is better to be a sports champion than a cabinet minister.

The human communion of sweat and competition creates ineffable bonds.

In the Swimming School, we lived for our five hours of daily training: eating, and sleeping, and again more training, eating, and sleeping. Nobody complained about Fidel, nor about the "situation."

The school admitted children of Socialist privilege, children of the friends of privilege, and a few children from the interior of the country who were very grateful for the opportunity to live among the elite, and to spend weekends in their homes as guests.

It was 1968 and fashionable to have long, straight hair and be skinny.

But who could be skinny with all of that privileged food! With the hair it was easier, because we used to iron our manes.

We had to rise early and shine. That was it. Studying was not that important.

And thank God! We didn't have to go to the Escuela al Campo.

On Wednesdays our mothers would visit and bring clean uniforms for the rest of the week.

When my mother came, the hearts of the polo players beat faster. They would even crowd together behind a wall to take a look at her. One particular Wednesday she was very nervous.

"Fidel is coming tonight. I'd rather you stay here, Alina, because I want to speak to him about you. About your problem. So it's better if you are not there. If he wants to see you anyway, let him come another day so that—"

"Do I have any new problem besides maladjustment, painting women from the back, fish-eye warts, and allergic bronchitis?"

"He doesn't take care of you as he should. That's the problem I'm talking about."

So what else was new! He had been doing just that—nothing—for thirteen years.

"Do you know how many people in this school do not even know their fathers?"

"I'm doing this for you."

For me? I was better off if she didn't do a thing. When was Fidel's last visit? Two years is a long time when your breasts are budding.

For the first time in my life, I was not living in his shadow. Nobody was exacerbating my guilt by telling me about executions, expropriations, jail abuses, and visas denied, or asking me for houses, shoes, hospital admittance, or exit permits to leave the country. Even Mom had by now stopped making sacrifices for him, like driving on weekends to Santa María del Mar so that we could go to the ocean and swim in front of his house and see if, by any chance, he would make an appearance. She once had come out of the water in Santa María shouting "Fidel! Fidel! Alinaaaa!" She kept this up until the Comandante had to rescue us from a beating by his personal guards. He finally engaged in a swimming race with her.

I had no problems now. While I stayed on Aunt Angelita's farm, I no longer had to serve as a go-between for Uncle Ramón and his new lover, who used me to deliver love missives that made Suli suffer. My crazy cousins held a grudge against me for years on end and kept their hatred close to their straitjackets. But now I was finally at peace.

"I don't want to see *him*. I'm not interested," I told my mom.

But adolescents have no free will.

*The following evening, Mom* was there, radiant, an archangel by the side of the Comandante, who was lying on my bed, hands behind his head.

"I have been too busy these past two years. I have no time for anything. It's very difficult to keep a revolution alive. Lately I have been negotiating with Japan to buy some machines to make ice cream, and I am very satisfied. In two months they will be installed. One in each neighborhood, at least. So people will be able to have some ice cream. It's so hot. The best part is that I also negotiated buying an ice-cream cone factory and we'll be able to produce them right here in the country."

How wonderful, I thought. At least the cones were not going to be imported. . . . I did not applaud because we were alone.

"The Japanese are also going to sell me a plastic-shoe factory with a production level of thousands of shoes per day. It's incredible. You drop a little plastic ball made from a petroleum by-product into the machine, and a pair of shoes comes out the other end, heels and all. For men, women, and children and in several models. I bought the machine at a very good price and I think that in the long run, this is going to solve the problem of shoes for the population."

I was in a trance.

"My other piece of news is that the modification to the Constitution is ready. The new family code is operative next week, so you can use the Castro family name whenever you wish. The only thing your mother needs to do is get together with Yabur."

I saw myself in formation at school with the sea in front of me, and astonishing everyone with this untimely news.

It would put me in a ridiculous position again.

It was going to deprive me of my favorite excuse: "No, no. I cannot do anything for you. I swear to you I am not his daughter. No way. Nothing. Not even a letter."

"I think I'm going to keep the name Fernández. It's been my name for a long time, and I don't like having to explain things to people."

He didn't mind one way or the other, he said.

When he exited, there was a pair of black boot-polish spots on my bedspread and, in the air, promises to come back soon.

*My brother Jorge Ángel,* born after one bewitched train trip, did not seem too bright. He was quiet, and looked nice. I somehow felt affection for him because of his disability and his state of dependency on his half brother Fidelito and on a perennial girlfriend named Ena Lidia.

He was accustomed to traveling, carrying all the gear, rifles, and food containers in the back of his Jeep every time his brother, the crown prince, condescended to invite him on some official trip. Jorge always had to stand aside without anybody bothering to introduce him in these situations. His personal identity and self-esteem were nebulous.

Fidelito's letters to me from the Soviet Union were nice but somewhat pompous. He had advice about discipline and Revolutionary behavior, complete with postscripts of affectionate greetings for my mother. My heart, though, went out to the neglected brother, Jorge Ángel, who was bewildered by the motley family that I kept, little by little, introducing him to. Why would Fidelito want to keep Jorge Ángel under wraps?

It was my mom who offered him unconditional affection. We got to be so close that, to the last detail, the plans for the wedding with his perennial girlfriend, Ena Lidia, began to take shape at our home. We had the right legal person to perform the ceremony, the flowers, her wedding dress, and the buffet all arranged, when all of a sudden our lovey-dovey relationship collapsed.

The guest of honor, and best man, was going to be Fidelito, who would be back in the country after his two-year stint studying nuclear physics in the Soviet Union. We did experience an epistolary disagreement when he was still in the Soviet Union: I had referred to our Old Man as "an S.O.B. who does not take care of his children," and Fidelito responded with an angry exegesis. I had forgotten the whole incident until the day I received a phone call from my aunt Vilma asking me to get dressed and be ready right away because she and Raúl were coming to pick me up on the way to the airport.

The Protocol House, which is where government guests and visiting celebrities stayed, was packed when my inimitable brother came in, accompanied by a Russian girl who was totally confused by this official and populous welcome. The Protocol House was full of men dressed much like the military officers she had left behind in her own land.

Just like my dog Guarapo, there I was with my tongue hanging out and tail wagging, waiting first in line to be kissed.

My brother Fidelito spent half an hour embracing and greeting other people. When there was nobody else left to meet, and everybody in the room was looking at him and looking at me, he walked over and shook my hand.

"Thanks for coming."

That was all.

Except for the superior half-smile that ran to the left side of his face. The conceited fool—who did he think he was? The next Roman emperor?

My aunt and uncle had not expected such a reaction. Since they did not know what to do with me at that point, they took me, together with their children, to Fidelito's seventh-floor apartment, where a cook in full regalia was putting the finishing touches on the scrumptious late lunch.

We were then taken to another area of the same building. There, by removing some dividing walls, a duplex of love had been prepared for the couple as a gift. We were shown the furnished premises and then taken back to the seventh floor. Both my surprise and my confusion stuck in my throat. If there are catastrophes one cannot swallow, this was one. It seemed that my next Socialist five-year plan would be directed to regain the love of my brothers.

After lunch came the distribution of gifts. Fidelito had brought records by the Beatles and by Raphael, his favorite singer as well as mine. He gave my cousins clothes and toys. Then, finally, he turned to me.

"I didn't know what to bring to you, so here you are." And he handed me a bottle of some nauseating Russian perfume from the Communist era.

I was desperate.

"Mommy sends you all her love. She can't wait to give you a kiss for all those nice things you said about her when you wrote to me. And she wants you to know that her home is your home. Come visit us anytime," I said to Fidelito.

"Tell your mother that there is nothing for me in her home."

My heart stopped. And I don't have a weak heart. I suddenly remembered Myrta, his mother, and the old letters switched by the noble jail censor. I thought that, though it was forbidden by Revolutionary principles, my brother had perhaps made a secret flight to Spain for a meeting with his mother, who was living there in exile. She was another member of the consortium of witches against my mother.

I put the perfume on the kitchen counter and left. I didn't feel like going home, where Mom was waiting, all excited, to find out how the meeting had turned out.

I stood on the street corner, waiting for the uncertain appearance of any bus that would take me far away. At my feet, all crumpled in a little imperceptible heap, were all my hopes. I picked them up, jumped onto the footboard of a 69 bus, and anchored the tip of my right foot there as I elbowed my way in a bit, on the backs of the people already on board. This was the only way to travel in Cuba when there were still buses.

Jorge Ángel called one afternoon to say that his wedding was not going to be at my home after all. It was going to be in a Protocol House in El Laguito. Celia had already arranged everything.

"I am sorry to have to tell you this, but Naty is not invited."

"Stupid bastard!" I blurted out.

Some brothers God had given me! One was a Fouché in diapers, and the other, the greatest opportunistic idiot on earth.


*"What does the world* have against my mother?" I asked my beloved cousin Mayito.

"That is none of your business. Mothers are not to be judged. Mothers are to be loved. It is the only right we have over them," Mayito said, with a sweet flicker of his ears.

I began to exercise my rights over mine at full blast. If she couldn't go or wasn't invited somewhere, I wouldn't go either. In a small way, I acted as her mother, because Grandma Natica was terrible, always criticizing her. She treated Mom as if she were mentally incompetent, and prevented her from bringing any friends home for lunch by making fun of them with her cutting, unerringly targeted remarks.

I had tried to return her to her proper hierarchy, but it became clear that not even Hercules and his Twelve Labors could break the ring of violent rejection around her. Even after being put on the rack, Mom was still intent on demonstrating that she was a true-blue Revolutionary, and that for her the Revolution had not been a passing uterine infatuation for the hairy guy, but a lifelong commitment.

I was seeing less and less of her now that she had managed to become a bona fide member of the Communist Party in triumph over Celia's dark machinations. She retreated more and more into her peculiar position. Alienated, she came to inhabit the world of a heroine incapable of feeling either the humiliation or the hypocrisy of the spite she had inspired.

Everything seemed overblown to me, and being both on the inside and on the outside of the situation, I couldn't save her from herself. I tried to convince her to accept one of the embassy jobs she was continually being offered, as some sort of spy or whatever, so she could escape this discord. Anything so that she could return to being the charming woman she really was. But she had discovered a new way of coping and was impervious to other people's opinions.

I finally left the field open to my brothers and their schemes. This exit of mine liberated me from Sunday lunches and my complex relatives' double standards.

Celia's harassment and evil intentions lasted as long as she lived. She continued to be as hard as flint, until the malignancy that attacked her lungs and reached up to her tongue left her punier and more vermicular than she had ever seemed before.

But by the time she died, ten years had gone by, and my mother was already a prisoner of her own fixed ideas.

The Castro family, as their expressive faces proved, had treated my mother better while she was the Bearded One's whore than when she became the Comandante's ex-mistress.

*In September 1968 we* all returned to the Swimming School, pretty and chubby because of our unbridled appetites during the long summer vacation without exercise. With our uniforms and our just-ironed hair, we were all standing ready for the first morning routines when the director spilled the news.

"Since aquatic ballet has not been declared an Olympic sport, we are sorry to inform you that the aquatic ballet swim team has been dissolved by order of the Ministry of Education, effective today. All participants in the program are to return the two bathing suits, the terrycloth robe, the cap, the nose clip, the shoes, and the school uniform at once. All of these articles must be left with the dorm supervisor, who will sign a receipt for you. Then you will have permission to call your parents. Have them come to take you home!"

That was the end of it.

I then took the tests to apply for the regular swimming school.

"Not physiologically adapted to water," said one of the judges.

"What does she need to be 'physiologically adapted to water'? Gills, fins, scales?" Mom was furious. We went to see the minister of education, Llanusa.

"Look, Naty, I can't do anything for the child. If she stays in that school, people are going to say that it's a special privilege for being Fidel's daughter."

"She is the best on her team, and they all know it. Her swimming test was fantastic, and look at what they said! Their explanation doesn't make any sense!"

"Their explanation is irrelevant. The order to send all of them home came from me. They are all considered to be spoiled brats. Children of privilege are not welcome anywhere."

"Then try to find a solution. This school has been the best of all worlds for Alina."

"Perhaps . . . By the way, my dear"—the minister turned and addressed me—"what's the name of that disease you say I have?"

"Gynecomastia," I answered. "It's an unusual growth of men's breasts. And I hope yours drag all the way to the floor, Señor Ministro."

I said this on behalf of all the students from my school who were imprisoned on the rehabilitation farms that this bosomy bumpkin had set up to reeducate their taste for tight clothing and long hair.

I returned to my old school, Ciudad Libertad, in a rebellious state of mind. The teachers there ended up not allowing me into their classrooms.

I swam for five hours every day until I held the top rank in butterfly and backstroke and earned the right to train with the preselected swimming team. Since I had my return ticket to paradise, on the day of the competition I was a no-show at the pool.

I have always been like that: when I am one step away from something, I quit.


*Our house on Twenty*-second Street began to crumble. Large chunks of plaster fell from the ceilings, exposing a rusty bramble of iron bars and rotten pipes.

Mom found a powerful executive capable of pulling strings with the *permutas* (house exchanges) in the "frozen zones." We were going to move.

On the nineteenth of March, when I was emptying the chauffeur's room and suffering from a pesky fever—I had a cold—a shelf came down, and I discovered a strongbox.

Before calling my mother, who had the questionable habit of donating all her possessions to the Revolution and Socialism, I called Grandma Natica, the preserver of lamps and other family treasures.

But Lala could not get rid of the Security agents in charge of supervising our move. They came to the room above the garage with her.

And they ended up violating the secret of that strongbox. With a blowtorch and hammer in hand, they finally opened the box, which revealed the grief of the former tenants. Before their desperate flight from the disasters of 1959, they had hidden their most prized treasures: property deeds, money, and jewels.

Grandma wanted to keep a gold-inlaid makeup case that was in the box, with the excuse that this was my fifteenth birthday. The Security people didn't let go of it.

"Help! Help!" Lala shouted, in sudden hysterics. I thought she had turned radical in that instant and was going to start a battle against the abuses of World Communism.

At her feet on the floor, swimming in turquoise fluid, was my blue homunculus.

One of my childhood jars from the laboratory had fallen out of her hands.

# 4

# REBEL, REBEL

*Our new house sits* on a corner on the shady side of the street, its limestone blessed by the late afternoon sun. The interior of the house has no doors but rather opens into salons, a dining room, and sitting rooms, as if offering itself.

Shy greenery climbs up the stone walls, and poinciana trees stand guard around the house. A jacaranda prays to the heavens, apparently foreseeing the tree-killing frenzy that would whip through the neighborhood a few years later.

The day we moved, I turned fifteen. If Tata had been alive, she would have recorded the fact, secretly, in the diary she kept for me.

The Comandante's emissary arrived late that night, dressed just like him. He was a virile *campesino* with gray hair and lots of muscle. Sosa was his name, and he was invariably the bearer of good news.

"Here is a gift from the Comandante. Congratulations!"

It was a little lamp containing a flask of perfume called Crystal.

And what about Fidel, I thought, when was the last time he came for a visit?

"Well, at least he responded. I was afraid he might not even receive my message," Mom informed me.

The perfume present was the first miracle. The second was a confirmed dinner reservation at Polinesio.

There were only three restaurants open in Havana. In order to secure a table in one of them, people sometimes got into street fistfights and rock-throwing contests until the police intervened. This usually happened after a whole frustrating evening of standing in line and then not gaining admittance.

The night we went to Polinesio, I wore a silver lamé suit, with pants and a sleeveless jacket, that Juana and Lala Natica had made for me. It was in the style of the seventies, my mother said.

I looked like a gift-wrapped walrus, and I felt like dying, but I was not going to spoil that special gastronomical luxury for my two matriarchs. There was no one else I could invite. Because of my exodus from several places, plus the changing of schools, I had no friends to ask.

Since the Mercedes-Benz was in its terminal phase, we decided to take the number 27 bus. We made a very strange trio.

"Hey, look, it's Carnival time!" was the gallant reference to my getup from a man in the street.

What can we do? We spend three-quarters of our lives doing something ridiculous.


*Every time Mom was* "transferred" to another job, I had to change to another school so that I could go to see her.

This time, she was sent to MINCEX, or Ministerio de Comercio Exterior (Ministry of Foreign Trade), where she was turned into a specialist for the GEPLACEA, or Group of Latin American and Caribbean Sugar Exporting Countries. In spite of her brand-new fancy title, she was given a desk inside a redesigned closet.

"MINCEX, MINFAR, MINCUL, MINIL, MICON! All these government acronyms sound like Vietnamese! Even the language has changed in this country!" Grandma Natica exclaimed.

On top of all this, the Party kindly forced Mom to study for a degree. She had to grit her teeth and pull all her energies together in order to secure a degree in French at the Workers' Schedule. She had to attend classes every night from seven to eleven. And she was almost eligible for retirement.

All that was added to her obligations as "union" delegate.

Life for her had become a B.I.G. mess.

Her Mercedes-Benz came out of its coma, but it was being held together by little pieces of wire and all sorts of grafts from a Volga and a Moscovich, and it was forever declaring itself on strike.

And then, her boss started picking on her.

Malicious rumors reached me in no time that Mom was often seen crying in the street. I decided to do something about it.

A couple of ideas came to mind.

I made her stay home to rest for one day.

"One day only, Mom, I beg of you! Since I've known you, you haven't missed a single day, ever. Please." She agreed.

I then went to have it out with her irrational jackass of a boss, Eduardo.

"She's always doing everybody else's job!" he protested.

He accused her of trying to help other people so much that she neglected her own work. He was simply not aware of the fact that she didn't belong to herself and that she felt a deep dissatisfaction with herself. She managed to bury this dissatisfaction only out of sheer willpower.

He also accused her of being obsessed with her studies, and of spending mornings at the chiropodist while leaving her eyeglasses on her desk so people would think that she was around.

"She's only trying to get a degree because the Party ordered her to. If helping others is a defect, well, she's got it. But she's incapable of a sneaky calculation like leaving her eyeglasses 'present' while she is absent. I will ask her to put her feet up on your desk. She has worked very hard, and has more corns than a cornfield to prove it. Do you know why? Because when idiots like you were still peeing in their diapers, she threw her home and her family out the window so that *you* could become what *you* are now. You know what else? If you don't leave her alone, I swear to you I am going to ruin your life. The woman is old enough to be your mother!"

My second option was like flipping a coin in the air.

I went to see my uncle Raúl Castro, who by then had given me a job as a French translator in his office.

"Did you know, Uncle, that I read all the letters you wrote to my mother before that bastard Pacheco swindled her out of them in the name of the Museo de la Revolución? They were beautiful letters."

Raúl was caught up in nostalgia for the old times.

"She was like a fairy godmother to all of us."

No kidding!

And since I had struck a poetic chord, I wrested out of my soul that "she has become depressed, and no matter how hard I try to lift her spirits, there's nothing I can do. She is like a sick flower, squandering its fragrance when you least expect it, and closing at the first light of day, instead of opening. And yet, she did display her full corolla for people who neither saw her nor appreciated her; and she helped them so much, pawned all her jewels without hope of retrieval, to buy weapons for the Moncada assault," and blah, blah, blah.

I then tried to get her Mercedes exchanged for another car "not really new, but in good shape."

"You do like Mercedes-Benz cars, and this one can be fixed perfectly at MININT's Workshop Number One. It's the same model as the ones you have," I told Raúl.

"I can't accept that, my niece. You sell it. So you can have a little money. You can get an incredible sum for it. And if you want my advice, sell it out in the country. With the black market, the farmers are filling their pockets with money and they have nowhere to spend it."

That was true, there was nothing to buy. Since he was in a generous mood, I made one last request.

"Uncle, what would you think if, to make her the happiest being on earth, you included her in the 26 de Julio celebrations? You know, every time she hears that the participants in the Moncada assault are having their annual reunion, but she's not invited, she just wilts."

"That I cannot promise you. I need to check on it."

As a result of my meeting with Raúl, my mother got a blue VW the next day and, a few months later, an invitation to the 26 de Julio festivities. There was a catch, though: she was not invited as an ex-participant, but as a relative of the martyrs—even though the only casualty in her family had been the coiffure, with its English-style permanent wave, that fell off Grandma Natica during her exploratory trip to Oriente province.

*   *   *

*I finally had gotten* the message and stopped the rigors of my useless training for competitive swimming so that I could attend the Saúl Delgado Institute, a college preparatory school in the Vedado. It was the absolute domain of a dark force of education, Mrs. Marquetti. With an Italian name made famous in baseball, a toothy mouth on a black face, and burning eyes, she had a visceral hatred for anything connected to Revolutionary "leaders." Since she couldn't get at them directly, she harassed their children.

Just by chance, Hildita Guevara and I met again at the Institute. Our friendship was unaltered by time or the distance of our unplanned separation.

Her mother had died of cancer, a disease that shows no mercy, in less than six months after being diagnosed. Hildita told me something that, in a moment of cowardice, I quickly buried in my conscience among the horde of detailed and desperate confessions from many other people, in the desire not to let go of my own innocence.

"Do you know what my mother told me before she died? There she was, her lungs half gone, about to breathe her last sigh. But she could not help herself. Do you know what she said to me? That the Cubans had let my father die in Bolivia. That it was all part of a scheme to create the Necessary Hero. That all those letters they say he left are fake, the product of expert calligraphers. Even my own letter! She warned me to be on the watch for the truth, because it would come out one day. Damn it, why can't people just die, and leave the living in peace?"

I didn't know what to say. Her mother, the Venerable Frog, had always seemed inscrutable to me, and besides, who wants to see sacred myths deconstructed?

*Not even my friend* Hildita could cope with Mrs. Marquetti at the Saúl Delgado Institute. She left after six months, but not before the Marquetti woman managed to humiliate her one last time.

Hildita married a Mexican who had been exiled in Cuba after a massacre of Mexican laborers by someone named Echevarría, later elected president of Mexico [1970–1976]. Echevarría was honored in Cuba with a red-carpet reception, but before his visit, all the Mexicans exiled on the Island on his account were arrested. This seems to be regular police procedure all over the world.

Hildita's husband was imprisoned around the same time, and disillusionment found its way into both their lives.

I went to see her, bringing a small suitcase full of clothes and a pair of shoes, because she was living now under the same conditions of poverty from which she had saved me when we were both eleven.

When I met her she had a newborn in her arms, a baby plagued by all sorts of tropical parasites. She accompanied her husband during his second exile—to Italy, heaven knows why. I heard again from her years later, when another defeat made her return to Cuba, gratefully. It was the only place where she could count on being able to see a psychiatrist, and on friends to bring food for her second child. By then she could no longer distinguish between a bottle of rum and a baby bottle.


*José Ramón Pérez had* overexcited all of the maidens at the Delgado Institute in the Vedado with his multiple charms.

He had mischievous green eyes, small, beautiful teeth. His hair formed a rebellious fuzzy plume on his perfectly round head. But what really made him stand out were his tie-dyed jeans, a pair of fringed suede boots, and a white Volkswagen. He was a fashion plate in a country of ration books. His Volkswagen, a white messenger pigeon, made him king of the road in the land of no traffic, at a time when waiting at a bus stop was about as useful as fervent prayer.

Besides, his father was in the Political Bureau.

Those were more than enough reasons for Marquetti to throw him out of the school, but he kept on being the golden charmer.

Imagine my surprise when he started to pay attention to shabby me.

Love's arrows are always unpredictable.

His illustrious father had exchanged his matrimonial bed for that of a female office manager twenty years his junior. The abandonment left his family in deep mourning and fostered in his son a muddled sensibility.

In other words, he was a tad sick. He was sixteen when he became the first man in our house. My boyfriend went from my knees to my grandmother's knees, and he liked to squeeze and kiss my evasive mother.

One of his rituals, which he made into an obligation, was to turn off all the lights and make sure the house was well locked before leaving me properly tucked in bed though sexually intact.

Every night, José would sit at the edge of my bed, introduce his left hand under the covers, and begin to touch me slowly. "To get to know your body by heart," he would tell me. Engaged in a detailed tongue exploration, he already had his head and half his body under the sheets by the time my grandmother awakened in the darkness from her hermetic snoring.

"José Ramón, are you still here?"

"I'm already closing the door, Grandma!" he would call back.

Like the Wolf in "Little Red Riding Hood," Grandma Natica would fall asleep again, dreaming perhaps of a miraculous cure for the sick mango tree in the garden, which aborted its enormous, seedless fetuses way ahead of season, or for the crotons and rosebushes she had grafted.

I would be disturbed, exhausted, and moist in the disarray of the fresh sheets when José left, walking slowly. He was not headed for home.

The more lies he told, and the more trouble he got into, the more friends he had. José Ramón turned the drama of being the traumatized son of a political leader into a profitable profession. Instead of paying his bills at the Hotel Habana Libre (formerly the Hilton), which was his domain, he used to sign for them. We called him "Baby Hilton." After leaving me excited and happy in a dream world accompanied by my grandmother's snores, he would go in search of release for his own excitement, straight into the arms of some night creature, in the hotel's cabaret. He never pressured me further, and for the time being I held on to my virginity.

\*    \*    \*

*José Ramón had an* obsessive ambition to enter the police corps of the Ministry of the Interior (MININT), just like hundreds of young men who thought, not without cause, that State Security was an elite corps. I don't know with what kind of ID card he convinced someone to lend him a Colt .45 pistol. But one night about ten o'clock, as we were leaving Polinesio, he drew the gun and shot a stream of bullets into the grass bordering the sidewalk. He did it to threaten two macho guys whom he had overheard making lascivious comments about my legs and my mother's inviting curves while he was paying the bill for our zombies and barbecued chicken.

We spent a long night at the preventive jail facilities of Zanja Street and Dragones, in the midst of Chinatown in Old Havana. My mother, thanks to her air of respectability and Communist Party membership, was allowed to sleep in a police patrol car parked across the street.

She lay down in the backseat of the car and stuck her pretty legs out the window. She was wearing a dainty pair of shoes from the old Paris days, and slept just like that all night.

Early the next morning, people on their way to work were stopping to look at her.


*A lot of time* had now gone by since the day that Fidel, triumphant and acclaimed, spent over nine hours explaining how he was planning to separate the regular army from his own troops that had just come down with him from the mountains.

A medallion with Our Lady of Mercy, syncretically also called Obbatalá in the Afro-Cuban religion, hung from Fidel's neck, while white doves pecked away at the birdseed on the epaulets of his uniform.

The anniversary celebration of the establishment of MININT and of MINFAR [Ministry of the Revolutionary Armed Forces] took place that year in Miramar, at the Patricio Lumumba Workmen's Social Circle, the former Biltmore Country Club. It was a day filled with the kind of music and homilies that would have altered the neurovegetative system of a llama. A tall, dark-haired man, beginning to turn gray, with a sardonic grin and catlike movements, crossed my path.

I suffer from a kind of esthetic Daltonism that makes people look either pretty or ugly to me. It is all based on my third eye, which has defied every effort by friend or foe to make me see things as they are. And I had all my eyes on Yoyi, the dark-haired man, and used all my wiles until we were properly introduced. I had such good luck that I let him, my future husband, take me home at the end of the evening. He had a beat-up Chevrolet, assigned to him so that he could fully attend to his missions as a counterintelligence lieutenant on his way to being a captain, and also be on time for his karate lessons. I was Cinderella in a government carriage. And just sixteen, with a prince twice my age.

He began to furtively write suggestive poems to me, and we started to meet secretly around the noon break.

But there are no secrets on the Island. An avalanche of unpleasant rumors exposed our relationship.

My boyfriend, José Ramón, still under house arrest after the shooting at Polinesio, showed me to the door of no return, and Yoyi, married to a black singer who still has the best voice in Cuba, had to start his uncertain trek, with a couple of suitcases full of clothes, papers, and shoes, counting on short stays at friends' homes.

And friends were the best thing Yoyi had. Mom and Grandma were simply delighted. His friends were all charming, full of exquisite possibilities like restaurants and nightclubs and, for weekends, houses at the beach, cabins in the mountains, fishing trips, and traveling.

The magical world of the Cuban military elite. We had joined the best in uniform.

This circle of friends made Lala Natica feel useful and happy again, thanks to her culinary offerings of gourmet concoctions. She resurrected old recipes in her kitchen, like her lobster *au chocolat* and her famous soufflé, and offered marriage counseling on the phone to his friends' wives, women twenty years older than I and with whom I had very few common topics of conversation.

Mommy didn't have to worry about things malfunctioning or breaking anymore, or about any kind of emergency, because suddenly, fortune was squeezing the good side of the horn of plenty. With Pepe Abrantes, recently named minister of the interior; El Gallego ("The Galician") Franco, chief of the National Police; and the De la Guardia twins from the Special Troops, together with their chief, Pascualito, at her beck and call, all problems and snafus could be easily resolved.[8]


*We were all having* lunch at L'Aiglon in the Riviera Hotel with the twins, Patricio and Tony, one day.

"What are the Special Troops?" I innocently asked them.

"It's an elite unit, the army's assault troops for all special war missions."

"Assault? What is Cuba going to assault? Aren't we an antiwar, pacifist country? Aren't we defending all nations' rights to self-determination and opposing Imperialist intervention in the internal affairs of any country?"

I knew the rhetoric by heart. I had heard it hundreds of times.

Yoyi grew livid. My mother urgently elbowed my ribs, and the twins looked at me as if I had just been beamed down from Mars. But I was not a Martian. I was just considered stupid.

As a result, they were never very cautious whenever they spoke of secret topics in my presence.

The trouble started when it was our own friends' lives that were endangered. After Fidel's campaign for Allende in Chile[9]—an affair they called Operation Salvador—Pepe Abrantes developed a chronic illness by having to run next to the Comandante's Jeep for a whole month. Besides leaving Abrantes with a permanent heart condition, the Allende campaign almost cost the twins their lives.

Things (the "conduits of penetration," or something like that) had apparently been well organized from the beginning. Tati, Allende's daughter, was already married, as planned, to poor Luis, a State Security officer. Getting him divorced from his Cuban wife so he could carry out his mission in Chile had been a problem. Allende had accepted one of the twins, Tony de la Guardia, as chief coordinator for the Grupo de Amigos del Presidente, or GAP, which was the future president's personal guard, thanks to the efforts of a Chilean agent known as El Guatón (the fat one), who had been trained and molded in Cuba.

I paid attention on and off to this specialized terminology. Fidel's prolonged campaign trip in support of Salvador Allende was an everyday topic on the television news.

One day, while the De la Guardia twins were in Chile, their wives were enjoying a luncheon with us, prepared by Natica. It was being served in the garden. There, after fifteen years of abstinence, the white wrought-iron tables could again be in pleasurable contact with curly parsley, grandma onions, cloves of garlic, and lobsters' deadly weapons, finally able to forget the privation of ration books. A voice suddenly interrupted all radio and television programs to break the news that army tanks were surrounding the Palacio de la Moneda in Chile, where Allende was making a stand together with his daughters. The GAP were ready to offer their lives in defense of democracy. Wives, friends, and I were all in a state of inconsolable grief when we were astonished to see on the television screen, in the pink of health, the twins and the Troops, and half of the GAP with their chief, El Guatón Marambio, on their way to asylum in Cuba.

The best part was that they all had time to pack their presents and drag along their television sets and washing machines, while we were under the impression that they were giving up their lives in La Moneda to defend the president.

A few days later, Tati Allende was found dead in Havana. She had shot herself. The gun belonged to her husband, the officer from the Cuban State Security. Soon after that, Allende's sister, too, committed suicide in Havana. She jumped from one of the top floors of the Riviera Hotel.

Fidel had achieved an ideological victory.

"A revolution cannot succeed without the violence of an armed intervention."

The twins, along with Yoyi and me, went to relax after all this stress, to one of the Troop cabins at Soroa Falls, a resort festooned with ferns and various wet creatures.

*Another stint at Escuela* al Campo interrupted my idyll. This time I had to spend two and a half months in the province of Pinar del Río under the Tobacco Plan.

Since I had no tonsils or appendix left to extirpate, no fisheye warts or any other juvenile warts to incinerate at the diabolical hands of Alonso the dermatologist, I had to report to the school immediately. I went with the usual bucket, hat, suitcase, and wooden flip-flops.

I started a one-person strike: "no bath, no food." In order to survive in the dietary meagerness of the camp, I fixed the peasants' shirt-sleeves in exchange for a plate of rice and beans. I covered my body with a layer of tobacco resin as an insect repellent.

One day, I was awakened before dawn by a flashlight shining directly on my face, blinding me. "You have an urgent meeting at the warehouse," said the Marquetti woman, sneering at me with the glory of all her teeth.

The warehouse was the domain of the mice, who disdained the brown sugar bags to go pee in the rice and the toasted corn flour. I found five of my friends perched on the bags: Hildita, Aimée Vidal, whose mother was a popular television announcer, and three other girls from the social class that made Marquetti's blood boil.

The argument started with hygiene. We were accused of not bathing. We defended ourselves, saying that with ten primitive overflowing bathrooms for five hundred women, one came out of a bath dirtier than before.

"And that's not all! You play baseball and, instead of going to sleep, you spend the night singing and scratching each other, picking off the fleas and lice that, unfortunately, we have not been able to eradicate from the school. This mutual pawing is despicable!"

With a knowing smile, Conchita Ariosa nodded, letting her eroded teeth show. Her buddy Luisa agreed. Conchita and Luisa were first and second secretaries, respectively, of the Communist Youth group. With the baths as point of reference, the whole issue had been turned to active homosexuality.

That Marquetti woman was determined to make pariahs out of all of us. In some ways she succeeded. Some of the girls lost their boyfriends because of these rumors. They were left with their adolescent fates twisted and falsified.

\* \* \*

*When I returned from* the countryside, I found Yoyi wedded to my matriarchs and conveniently installed in my home.

It was a pleasant surprise to find his shaving cream on my wash-bowl and a man's disorder, instead of mine, in my room and my bed.

Despite Grandma's acid commentaries—"Alina, how can you sleep with a man who has done it with a black woman? That's a step back-ward, m'dear child!"—she herself had made room for him.

In the meantime, I had to sleep in a bedroom in the back of the house.

Of course, this did not prevent a lot of masturbation and innumer-able steamy situations which seemed to me something more properly enjoyed later, after consummating the nuptials. I went into his room one night and made him break down that uncomfortable barrier that was putting rings under his sleepless eyes.

"You can go ahead now, everybody's sleeping!"

It was all very romantic, and I got pregnant.

Fearing the usual malicious gossip, my mother took me aside.

"A child, you? When you can't even finish anything you start?"

My matriarchs threw everything at me—my social maladjustment, the women I drew from the back, and all my traumas as a child aban-doned by an elusive father. So I let myself be taken to the Best Hospi-tal for Gynecology in All of Latin America, as they called it. But something must have happened in the abortion room, because after-ward I would wake up howling every night, and every day exactly at noon, in the middle of class, I felt a hand ripping my inner core and then doubling me up in pain, making me sweat in silent terror. It was as if that rejected soul could not, and would not, forgive me.

Nevertheless, we all continued preparing for the wedding.

From a trunk that had made it across the ocean from France, Mom unearthed a yard and a half of embroidered Swiss linen. With this, Juana the seamstress fashioned a wedding dress for me. She made the slip for it out of one of Natalie's linen batiste dresses.

We set the ceremony for March 28. It was to be at the beach, and our friends had organized a perfect evening for us.

*   *   *

*One day, the phone* rang.

"I want to talk to Alina!"

"Speaking."

"Well, this is Leivita, chief of your father's Personal Guard. I'm so pissed off I can barely speak! You ungrateful daughter! Yes! You're an ungrateful daughter with no respect for your father, for El Comandante!"

I thought it was a prank, so I hung up. The oddly named Leivita called again.

"Put your mother on the phone now!"

"Me? A bad revolutionary? Compañero, get hold of yourself and show a little more respect!" I heard her counter.

Leivita went on to threaten Yoyi with the Counterintelligence Service's eternal displeasure, and shouted (at me, again) that I couldn't leave the house until El Comandante found the time to send for me.

"Do you think I'm going to be here just waiting for him to have some time for me? I'm getting married in four days, you know. The best I can do is let everybody know where I can be reached." I hung up.

Every time I went out, and wherever I went, someone from Personal Security would show up to check on me. It terrified the people I was with. It was even worse for my mother, for my future husband, and for all his friends, who suddenly didn't know whether he had fallen into disgrace and they should break off their relationship with him.

We were once at the Bodeguita del Medio, an emporium of indigestion with its mojitos and *chicharrones* (fried pork rinds), and struggling with our postprandial avatars, when Leivita materialized, all five feet of him. He respectfully mistreated me until he succeeded in getting me into an Alfa Romeo bristling with antennae.

"Yellow calling Blue! Yellow calling Blue! Heading for target with objective."

His objective was fuming from every pore.

Judging by the unpleasant demeanor of the guards at the basement doors of the Palacio de la Revolución, I concluded that during the previous seventy-two hours I must have altered the pulse of Cuban history.

I was led into a rectangular office with a luxurious parquet floor and an abundance of tropical plants, and was directed to sit facing a large desk, and shelves holding jars filled with seeds and a few books.

It was two o'clock in the morning. Due to my digestion and the deadly $CO_2$ emanating from so many locked-in plants, I was dozing off when the Comandante came in. He was both uncomfortable and terse. I took a look at him from head to toe. His boots were a new model, black patent leather with squared toes, which made his legs look thinner. I smiled at him and was first on the attack. With a kiss.

Silence.

Then, dialogue.

"I sent for you because of your wedding."

"Oh."

"What date have you set?"

"We're still planning on the twenty-eighth of March. And you're invited, of course."

"There is something I don't understand, that I can't figure out: why you haven't asked for my permission."

My first impulse was to grab him by his lapels and shake him, but I didn't.

"Permission? And how do I do that? By praying? I have never had even a telephone number where I could reach you."

"I know. I'll admit that I haven't taken enough care of you. But getting married at sixteen!"

"Seventeen, since last week."

"What difference does it make? You hardly know this man."

"He's been living in our house for months, and he takes care of everything. As you well know, we are all women, and everything is so difficult. We have even found footprints in the garden under the windows. People have been watching us and trying to break in and rob us."

"But this individual has nothing in common with you. He was married to a singer!"

"You're not going to start in on me with my grandmother's argument, are you? That the woman is black and that if—"

"Stop interrupting me, please! I think this individual is an opportunist!"

"Opportunist? There is nothing in my home but troubles and misery. He was the one who caught the maid after she stole the silver samovar, and . . . Look, it's very late, and I don't want to keep on talking shit."

"Watch your language! I'm not using that kind of language with you!"

"I'm sorry. Are you really serious about this?"

"I don't know if you know this man has been in jail."

"Yes, for fraud. He was in charge of a warehouse and he distributed some television sets among his friends. People can change, you know."

"People don't change. I'll give you an example. A man once attempted to assassinate me. This was ten years ago. I saved him from being executed and gave him a minimum jail sentence. I talked with him several times. We even, personally, took care of his family. He was set free, and in less than three months he was in jail again."

"Did he make another attempt on your life?"

"No. He was trying to leave the country illegally, with his entire family."

Maybe it was because the many plants rarified the air in the room and I was not breathing enough oxygen. The truth is I could not follow his reasoning.

"I still can't figure out why on earth you have not asked my permission." The discussion was taking a rather byzantine turn. "You have not known this man long enough. An engagement should last two years, at least. I'm not even going to ask you whether you've already . . . I don't want to discuss those things with you."

He was, of course, referring to my virginity. He was not making much headway, so he launched a deeper attack.

"And it's not only stealing. That man has also committed rape!"

"What?"

"Yes! Everybody knows that when he was an interrogator at Villa Marista, he raped several of the women in custody."

"It really disturbs me that this regime has chosen a convicted thief, suspected of rape, as a Counterintelligence officer."

With that, I ran out of arguments.

"If you marry that man the day after tomorrow, do not consider me your father any longer!"

"I won't notice much of a difference."

"If you don't marry him, I promise you that things are going to change. I am only asking you to wait a little longer."

My progenitor managed to win the negotiations with the promise to provide food and drinks for the wedding party, if such a thing ever occurred.

He then took me home along the Malecón Drive, making promises of a more militant fatherhood. When we reached the Nuevo Vedado and I opened the car door, Mom, Yoyi, and Grandma saw him by my side and stood at attention. Poor Yoyi, standing there in his pajamas and his wooden flip-flops, gave him a military salute. Grandma turned away in disgust, and Mom recoiled in awe and began mumbling things like "You look fine" and "How's everything?"

Fidel came in and made a phone call to Lupe Véliz, wife of Antonio Núñez Jiménez, author of the very popular official geography of Cuba. She was getting some sweet reward ready for Fidel: an actress, a journalist, or a foreign ballerina. It was almost dawn when I accompanied him to the door.

"He doesn't seem like such a bad guy after all," Fidel conceded.

"You see? Listen, where did you get such beautiful boots?"

"Ah, they're handmade. Italian. Celia had them made for me."


*We postponed the wedding* until further notice. Fidel tried to fulfill his promise to change and become a father.

The day Brezhnev arrived in Havana, Fidel stopped by our house in his gala uniform. We kowtowed to him and revered his magnificent presence.

Then he went to Eastern Europe, and when he came back, just like when he returned from Chile, there was a family welcoming party at

Protocol House Number One. This time, Fidel made a futile attempt at reconciliation between Fidelito and me.

For his sisters, sisters-in-law, and nieces, Fidel brought back luxuries not easily found in Cuba: bottles of shampoo and small boxes of Russian chocolates. Even Mom got a present. For all the men he brought Bulova watches.

A few days after the party, Sosa, the army officer bearer of good news, paid us a visit at home. He came with a big smile and a set of bracelet, necklace, brooch, and earrings, all presented in a fancy Russian box. They were not diamonds, but Russian "glassmonds." They were worse than the gift perfume of the same provenance.

Less than a month had gone by when Fidel sent for me to invite me to the movies in another one of his houses in El Laguito. He sat me in the theater, wrapping me in a velvety coat because outside it was the kind of cold weather only otters enjoy. What we saw was a big surprise, a documentary of his trip through Eastern Europe. Silly me, not going to the movies lately, trying to avoid the hoopla of the newsreels!

Fidel was fascinated by how well people dressed in Europe. He had noticed how different it was in Cuba.

How could it not be different, when in Cuba people were making their clothes out of hand-painted burlap bags? When I mentioned the ration books with their allotment of only two yards of fabric and two spools of thread a year, he changed the topic.

*Yoyi and I were* married in August, five months later than the date we had originally set.

For the wedding reception, Fidel contributed food and drinks: a pasta salad with bits of pineapple; pastries; and ten bottles of Havana Club rum, plus one bottle of whiskey for him. Everything was served on little silver trays by Personal Security staff, who had also taken care of crossing all my guests off the list, including Hildita Guevara and her undesirable husband.

My wedding was a political event, with a toast. Even the female notary who performed the ceremony was from the Ministry of the Interior.

Fidel arrived on time, authorized the marriage with his signature, and had his fun. But it was no fun for me, and even less for my poor husband. To make the situation bearable, Yoyi drank, and I had never seen him get so intoxicated. Our honeymoon, decreed by the Wedding Palace, consisted of three days and two nights at the Habana Libre. It was a horrible ordeal full of disillusionment and vomiting. Just before leaving the wedding reception, my father had taken me aside and given me warning:

"Don't let me know when you get your divorce."

"Don't worry. I still don't have your phone number."


*Yoyi and I tried* to make up for our failed honeymoon with a trip to Varadero: a week of lying in the sun like two harbor seals, and as bored as two alligators in a flower vase.

Grandma Natica reclaimed her role as vigilant champion of the female honor of the family, as she had done before when her daughter got out of hand with the bearded rebel.

"Yoyi, my granddaughter is too pretty and too young for you to be sleeping with that filthy fat woman. Shame on you!"

The "filthy fat woman" was the person in charge of the frozen zone of real estate in the Nuevo Vedado. She was also responsible for decorating the homes of political leaders with furniture confiscated from other homes.

Yoyi and I moved to an apartment decorated by the filthy fat woman. I couldn't sleep at night. I missed my room, my bathroom, my bed, my pillow. One night at two in the morning, I trekked home in the dark down Twenty-sixth Avenue to my family's house.

The fat woman had nothing to do with the bunch of little devils planted in my head the night my father accused my husband of being a rapist and a thief.

I was still mystified by the awed worship and reverential fear of those who applauded Fidel, shouting "Viva! Viva!" as if the compass of their thoughts had gone haywire and lost its bearings.

The following August, I was an eighteen-year-old divorcée. It seemed that all the Counterintelligence officers and the entire elite unit of the Special Assault Troops had agreed on a joint mission: trying to sleep with me. I was constantly finding one or another of my husband's "best friends" at every corner, and even inside our house. The problem was that Grandma Natica, reluctant to abandon the social and culinary activity she had enjoyed, would open the door for them. She continually urged me to pick up the phone to talk to their wives.

The best solution I found was to try to get away.


*The new Escuela al Campo* had become the perfected version of José Martí's dream. To attend was no longer a matter of staying to work for two and a half months, but of living and studying right there.

Throughout the Island, gray buildings called *albergues* went up. The students would live in them six days a week, with classes in the morning and farming in the afternoon.

Silvio Rodríguez, the national singer-composer laureate had been assigned by the government to lure the masses. His latest pedagogical invention was a chant.

> *This is the New House.*
> *This is the New School.*
> *New House and New School,*
> *Birthplace of a New Race.*

In spite of which, Silvio is a great poet.


*"Your uniforms have been* selected for their comfort and practicality," Fidel announced. "Synthetic fabrics are hot, but they don't wrinkle easily. This avoids the need for ironing, thus reducing the chance of accidents and fires. The style of the shoes can easily be changed. . . ."

The shoes were plastic ones from the Japanese factory that Fidel had bought in 1967; they had been covering the feet of the country with fungi ever since.

"It is not true that students quickly pay back the cost of all our investment with the work they do. It takes three years," he tirelessly repeated.

The relief I gained by leaving home and going to a new school called Leoncio Prado, a prefab building an hour and a half from Havana, didn't last long. There was no end to the unbearable communality in the bathing, the sleeping, the shitting, the fucking, the witchcraft, the vulgarities, the snitching, the stealing, the Communist militancy, and the double standards.

At Leoncio Prado, we were assigned to the Pineapple Plan. It involved plantings full of murderous barbs. For months we slaved away with our mouths watering, our asses melting, and our anatomy tortured by gashes and scratches from the spiny pineapples. We all were eternally hungry, and waiting for harvest time to be able to fill our bellies.

Teachers and principals had simplified cheating so that their schools could win in the Socialist Emulation. They wrote the test on the board for us the day before.

We were offered preferred admission to the university anyway, and I was still obsessed with a medical career. One afternoon a friend of Yoyi's appeared on the school grounds. It was Honduras, the most persistent of the deceptive horde of guys on the make who wanted to get on top of me after my divorce. He was a Central American Indian from Honduras, and it showed.

He was an orphan abandoned in Cuba. His mother had sent him to Havana to spend his vacation with an aunt. One day, coming home from the tireless, playful world of a twelve-year-old, he found his house empty. His aunt had suddenly fled the country, without leaving word, when she saw the Revolution coming.

I could imagine that Indian boy alone in Havana in the midst of mass hysteria and shouts of "Viva! Viva!" and "To the Wall! To the Wall!" suddenly struck by the realization of his situation crashing down on him like a freezing waterfall.

The army took care of him. He fared well until, as a teenager, he found himself with a weekend pass in his hands and nowhere to go.

"It was then that I discovered funeral parlors. One can stay there all night, and there is always some female mourner to console," he told me.

Honduras was a junior lieutenant in the Special Troops and he had a feverish imagination. We were a healthy and joyful pair, and, of course, we began seeing each other secretly. Good old Abrantes found out and sent him ipso facto to Japan to become fourth *dan* in karate. From Japan he wrote me beautiful letters that filled my life and my heart with misspellings and mistakes in punctuation, syntax, and many other things. They were missives without shame or pain, with love and need of me so joyful, so basic, and naked that I can hardly forgive myself for not having continued to live in that chapter of my past.

One evening, when Fidel sent for me to forgive me for my first divorce, I was ready to expose him to the prospect of a second one, but he didn't give me time. I was sitting there, listening to him talk about hydroponics and the new Five-Year Plan. He was still talking about growing grapes, strawberries, and rice out of sea spray.

Suddenly, a perverse kind of energy distorted my vision. I saw his skin begin to disappear as he became a bundle of tendons and nerves tied around an evil aura, and then an enormous and bloody third eye appeared on his forehead.

I shook away my horror, but ever since that evening I have felt that something broke inside me. My menses stopped, and my intestines became paralyzed.

In spite of Honduras's passionate love, which I returned, I began to deteriorate and to hate my body. It was not responding and seemed instead to be making faces at me like a renegade.

So I began punishing it and depriving it of food.

I attended the celebrations at the end of the school term and of my admission to the School of Medicine, as well as the long-awaited return of my epistolary boyfriend, weighing only eighty-eight pounds. Honduras had just landed at the José Martí airport. As I stood there with the help of four pairs of socks inside my panties and some rags stuffed in my bra, my letter-writing boyfriend passed me by and kept on walking.

He had been unable to recognize that spatula of a woman who smiled at him with her ghoulish, death-mask grin. But love made him lucid. He began by putting bits of half-chewed food into my mouth, the way one does with a sick bird.

Anorexia was an unknown disease in Cuba then. Honduras had discovered what many psychiatrists had not: a disease that is caused by lack of love can be cured by love and attention.

Mom got some medical expertise out of a few back issues of *The New York Times* that had come to her office, rather her remodeled closet space, at MINCEX. It specifically was advice out of the "Open Letters to a Doctor" section. One day she came up to me on the porch. I was lying in a hammock, and I lifted my head to hear her translation of the articles.

" 'Dear Mrs.————: If your daughter's obsession with losing weight is out of control, she is suffering from anorexia nervosa. This disease is directly related to the kind of bond established with her mother during infancy.' "

"You're not to blame for anything, Mom, if my word is good enough for you."

For Mom, guilt is a familiar, comfortable feeling.

"Maybe. But why do you stretch your neck all the time, like a chicken, while you listen to me? Do you never lean back?"

"I suppose. My neck doesn't feel tired."

So she went inside, then returned to the porch, this time with a book on psychiatry.

"When people are able to hold their heads up without a break for a long time without feeling tired, we have what is called a psychological pillow. It is a characteristic of the 'paranoid personality.' And by the way, if you want Honduras to continue living here, you'll have to get married. I won't allow shacking-up in this house."

She got up and walked away, leaving me with a weakened neck for the rest of my life.

Cohabitation was not the real issue here. The Committee for the Defense of the Revolution had already come to our house asking for the RD-3 form from OFICODA[10] and the Certificate of Employment "of the *compañero* living in the premises. You know that you cannot 'aggregate' a citizen to the household, *compañera,* unless you notify the Committee."

*It was easier for* Honduras to charm Natica than it had been for Yoyi. Because of the black woman in his "obituary," she had written him off. Besides, Honduras, on the other hand, was bringing home lots of food and whole tins of almond ice cream that he took from the officers' mess hall of the Special Troops.

The best part for me was that he brought home the same friends we had before. The De la Guardia twins had been sponsoring him for a long time. He had come to be like a third son for their parents, two adorable old people nicknamed Mimí and Popín.

Fidel liked this new, unheralded husband of mine so much that he invited us to the New Year's Eve party to be held at Abrantes's house.

After that successful evening, Abrantes himself named Honduras his new assistant and personal chauffeur.

I kept studying at the School of Medicine.

Everything was going along fine until the war in Angola broke out and the Island became hysterical with a sudden war fever.

The first line of action was to empty the black ghettoes. They were the same old ghettoes from before the Revolution: La Dionisia, El Palo Cagao, Llega y Pon. The black platoons were the first ones Cuba sent to Angola.

It reeked of racism from all sides.

I became very difficult with everyone. I wanted someone to explain to me how Cuba had all of a sudden turned Imperialistic after so much preaching in favor of "The Right of All Countries to Self-Determination" and against "Intervention in the Internal Affairs of Other Nations."

I remembered the reactions I got: I just seemed like a Martian to them.

Frustrated, I went to the Palacio de la Revolución to take my turn in Fidel's waiting room and see if he could finally give me his Reasons of State. After waiting for a while, I met him in front of a map filled with glass-head pins.

That was how he moved his troops. He moved the pins.

At last Fidel had a real war. He was bored with the minor skirmishes in Syria, Algiers, Namibia, Afghanistan, and Latin America. This was going to be his emancipation from Russia. He did not even hear me when I asked him how, if we were living under the constant threat of Yankee invasion, he could leave the Island bereft of its army and its weapons of defense.

I left the Palace with the bitter conviction that my conscience had been swindled, and that the Yankees were delighted to have Fidel ninety miles away, planting subversion in the rest of the world. As long as Fidel was there, the United States could always find employment for its blond, gum-chewing army, idle since Vietnam and Korea.

The setup was like having a fumigation team ready to be sent wherever Fidel fostered Communism.

The Yankees couldn't have designed a better arrangement.


*Our friends in the* Special Assault Troops who had survived Chile left for Angola after the black platoons. That is just what they were: a movable Cuban army.

I was still obdurate in my stance that defending Communism by violating Communist principles did not make any sense at all.

That's when I started picking on Honduras.

"You're not going, are you? You're going to refuse to be making new orphans in Angola, aren't you?"

"Are you crazy, sweetie? How would I look playing a martyr, and a coward to boot? How on earth am I going to say no? And what about the Revolution?"

"You too? Don't give me that line about going to Angola to defend the Revolution! The Revolution is here in Cuba, it seems to me!"

My life had turned into fishing trips, houses at the beach, clothes, and watches. I finally came down from my sojourn in the clouds and got over my temporary comfortable blindness.

I had an attack of principles.

"Why do you call yourselves soldiers? You are mercenaries really!"

My dearly beloved scratched his head, thinking.

"I shouldn't understand you, but I do," he said. "The truth is, Alina, that for a blockhead like me, thinking is a dangerous thing. Let's leave the thinking for those who can. I have been a nobody for a very long time."

Honduras had taught me a lot of things, though. Like the times when we had to put aside so much of our romantic love and face the everyday miseries that eat up all the magic. Whenever he felt I was pushing him away, he would tell me:

"Hold my hand, and never let it go. Love creates its own needs little by little."

And I responded, "Don't worry about it. Maybe I can learn to live with twisted truths."

Though it would never occur to many of those who fought in Angola that they were mercenaries, they were really just that: Cuban soldiers paid by Agostinho Neto. He even paid our government for the stays in port of the Cuban ships.

In the end, Cuba was left a little poorer and a little more naked. And in mourning.

*Abrantes, who was already minister* of the interior, was then assigned to inspect the troops in Angola. I had a premonition that if his lowly assistant Honduras accompanied him to Angola, he would not be able to return. He would have to face the recriminations of his friends and fellow soldiers from so many combat operations. The gossip and resentments in the barracks were no different from those in a whorehouse.

My ovaries were on strike, my digestion was paralyzed, and I had a multitude of other health problems that were completely psychosomatic. Honduras was afraid I would starve myself to death if I was left alone at home without his pre-chewed food and his loving care, so he convinced Abrantes to put me in the hospital for a checkup during the time of his scheduled tour.

I waited for him in a room of the enclosed preserve commonly called the Clinic. There the Politburo people and their relatives are taken care of. For legal purposes and medical certificates, its name is the Surgical Unit of MININT.

Abrantes returned from his tour in three weeks. He came straight from the airport to tell me that Honduras had to stay in Angola because there were rumors among the troops that he was off the hook in his share of dangerous assignments only because he was married to the Comandante's daughter.

"Being a soldier, he should have taken that defect of mine into account," I said.

"A designated officer will bring you his pay, and his letters as they come. He has already authorized you to receive his pay, and he asked me to take very good care of you."

That evening I discharged myself from the hospital and went back home.


*His letters from Angola* left me in a state of fear:

I belong compañera to the scout team now imagine and yesterday I was more than six hour under a rock and under fire but from our own troops which is what happens when you go in the advance party but you already know me your other self I am a surviver and after we went on an inspection mission to the nearest villege and some poisonus bug had fallen into the food kettel of the tribe with something they eat here that they make with rotten casava they call fermented and I dunno it's name and the vermin was like a fat lizard of many colors with legs twisted this way and sticking out it's evel tong and has a tail that ends in a little ball where the poison is and its the ugliest critter I ever seen When we occupied the town or rather the tribe to speak correctly with houses with a dirt floor and a thatch roof and no windows people were allreddy stiff poisoned there was a big ruckus with Pedrito you remember him he is now in unit 3 he wanted to jump an Angolan woman still alive I dunno why in some people the animal comes out when the shooting starts you can see their not professionals but things like that happen in war as you allreddy know I keep thinking of you and in the tag they gave me I glued a photo of yours the one where were together at the wedding of nuñez jimenez daughter with el Guaton because I dident have time for nothing when I found out I had to stay hear and you know I dident want to but as you say in this Troop there is more talk over the back fence than in a whorehouse and they was saying I had turnd coward because of you or something like that Pepe tolled me and since your always right this is a shitty war and it dident need to happen but wait until I come back sweety cause this should not separate us on the contrary. . . .

I grew tired of waiting for his "killed in action" notice.

Life is not a straight line traced at birth from the sidereal star. It has been said that this star, by the year 2000, will become atemporal and impervious to any account of the bright moments and secret blunders of our destinies.

The little war in Angola caused more than twenty thousand deaths in an army of one hundred and fifty thousand men. On the Island it caused the breakup of almost all the survivors' marriages. The Communist Party devoted itself to the persecution of unfaithful wives. The militant nucleus of the Centro Laboral was in charge of meetings in which the cuckolded husband would be harassed and given an ultimatum:

"*Compañero,* you must choose between your wife and the Cuban Communist Party! Now!"

Those who opted for an understanding kind of love lost their membership card.

*The examinations that five* hundred of us in medical school took that year were very complicated. "De tests" students called them. For each group of seventy questions, we had to choose only one among four contradictory answers.

Upon leaving the examination room, we could see the "answer key" on the board, seventy numbers in rows, to find out if our answers were correct.

In the whole school there was not one genius who could answer ten of those questions without getting confused.

Besides psychology, we studied a lot of Marxism, anatomy, and biochemistry.

We skipped genetics because the teachers were following the "Internationalist Plan."

The technician in charge of the cadavers was named Bolívar. He took care of the dead without gloves because there weren't any. As a result, the fungi in his nails were thriving.

These peaceful unclaimed corpses were resting in wooden tanks filled with formaldehyde, just like the forgotten fetuses of my childhood, and like them, they did not complain about anything. Never have I seen a man take care of the living, before or since, with the dedication Bolívar bestowed upon his dead.

Good grades alone were not enough for admission to this field. One had to face a jury of Communist Youth and pass a political test.

"What do you think about the OLP?"

"And about the OPEP?"

"And what about the Brazilian Miracle?"

"Explain who Ben Bella was and discuss his historical importance."

*We used to study* in groups of friends who had things in common. One of the students in our group had a great idea. Did anyone know the person in charge of the faculty printing office? Yes! Well, then, for five hundred pesos we could surely get a copy of the examination.

In this way we would not have to kill ourselves studying on coffee and amphetamines.

We thought we were geniuses, way above everybody else.

We were amazed to discover, when we reached our third year together with the five hundred other students, that the little guy at the printing office had made a killing selling exams.

Luckily, medicine is not learned taking tests on paper. It is learned out of love for our patients and by giving them a share of our lives.

\*   \*   \*

*It was because of* the war in Angola that I met the ballet dancer.

I still don't know how Panchi had become part of the official guard at Children's Hospital in Havana. I was there with my mercenary husband's sick daughter, who was a lonely and gloomy girl.

Did we know the same doctor?

I don't remember. Does it matter? After all, love is the only important milestone in a chronology.

He had a blondish, boyish fuzz on his head, a bulbous nose, a complexion still under attack by the termites of youthful acne. But his legs were like Doric columns. That was how he walked. As if his body were a temple being carried on a float.

He was stunning!

Ours was a shared madness. After we left the sick girl at her home with a rather drastic treatment plan to kill the germs clustering around her tonsils, we sat on the curb to talk.

Panchi told me that around 1962, his mother had gone to the Cuban National School of Art with the intention of turning her oldest daughter into a ballerina, and her two sons into musicians. They were sitting there quietly, the mother and the two boys, waiting for the verdict, when suddenly Laura Alonso appeared beside them. She is the daughter of that great ballerina and great-grandmother, Alicia Alonso, the living legend of the Ballet Nacional de Cuba.

"Two boys! Let's see. Stand up and show me your insteps! Oh, my God, they're perfect!"

Well, not really. But in the sexist, Cuban machismo of the sixties, anything that either danced or acted and had balls ended up in UMAP's sinister sugarcane-cutting brigades, together with the few remaining priests and my long-haired classmates from secondary school. In the arts, men were conspicuous for their absence.

Laura convinced Panchi's anxious mother that dance offered her two sons a brighter future than music did.

"You see, in Cuba you need only to stamp your foot, and you'll have a thousand rumba dancers," she said. "But ballet dancers? To be a ballet dancer one must have an almost perfect body."

The daughter did not make it and the sons were taken in.

"My acne was so bad," Panchi said, "that to force me to dance for an audience at first, they had to threaten me with expulsion."

I told him I had to give up ballet because I had been given a life sentence in chemistry, a discipline in which I was incapable of even defining "electron." This had inspired my mother to turn me over to Ledón as a private student, to see if the chemical supergenius of the National Center for Scientific Research, and of the whole country, could manage to illuminate this part of my gray matter three times a week. At great sacrifice she abandoned her office to take me to him. I told Panchi how Ledón, wise in matters of ineptitude, from the moment I first stepped into his house, had provided me with colored pencils and paper to draw landscapes to hang on the walls or to create illustrations of the laws of physics as applied to pirouettes and fouettés. The professor and I had agreed to take this secret to our graves.

In less than a month Panchi and I were dancing our own pas de deux in a rented room at the Capri Hotel, thanks to the wife of the minister of the interior, Abrantes. It was my birthday present from her. I clearly remember every detail of that afternoon, which was, for all its pleasures, no less stressful. With all the love in the world, we conceived our future troll.


*My husband the legionnaire* had returned to Cuba a week after the victory over the staph invasion in his daughter's throat, and exactly three weeks before Panchi and I conceived Mumín Person.

His consolation for my leaving him followed the same wise principle he used to apply at funeral homes: there is always someone to be consoled, and there is always someone willing to do the consoling. My best female friends took care of easing his pain.

This would have been the end of the story, had he not also elicited my father's sympathy by underscoring his suffering as the deposed husband. Leivita, the loud-mouthed gnome, was in intensive psychiatric care, a fate he shared with many other former chiefs of the Personal Guard. It was someone else who called me and asked me to stay on hand "until the Comandante is able to send for you." He sounded offended.

A new driver took me to the Palace.

"I can't believe that you have left an Angolan war hero for a ballet dancer!"

"I did not leave him, Fidel. He left me two years ago to join a weird war."

"But for a dancer? If he is a dancer, he must be queer. What about your career? Now that I have turned Cuba into a medical power!"

I realized that I would sooner be thrown into a snake pit than tell him I was pregnant. Who could possibly talk to Fidel, the eternal bachelor by choice, about love? Or, for that matter, to Mom, the eternal sweetheart? As soon as she learned of my happy news, she evicted me.

"If you want to bear that bum's child, you better have it where you got it."

*To get to the* School of Medicine from where Panchi lived required a three-hour bus trip. And even the guards' quarters at Children's Hospital were prettier and cleaner than the tenement room with kitchen where Panchi lived with his sister and her husband and daughter.

So I began scraping pre-Revolutionary filth off his bathroom with a razor blade. I also tried to get a toilet: for years, only the hole had been left. As a memento.

To acquire a toilet, I had to get my name entered on a list of "primary needs" drawn up by the Assemblies of Popular Power. To get a secondhand, halfway decent one, I would have to wait over five years for the bowl, and a little more for the tank cover—"harder to get because they break more often," I was told.

That began my first serious quarrel with my mom.

"I am going to have my baby in your house because, God knows, you'd be living under a piano lid if it weren't for me. You gave away everything you had, though nobody ever appreciated it. If that bum of a dancer were in another country, nobody would steal the sweat of his labor. This is the only country in the world where the State keeps your whole salary and also makes you shit in a hole!"

"That's because the State gives you everything for free!"

But this was not a political discussion.

We got married so that we would not lose the privileges the government grants to newlyweds, which were: to be able to buy at the Wedding Palace two pieces of flatware, a bedsheet, a towel, his and hers underwear, and a coverlet. With luck, a woman could also get an extra pair of shoes.

*I already had a* bulging lump in my lower abdomen on my first day at the Manuel Fajardo Teaching Hospital. Our fraudulent group was assigned to learn medicine by practicing it.

Professor Wagner welcomed us with a speech.

"Our Internationalist mission in Angola has priority for our government. Consequently, we lack some materials and instruments that our army needs more than we do. For example, in our hospital we have had to improvise urine sample collectors. Our nurses took the initiative. Let me show you."

Then he introduced a horrified, unfortunate fellow, whose penis was stiff with adhesive bandage, its head covered with a cut-off finger from a rubber surgical glove. There was a little more adhesive bandage and a catheter resting amid bloody urine bubbling in a Doña Delicias mayonnaise jar.

"We are going to assign one patient per person," the professor continued.

He sounded a lot like our ration books.

The hierarchies at the hospital were all reversed. The most important person was the one in charge of the pantry, the Goddess of Food. Then came the nurses, who knew all the unspeakable secrets. The physicians (we, the students) were next, and last came our patients.

That same week we had our first teaching session. Meister Wagner was speaking about inguinal muscles and sperm conduits with weak walls when a patient entered the classroom. A sweet old man, he walked gently kicking forward his gigantic testicle. He had been told that his treatment and cure at the hospital depended on that act of exhibitionism.

The old man swallowed hard and lowered his pajamas; as if putting a baby to sleep, he rested that monumental gray-haired testicle on the table, regarding it like an alien creature.

"This is an inguinal hernia. You can come close to see it and touch it," urged Wagner.

*Less than three weeks* after classes started, Conchita and Luisa, the big-time duo who were the secretary and second in command of the Communist Youth, received matching telegrams. They had to repeat second year because they had not attended gym. The three hours of gymnastics a week that they had missed were going to cost them the whole year of study they had just completed.

Three days later I got the same telegram.

Like the old man with his testicles, I took my belly out of my clothes and placed it on the faculty dean's desk.

"Does this look like a pillow to you?"

"No. Definitely not," she said.

"Then why do you insist that I become the first pregnant woman in the School of Medicine to do Swedish gymnastics?"

"The fact is that two female students are accusing you of intimidating the faculty of Physical Education."

"The whole faculty? Me, alone?"

"Yes. With photos. Photos of you with Fidel."

Conchita and her aide-de-camp, Luisa, were a recurring nightmare in my life. They had been dogging my path since I walked into the pre-med course. They had moved with me from school to school. I remembered them with Marquetti, sitting on the brown sugar sacks in that Escuela al Campo, accusing us all of being lesbians. I also remembered Alquimia's father, who, to save his daughter from a more severe sentence for larceny at Leoncio Prado, told the police that I was her accomplice. "Fidel's daughter" here, "Fidel's daughter" there. Every time there was a little problem near me, either the parents or their children managed to involve me, hoping that if I too was implicated, the authorities would overlook the whole thing.

"The only photos I have with Fidel are from my wedding," I told the dean. "I would not show them for anything in the world. I am the fat girl in the lacy gown costume. Anyway, *Doctora,* shouldn't you be upbraiding your faculty instead of me? The last thing you need, it seems, is ten addlebrained teachers intimidated by a photograph!"

With that I returned to the Fajardo teaching hospital, exonerated, after a week of paperwork that also included exhibiting my belly on other desks in the Ministry of Education. There, luckily, the bosomy Llanusa was no longer in command. He had been dismissed and was now on a State farm, raising pigs.

Even though I was able to prevail, my spirit was thin and my hopes for the most minimal human loyalty were now dead.


*The patient assigned to* me by the Wagnerian distribution died on account of a couple of radiology tests, one useless, and the other badly done.

One of his lungs had been eaten away by cancer. He had been kept waiting for weeks while the old bronchoscopy machine was being repaired. The technician, misunderstanding which organ was in question, returned him to us with a stomach X ray. Since Meister Wagner never admitted defeat, he ordered the bronchoscopy again, which ended up killing the man after he had to lie in bed for days, with his head hanging down, trying to spit into a basin whatever had been forced down his bronchial tree.

I had just sent my patient to the morgue when my sweet neighbor Estercita was admitted in a diabetic coma. For days, her eyes kept rolling back; she was trying to escape this life. For her first meal as a survivor, she was served a tray full of carbohydrates that could have sent her to the hereafter. At the foot of her bed, hanging from the peeling, twisted rails, there was a medical case history—blank. I earnestly tried to find the party responsible for this, and wrote the hospital director an irate letter.

My next patient was a nice old lady with Parkinson's disease. She was given a few dopamines and sent to the operating room. It seems the brain gets better when the damaged areas are implanted with sections of human fetal tissue.

I did not know then that Parkinson's disease could be surgically treated, and I found it difficult to understand how this conclusion could ever have been reached, since there is not a single guinea pig in the world, nor mouse, rabbit, or monkey that suffers from it.

Around this time, I first noticed a big change happening in our medical ethics.

The dead in formaldehyde boxes never disturbed me. Like Bolívar, I had thriving fungi in my fingernails because I touched the cadavers with my bare hands. But I was not quite ready to deal with live patients, or with hospitals.

Besides treating hospital patients, we had "field" duties—checking on pregnancies and venereal and tubercular cases. I was assigned to the old Chinatown in La Habana Vieja. I arrived at Zanja Street with the notion that of those Cantonese immigrants who had come during the last century as cheap labor, the ones who had created—and then lost to the Revolution—laundries and neighborhood eateries, only a decimated community remained.

I was surprised to discover that they were still there, heaped in the same slums of old, and growing up and having children, practically isolated from the rest of the Cuban population. Naturally, under those subhuman conditions where food and feces kept company, the Koch bacillus was healthy and thriving. The Revolution had not yet happened for Havana's Chinatown, just as it did not exist for La Dionisia, Palo Cagao, and Llega y Pon. They were still the same open sores of unspeakable poverty.

I kept my horror to myself until one day an emergency case was brought in. It was an ageless man, because people can grow old very quickly in cases like his. A bad fall had paralyzed him from the waist down. He was lying there, dejected, his enormous blue eyes lost in a sea of anguish.

Wagner took us aside.

"With care and good judgment, though the procedure cannot

cause any harm, practice rectal examination on this patient. Some of you could also do a lumbar puncture. Not all. Only those who plan to become surgeons."

There were twenty of us in this flashy group of apprentices, and eighteen of us stuck their fingers up this patient's ass. To Wagner's credit, he allowed only eight lumbar punctures.

I couldn't get over it. The next day, the poor man began to tremble as if possessed, in a hospital wing where at two in the afternoon there was no doctor or nurse in sight.

I looked for help but could not find anybody. I even looked in their usual secret trysting places.

At last I located them in a Communist Party meeting, which was being held early so as not to cut into anyone's time off. They were all studying one of the Comandante's speeches in which he talked about medicine with the same prioritizing zeal he had used to promote his cattle breeding.

Dragging my big belly around, I had lost half an hour trying to find them, while I dreaded that the devil might snatch away the soul of that trembling Christ. My pity transmogrified into rage, and I let out a stream of concentrated insults.

"Opportunists, idiots, murderers!"

I was gasping, big with child, and bedraggled. A grotesque mater dolorosa gone berserk.

*That Saturday Panchi took* me out to dinner with Antonio Gades, a Spanish dancer who was staying in Havana to choreograph a ballet combining rumba on pointe and flamenco.

Gades was intense, sociable, and charismatic. It was a fun evening with good music, good dancing, and good wine.

By dawn on Sunday I was awakened by vivid, unmerciful, and relentless contractions. The fetus had begun to painfully open up its own escape route from my body.

I woke my Sagittarians up at a time when their brains were not functioning yet. Mom and Panchi began shouting orders at each other and running around the house in circles. I watched them with resigned patience from a chair next to the kitchen door, my satchel of hospital and baby needs on my knees.

I was unaware of the breathing and other techniques to help delivery, so at the hospital I started walking. I was sure that gravity would help my child, whom I knew to be a girl, and already annoyed at the dark, enforced communion of our shared space.

But, just my luck! The team on duty at the Best Hospital for Gynecology and Obstetrics in All of Latin America looked anything but Cuban or professional. They were part of the famous Internationalist exchange, students from all over the world. They were younger than I was and even more frightened and confused.

Two other women in labor were screaming all the cusswords in the Spanish language at the top of their lungs.

In these surroundings, my expected torture started. A claw pierced my insides, and in the midst of contradictory sensations, in a paroxysm of love-hate, a heavy contraction like an earthquake delivered Mumín to the threshold of life. Meanwhile I, obsessed with the baby's astral time and the perfection of a round navel, watched the clock and threatened the nurse with sure death if by any chance she allowed my baby to have a protuberance like a pacifier in the middle of her tummy. Outies were prevalent among the new Cuban generations for some unfathomable reason.

## 5

# MUMÍN, MY TROLL

*Mumín was born that* December Sunday in mid-morning. To prevent any astrological spells, I won't tell you the exact time; there are people with enough power to interrupt the peaceful and prophetic transit of the stars.

She was a troll. With her flattened nose and bushy black hair all sticking out and reaching down to her eyebrows, she would have been perfect for scaring people under bridges.

Natica had trouble accepting that.

"When they took me to the nursery," she said, "there were two pink babies, blond and beautiful, and I told Panchi, 'She must be one of those.' But he pointed to one with dark hair and a Negroid nose. 'Are you sure she has not been switched?'"

Grandma Natica belongs to the Encouragement Commission.

Mumín has not changed since she came into the world that morning, except for her aesthetic progress. She never cried out of hunger or anger. My breasts were painfully overflowing with milk, but she didn't care about that. She wanted to sleep and be left in peace. She was so tired!

Mumín survived all the experiments of my ignorant motherhood with the same happy disposition. She would always open her eyes in the morning before anybody else, and I always found her flinging around toothless smiles. She had no complaints. She would wave her arms and dazzle me with her pair of day stars.

While Mumín sucked at my breast, I prepared for the exam on the respiratory system, together with a friend who had been studying with me since we had lost our darling printing operator due to changes in the faculty. With the stitches from the delivery still fresh, I took my seat in the exam room. Here, Professor Wagner had a gigantic, vengeful surprise for me.

Distributing the exam papers, he walked in front of me and behind me as if I were a ghost. Finally I protested.

"I'm sorry. You cannot take this test. You don't have the required attendance."

"But I only missed a week! God, I was having a baby!"

"That is not my concern. Please, leave the exam room."

I left, dragging my morale, which was sliding down my legs like underwear without an elastic band.

My aunt Vilma forgot all about the mother's helper from the Federation of Cuban Women that she had promised me during an unexpected attack of family generosity.

The only help I could get was as pure as an immaculate conception, but she had more fungi under her nails than Bolívar the technician. Mumín developed a red abdominal rash in response to the contagion.

Grandma Natica declared herself a sympathetic observer only, and Mom could not abandon her job.

I asked for maternity leave and received instead a resolution whereby I had been expelled for having abandoned my field of study. To this day, the medical school turns a deaf ear when I ask for a copy of my academic record.


*Motherhood and Ration Books* are irreconcilable enemies. The troll didn't even have a mattress when I got home, because I couldn't get one at the hardware store without a hospital certificate stating that she had been born alive.

Our monthly ration of laundry soap was not enough for the inexhaustible pile of dirty diapers; nor was the fifteen yards of absorbent fabric enough to make the number of diapers needed.

There had been no water at home since the minister of transportation had a swimming pool built in his garden a few blocks down. And bananas, pumpkins, and *malanga* (taro roots), the traditional baby foods, existed only in our memory.

The pilgrimages necessary to obtain enough food for the troll included a trip every two weeks on the bus to my mother-in-law's, which left me exhausted, and much shorter trips to see an old man who gave me a few vegetables from his garden in exchange for fondling my breasts.

Panchi was always away on his endless, unpaid tours with the ballet company, flying Cubana de Aviación. Mom was tirelessly flying from office to classroom to meeting in her VW bluebird courtesy of Raúl Castro. Grandma Natica traveled through the ether via her telephone, and I went from one side of the house to the other, watching over the boiling water with the diapers, and baby bottles, and my baby's unperturbed peace. One day my very dear friend Sosa [Fidel's emissary] came to visit with a congratulatory smile and a gift box wrapped in lilac paper. It held a box of talcum powder, matching cap, jacket, and woolen booties for the baby, and a housecoat for me, the same cyanotic color as the wrapping paper.

In my opinion Fidel does not choose these gifts. I manifested my gratefulness, but busily continued washing diapers in water with lye to get them really white, while devising new recipes of mush to help the troll grow. She had become something of a glutton on her way to being a gnome.

The troll disciplined my life with a sensible schedule that she didn't want to alter for anything in this world. I wanted to be her mother above all else in my life. But her mother also had to keep studying, because even my own mother reminded me once in a while that she had a diploma on her wall, adding that she had been able to earn it even though she was past fifty. Why couldn't I, she wondered.

Her sweet pressure was nothing compared with that of the Federation, the Committee for the Defense of the Revolution, and all the people's organizations wailing their slogans, all of which had definitely turned Cuban women into beings in pants that juggled work, study, the vicissitudes of public transportation, and the lines at the grocery store, with no time whatsoever left over for themselves.

\*    \*    \*

*Twenty years ago, a* resolution from a Revolutionary ministry had left Uncle Bebo, Grandma Natica's brother, unemployed and unable to return to Cuba. He had been "the best-dressed man in Jamaica," with his morning coat, high boots, gloves, and top hat.

Uncle Bebo was now returning for the first time since his debacle, and his plane was about to land. He was representing the Cuban Community in Exile, the new name devised by Fidel to replace *gusanos,* for that multitude of people burdened by their past and by the painful amputation from land and family.

Fidel was now allowing the reunification of families, and obtaining some convertible cash in exchange. The "worms" were returning for a visit to the Island, transformed into generous chrysalises wrapped in dollars and bearing numerous gifts.

Exclusive stores (*diplotiendas*) for the visiting exiles were set up in the hotels. There was total confusion. Party militants had to be forbidden to receive or have any dealings with their visiting, exiled relatives. As a result, they sent their children and other relatives, in a state of anguish, to beg them for things sold only in those stores.

The whole affair became a cause for denunciations and family quarrels. The younger generations, nurtured on anti-Imperialist slogans, experienced love at first sight for those uncles, aunts, and cousins capable of solving the urgent problems created by the scarcity of food and clothing.

Bebo still looked like an English lord. Never married, he had a Hindu servant and did yoga exercises quite early in the morning, mitigating his diabetes with that discipline of the spirit.

He introduced into my mother's home certain imported advances of civilization, such as paper towels and solid detergents, as well as ancestral family rituals like the evening whiskey libation.

But he was frustrated in this, because at seven o'clock his niece Naty was still working, and his sister Natica had long ago lost the taste for good and virtuous drinks.

He and I went to the diplotienda to buy the whiskey and the soda, and in the name of my matriarchs, I volunteered to satisfy his cravings. Like clockwork, I had his ice and syphon ready at the exact moment when the sun begins to sink in the ocean and the enervating sunlight starts to melt into the sunset.

Bebo took the temperature of the household with his personal thermometer, and didn't hesitate to give me a reading.

"I have never seen a sicker situation. What could possibly have happened to my sister and my niece? They eat such awful things with apparent relish! Things that in my time, and certainly in theirs too, were fit only for dogs and pigs. . . . And let's not forget that my sister and your mother were once two very refined women!"

"Did they give you toasted corn flour for breakfast?"

"Not only that, but what a way they have of treating each other! Instead of speaking, they bark, and they both give you orders as if you were their husband! They don't listen to anybody and have made a habit of it! I didn't have great expectations when I came, but the truth is, dear niece, what I found is . . . Well, I'm really sorry for you."

"You know, Uncle Bebo, I'm really worried about Mumín. I would give anything to be able to take her far, far away."

"Well, let's see. What is Natica doing in Naty's home all day long, when she has her own apartment right across the street?"

"Oh, I don't know! She doesn't like to be alone. She comes in at nine in the morning and leaves at ten at night."

"As soon as your mother comes home from work it seems all hell breaks loose. Do you know how they want me to take my bath? Sitting on a bench, with a pail of water and a candle! I feel like I've been thrown back into the Middle Ages, but they see it all as fine and dandy."

The fact was that, since the electric power was often cut off for hours, and so was the water, after serious thought Natica had decided that, considering how tall Uncle Bebo was, it would be easier for him to sit next to the pail and scoop out the water rather than having to bend down for it.

"And you, how are you doing?" he asked me.

"As well as I can. I am trying to solve some of their problems. I brought them a couple of husbands, but with this third one, it's as if I had brought the devil into the house. They won't even watch Mumín so I can go out for a couple of hours in the evening."

"That will change. As children grow, people quickly learn to love them more and more. Why doesn't Natica give you her apartment? Couples should live alone."

"Well, I don't know. . . . It's her apartment."

"She is not using it. Leave this to me." Uncle Bebo was a master of yoga and a master of diplomacy as well. He used to say that the only one in somebody else's hands was Fidel, while the Cuban people were all in Fidel's hands.

"Look, Alina, now tell me the truth. You're not seeing Manley, the president of Jamaica, are you?"

"Only on television."

"Well, you see, the rumor is going around in Jamaica that he comes to Cuba often to be with Fidel's daughter."

"We don't need to go that far, Uncle Bebo. Right here in Cuba there are people I don't even know who claim to have some kind of relationship with me, only to see if that would get the police off their backs."

"I am not surprised. The way things are, so many people live in fear. Tell me, what are you going to study now?"

"Diplomacy."

"Are you out of your mind? The moment this administration changes, you're out of a job." He knew.

Thanks to my uncle's expert handling of the situation, I inherited from my grandmother, while she was still living, a place to be on my own with the troll. Mumín had turned beautiful and mischievous, and was learning to use her charms to her advantage. By the time she was a year old, she could take the telephone and call home from her grandmother's and vice versa, and would keep at it until she found someone willing to do what she wanted.

*The powerful widow of* a martyr of the Revolution, who was close to retirement but had extensive and deep connections in the Ministry of

Foreign Relations, finally found a solution to the unwilling unemployment of my intellectual capacity.

"This girl is perfect for a diplomatic career!"

This widow was a stentorian woman. She imposed her decision to sponsor me at the top of her lungs, and that was how I found myself in Cuba's most elitist school, which was reserved exclusively for Communist Youth militants who were also National Vanguards.

The dogmatism there was so thick you could cut it with a knife.

So far, thanks to a series of very convenient illnesses, I had managed to get away every time I was pressured into joining the militant ranks, and I suddenly found myself surrounded by Cubanologists and brave defenders of Marxist ideology.

The "Varnishing School," as we used to call it, attempted to civilize those people a little, so they wouldn't eat chicken with their hands while representing Cuba somewhere, and also helped them learn how to say *merci* in several languages.

We studied languages, world literature and art, Marxism and protocol.

The protocol teacher, who had served as ambassador to the Vatican, taught us how to match the color of neckties with that of suits, shirts, and socks; how to set luncheon tables for single men; how to eat snails and other specimens in the shell; how to crack open, with elegance, hard shells like those of lobster and crab; and how to rinse our greasy fingers with "rose water for the women and water with a slice of lemon for the men." I had already assimilated all these matters while Lala Natica was educating me on foods of noble rank, such as lentils served on silver trays, and on nonexistent servants who served *à la russe* or *à la française*.

To vegetate among those twenty-year-old ideological gendarmes was deadly boring. My other problems had to do with the damned early morning punctuality: the troll always had last-minute whims before she left for Poland's Little Friends, her day care center. An invincible sleepiness came over me, as soon as my rear end connected with my classroom desk. Not even amphetamines or a cup of bitter, thick black coffee could dispel my narcolepsy. The bell would wake me up at the end of the class. That is how my eight hours of class were spent, in the stupor of a zombie caught between two different metabolisms.

Marxism ended up disturbing my life. I began to adopt those dialectic laws by which everything is proposed to be both itself and its opposite, every event negates the preceding one, and thus everybody has an identity and, at the same time, is a battleground of conflicting opinions.

*Das Kapital* explains with grace how to exploit people by paying them less. So the only notable difference between the United States and Cuba and Russia is that in some you know whose pocket gets filled with money, and in others you don't. I could never figure out where the money earned by those of us doing voluntary work went. Everything was going from bad to worse; the people were poorer and more raggedy, and paint was peeling off the dilapidated houses.

If Fidel had not suffered an attack of megalomania, and we had not worked so much to pay for the Angola war and all the guerrillas, maybe we still wouldn't be happy, but we wouldn't be so dirt-poor.

Philosophy is to blame for the fact that there are no books on the Island. When we start reading about universal issues, and meditating on them, our brains fill with oxygen and wild ideas that transcend and elevate us above the predatory and agitated slogans and the everyday reality that wrap around us. Fidel knows this very well, because he read widely, and more than he needed to, the whole time he was in jail. He thought that life was passing him by while he was in his stationary journey; ironically, there seems to be more freedom in jail than there is when one is trying to whip up a collective soufflé that never rises.

I am not going to blame philosophical ideas for the fact that when Panchi came home from his tours, he found me exhausted.

In the little time he spent in Cuba, he took his place as relief runner in the eternal food search for the troll, and in other chores, confusing all my scheduled routines. Whenever I started getting used to his presence and his lifestyle, another tour would take him away.

Gradually, I became detached from him, incapable of balancing his world of open spaces with mine.

By the time the term ended, we were divorced.

Mom reacted in quite an unexpected way.

"I am not going to allow my grandchild to grow up without a father!" And she took Panchi to live with her across the street.

"You're going to mess up all of our lives."

But she paid no attention.


*The only Varnishing School* teacher engraved in my memory was my professor of world literature, José Luis Galbe, a Republican Spaniard who was residing in Cuba at the time. When he soared in poetic exaltation, he was able to evoke the miraculous green ray of light in a sunset on the Aegean Sea. He blended in quotations from his own surrealist oeuvre, and he delivered his tremendous tales in strong Castilian tones.

"Intellectuals should commit themselves to the social processes, but not at the cost of their own identities. And this is exactly what is happening in Cuba. I am going to tell you about the day I was invited to a poetry reading at the Cuban Writers' and Artists' Union [UNEAC]. All the Revolutionary Cuban writers were there: César Leante, Fernández Retamar, Pablo Armando Fernández, Ezequiel Vieta, and others. Each one read a poem. At the end they asked me to read mine. After they finished applauding, I told them: 'Listen. My poem has been written with a phrase from each of the poems you have read this afternoon. Gentlemen! Allow me to tell you that you have all fallen into mediocrity. I consider originality in art as an infringement of ordinary traditions. It must be acknowledged that you don't have even an iota of creative courage.' "

That old man Galbe, who had no children, no grandchildren, no family with whom to share his epiphanies, was a delight.

He was once talking about Balzac and the Illuminists.

"Let's see! Who among you has read *The Human Comedy*?"

I lifted one pale, shy finger. Fidel had given me Balzac's complete works in French. Ten volumes, onionskin, which I had dutifully read.

"Well, I congratulate you! Obviously you had a lot of time to waste!"

This professor of literature was right. I spent my time reading about other people's lives thanks to St. Termite, patron saint of bookworms. My life was not a normal life. I was stuck in the feminist phalanx of the Revolution, going after university degrees, and over-extending myself in the miraculous task of providing even the barest minimum for my child.

And I was alone, even more than the last of the Mohicans. We matriarchs were the only ones left when the normal thing should have been for the whole family to push life ahead.

*I was in my* second year in the varnished lowlands of the School of Diplomacy when a shameful scandal occurred at the Peruvian embassy, a building located in a frozen residential zone facing Fifth Avenue in Miramar. Like all foreign fortresses, it had the institutional right to grant asylum to Cuban citizens, and was therefore guarded by a wrought-iron fence well over six feet high with arrow tips, and defended by Cuban soldiers stationed at nine-foot intervals, in order to defeat any attempt to ask for political asylum.

One night, some men killed a guard while forcing entry. Cuba requested the return of the men, but the Peruvians, who had granted them asylum, refused.

A dialogue started between the Cuban government and the embassy. Peru insisted on its right to grant asylum, and Cuba withdrew its guards from the embassy.

An incredible thing happened then. A crowd asking for asylum toppled the fence. Hundreds of people rushed in, crossing over from adjoining backyards. Bus drivers stopped their buses, shouting:

"This is our last stop, ladies and gentlemen!"

Some of the passengers were stunned and remained sitting, and some got out and ran through the destroyed fences to join the others inside the embassy. So many cars were abandoned in front of the embassy that black market auto prices slumped. In less than three days the grounds were jam-packed with thousands of Cubans, heaped on top of one another.

The government could not allow such an absurd situation to continue. It had the embassy surrounded with barricades that started miles away. But they couldn't stop the human torrent that kept on flowing in.

In order to prevent being accused of genocide, Fidel had no choice but to provide the embassy with water and some food for the people, who even crowded the roof and the window gratings, and the gardens and tree branches.

That desperate multitude was given the moniker *escoria* (dregs, scum).

It was Fidel who personally attempted to turn this seeming defeat into a victory with the infamous *actos de repudio a la escoria* (acts of rejection against the scum).

The Cuban government and the Peruvian embassy came to an agreement regarding the future exiles. They would be returned to their homes until an orderly exit from the country could be arranged.

The street disturbances caused by all this left me with one of my most horrible memories, and upset any trust I had in the human race. Cubans shouting "Escoria! Escoria!" indiscriminately at their own countrymen. Hordes of people provoking, hitting, humiliating, and lynching others, while the police watched and did nothing.

Once I saw from a bus window the strange and fleeting image of a woman wearing sandwich boards like those for advertising lottery tickets. The word "ESCORIA" had been written on the front and back boards. I cannot forget the irate, twisted expressions of those who were attacking her.

One of those acts of rejection was organized in a building at the corner of my block. It lasted for weeks. People cut the electric power and the water supply to the target family, and through a public-address system, specially installed for the very purpose, they shouted: "Whore! Butt-fuck! They rammed it up your husband's ass at the embassy!"

Relatives from Miami came to the rescue in all sorts of boats, either their own or rented, because Peru alone could not cope with so many refugees. These boats were forced to take several trips with loads of abandoned mental patients, criminals who had been taken out of jail and whose eyes were not yet accustomed to daylight, and young, smiling, handsome men who were either real or fake homosexuals.

It became a requisite for the refugees to get an official discharge from jobs or schools, but not even that managed to slow the people's desperate exodus.[11]


*One day at noon* we had to assemble on the main floor of the School of Diplomacy to attend a "nonviolent act," we were told, directed at a young fifth-year student who was leaving the country.

He and his mother were walking past all the silent and hostile faces when a handsome first-year student, applying all of his acquired diplomacy, slapped the woman so hard her head turned. All hell broke out.

Behaving like damned Nazis, the more than two hundred students, irate revolutionaries primed for the hunt, pursued the mother and her son up the street and would have beaten them to death if a citizen had not rescued them just in time. The rescuer had to surrender the shards of his windshield on the asphalt.

I went berserk.

I grabbed the first-year student, the mother-slapper, by his shirt collar, which was filthy and soaked with sweat.

"You bastard, son of a bitch, chickenshit, hitting a woman in front of her son! If you touch me, I'll bust your balls. Try me." I assumed full combat stance. I hadn't been married to two karate national institutions for nothing. I must have looked like a hysterical crested hen.

The student became sheepish.

" 'Behind an extremist, there is always an opportunist,' " I blurted out. I was an expert on Lenin. "Maybe it's you that wants to get yourself out of this shit and you don't have the nerve."

Those watching us did not applaud.

Professor José Luis Galbe's reaction did nothing to change the other students' attitude. When we returned to the classroom, he was somber. Despair was coming out of his pores and tightening his vocal cords. He repeated the same famous phrase I had quoted from Lenin, and called them all cowards.

\*   \*   \*

*It was around this* same time that my body began to swell. I was all right when I got to school in the morning. As soon as I sat down, I would fall asleep, wake up, fall asleep again, and that's how my whole day went until I was a sleepy Buddha. On my way home, I picked up the elf at her day care. By the time I took my shoes off, my swollen feet looked like hams.

All through the night I could hear the insults coming from the loudspeakers installed on the corner building for the *repudio,* or public act of rejection. Even the drunkards passing by in the middle of the night would stop to let the bad blood out of their system in phrases that should not be repeated here.

Mumín was sleeping peacefully, but I could not escape the thought that bringing her into this world had been like mailing a letter to the wrong address.

My guilt feelings kept piling up.

I was admitted to the Surgical Unit of MININT for the second time, to try to identify the unnamed condition that was making my body absorb fluids like a sponge. The first week, for no apparent reason, I lost around eighteen pounds—all water—causing confusion among the doctors and nurses.

But I knew what was wrong with me. I was absorbing everybody else's shit by osmosis.

It was all psychosomatic.

I was referred to a psychiatrist suffering from arthrosis who had to roll his words in order to prevent his outsized tongue from hanging out. We fell for each other right away.

I convinced him to do a narco-hypnosis on me, to see if a thiopental-induced trance might help reveal the arcane mysteries of this disorder that in the course of the day was capable of turning me into an edematous Buddha. During this mesmerizing experience, I didn't speak at all, or if I did, it was not in any identifiable language.

After the session, I ended up accompanying my doctor for drinks at his mistress's place. After all, even psychiatrists need to be listened to.

I stayed four months at the Surgical Unit, but I could have stayed forever. I was having such a great time.

Due to my obvious absence, I was liberated from the acts of public rejection at the Varnishing School.

A retired boxer was converting me into a long-distance runner, a future champion for MININT. I trained twice a day.

The Castro family made an occasional appearance. On my birthday, Uncle Ramón, still bewitched and strumming the same sad songs on any guitar, woke me up with a humongous cake that he rolled in on a hospital gurney.

Even Fidel paid me a surprise visit with a gift of two crates of hydroponic cauliflower. Espina the cook seasoned and prepared them for me according to Fidel's specific instructions.

His visit must have affected my situation because, soon after, I got a very easy job. Núñez Jiménez turned out to be a literary person, besides being a geographer and a speleologist, and he needed to increase his staff of editors and proofreaders. Following Fidel's footsteps, he materialized in my room at the clinic one day with a proposal for editing a book about Wilfredo Lam, the international glory among Cuban painters. From my hospital bed, I began to make some money.

I was now classified as "having a nervous condition," and decided to use this status for the rest of my conscious life. In Cuba there is nothing better than being considered unstable or crazy. You are then excused from having to do a lot of things.

I even had a television set and a VCR in my hospital room.

In the evenings I could get a pass and go out to act as an extra in a Cuban film starring the Spanish actor Imanol Arias. What I really enjoyed was the care of his makeup person, Magaly Pompa, who taught me the secrets of contour shading with makeup. I would return in the wee hours of the morning, sleepless and tired but happy and just in time for my training with the black boxer.

I had become the darling of the Surgical Clinic, but I missed the troll and her cute ways.

*It was because of* the troll that I found myself in the Palace again, after emerging from my paradise of the last four months. Fidel's curiosity about the recurrent part his genes were playing in my lineage was not yet satisfied, and he detested imperfections.

"How skinny you are! Why are you so skinny?"

"It's because the boxer Regoiferos has turned me into a long-distance runner."

"That's terrific! Do you want me to send for a sandwich? They make very good ones here. A café con leche, maybe?"

"At this time of day, wouldn't a little whiskey be better?"

So we both had our whiskeys.

"How's the child?" he asked.

"Well on her way to becoming a goblin. She's losing her baby fat."

"Does she eat well?"

"She has a sweet tooth."

"Children should have their own refrigerators. It's more hygienic. Food for a child should be kept apart, free from contamination. Not where everybody keeps handling things. I'm studying medicine, did you know?"

I didn't, but it was no surprise. I envisioned his next speeches. They would be filled with medical references.

"I'm going to send you a refrigerator to keep her food in. I want you to know that I am going to pay for it out of my own pocket, though I don't have much money now. I have had a lot of expenses lately. Fidelito and his wife are coming back from the Soviet Union. They need a house, and money to have some fun."

"Of course, of course."

"This thing about the refrigerator is something else, though. I want to help you with your child. Does eighty pesos seem all right to you?"

Oh yes! With triple that amount I could pay my electric bill.

"Perfect!"

"Now what is this about your having problems with your nerves?"

"I don't know. I got all swollen up when a series of things went wrong, and when things improved, I stopped retaining water. It was that incident with Peru, and all the acts of public rejection. . . ."

"How silly of you! We got rid of a lot of chronic patients, not to mention criminals. Let the Yankees deal with them. Mental disease is a weakness, an imperfection."

"I keep having the impression I am in the wrong place. I want to leave."

"Leave? Where? Leave the country? That would have political consequences. Forget it."

"You told me the same thing when I was eleven, three years after I had returned from Paris, and Wilfredo Lam's family invited me to visit them in France."

"What you need is a rest."

"I've been resting for four months."

"You're going to stay here in the Palace until the end of the school year. Then we'll see what you're going to study next year. The idea of a diplomatic career is sheer nonsense."

At least he and Uncle Bebo agreed on something.

He picked up his telephone and asked for my official release from school.

My stay at the Palace followed a plan that Fidel had especially designed to help and rehabilitate Willy, his new protégé. Willy was the son of Guillermo García, the man who had emptied several cisterns in the Nuevo Vedado in order to fill his own swimming pool. My assignment was to have lunch every day with a select group and, in the afternoons, to study Russian with a teacher.

"If you want to help the boy, get him a good psychiatrist. He's a professional liar," I commented, speaking of Willy.

"I didn't ask for your advice. I asked for your help. What is a good time for me to see your child?"

"It's better if I bring her to you." I wanted to avoid the horde of supplicants that he would attract.

When I took the troll—looking like a large, frothy, synthetic meringue—to him, he was waiting for us in the hallway. He bent over, the way Daddy Orlando used to do, with his arms open. Mumín ran to him, stopped, took a second look at him, and then turned around to cling to my skirt.

\* \* \*

*The lunch habitués of* the small dining room at the palace were Osmani Cienfuegos, the brother of a Hero of the Revolution; Jesús Montané, who headed the Ministry of [nonexistent] Communications; his son Sergito, who had been much sought after by women until a recent brain operation left him convulsive, babbling, and lost in a childish world from which he was emerging slowly; Faustino Pérez, the father of my former boyfriend who drove everybody crazy with his lies, a generation before Willy inherited his position; Chomy, Fidel's new chief of staff, a kind of Celia Sánchez in a Mao suit; Willy himself, nicknamed *Macha Papa* ("mashed-potato head") in reference to his cephalic expanse, where his charming lies originated; and I, who swelled up according to the undifferentiated dictates of my psyche or my soma. I was the only woman to be present at those fetes, except for the federated employees who served us lunch.[12]

Everybody was delighted with me. So much so that I began to put my hair in topknots, and to wear long dresses with lace shawls in the old hippie style so it would not occur to them to take me seriously. The table, set for eight, was in a small salon. To the right of every plate there was a selection of pills that were taken to increase mental acumen, powers of concentration, and virility. The main ingester of these was old Montané, who had a brand-new wife.

The conversations sometimes got lofty. For example:

MONTANÉ: Carter is going to be reelected! That guy Reagan doesn't
  have a chance.
SERGITO: Bb . . . bb . . . but, Dad . . . Daddy, what are yy . . . you saying?
SOMEONE ELSE: Carter has all the Jews and blacks against him since
  the Andrew Young scandal. Money is against him! He won't be reelected, not in this life or in the next.
MONTANÉ: Just you wait and see!

We saw: Carter was not reelected, and Montané was named Fidel's political advisor for Latin America. I went on inventing new topknot combinations for my hair every day.

\*   \*   \*

*My Russian teacher was* an albino who, every day, came in half blinded by the bright sun after a bus trip from the other end of the city. His duty was to teach the language to two privileged students, and he knew of no mission that could make him feel more honored, especially after Fidel began to inspect our class. When Fidel visited, the teacher turned red and then transparent, depending on whether it was his arterial or venous blood running under his cellophane skin.

Some moments of joy have come late for me. At last I had my father visiting my school and watching me study! But there was no way to transcend my lost childhood, and he ended up sending for me to come see him at his usual office.

The penumbra of his plant jungle, combined with some whiskey, was conducive to personal disclosures. In spite of the topknots in my hair, I became Naty II in costume—perturbed, however, by my social conscience.

"You can't be serious when you tell me that Montané is now your political advisor! You must have appointed him so that you can disregard his opinions, right?"

"What do you mean? Chucho's a really hard worker!"

"Mom works much harder and longer than he does, and she has to do it inside a closet!"

Montané did not last long in his position.

Editing Núñez Jiménez's books continued to be my main source of income.

"That book, *En Marcha con Fidel,* which your pal Núñez Jiménez is writing, is shameful! It makes him look like the Father of the Revolution."

"What do I care! It's three hundred thousand pesos in royalties, and half of them are mine. What's your problem with Núñez? He's very intelligent. Did you know that eels spawn in the Sargasso Sea? I bet you didn't!"

"No, I didn't. But if in order to entertain you, one has to read two or three encyclopedia entries before coming to visit. . . ."

My real objection was that very late at night, Fidel used to spill out all his deep concerns, and by the next morning they were all on the Havana grapevine.

"You're not going to let Núñez Jiménez publish that little book *Conversaciones entre Fidel Castro y García Márquez,* are you? You two talked about nothing but food. Lobsters 'going up Gabo's furniture.' Cubans have to go to the aquarium to see a lobster."

I grew very persnickety.

"Why have you sent that bunch of artisans to jail? Is it a crime to sell homemade clogs or dresses made out of material that was used to cover tobacco crops?"[13]

"The State can never give up its absolute control over business transactions!"

I started trouble when I asked him if the State was really supporting the black market by having stores that only accepted dollars, when Cubans were paid in pesos.

Being the spokesperson for public opinion and the nation's miseries was not bringing me any benefits.

"Why don't you take me fishing some Sunday?"

"Because I go fishing to get a rest!"

Gradually, I went back to my position as listener. It was smarter to let him tell me about the latest achievements of his cow White Udder, which continued producing milk until it got into the *Guinness Book of World Records.* He also bragged about the achievements of his youngest son, Angelito, who was undergoing a new accelerated plan of education at three years of age. Or he went on about his new culinary acquisitions. My succession of marriages seemed to hold little interest for him.

"I wanted to tell you that I'm going to get married."

"Take a few cashews with you. They are fresh. Agostinho Neto just sent them to me. I can't give you any more because he sent only one can. I'm sure you never had toasted pumpkin seeds! Here's what you do. You spread some oil on an iron pot as if you were going to roast coffee beans. Then you brown the pumpkin seeds slowly until the shell almost comes off." Our dialogues shifted from seductiveness to theatrics. "By the way, who is your next matrimonial victim?"

I left very late that night, with my two Doña Delicias mayonnaise jars full of cashew nuts and pumpkin seeds, which I chewed like a sybarite while meditating on a proverb of Mom's: "Brilliant minds think alike." My mind must have been very pedestrian because it cost me a huge effort to follow the Comandante's reasoning.

This was no way for me to live. I was a baby-sitter for Macha Papa, and a plaything for the libidinous old men of the cabinet. I was a portable complaint and suggestion box, a magnet for everyone's envy and vengefulness. All this time I was up to my ears in surveillance, because anyone who's near the boss is subject to a protocol of unbreakable Personal Security rules. I was being followed twenty-four hours a day, and my phone was always bugged. When Fidel sent for me one afternoon to present me with his plans for my next year in school, which included subjects like computer science or programming, I was already beginning to have my old symptoms of water retention and sudden sleepiness during class. Following wise Willy's tracks, I was no longer attending the luncheons. The time had come for insurrection. I intended to drag around all those who spied on me and give them a whole night of entertainment and Havana-style rumba. I wanted to keep them up until the crack of dawn.

One never learns to be afraid of sudden decisions. I was sick and tired of playing the Palace courtesan.

My "next victim" was going to be a loving Nicaraguan who had taken in Sandinista ideals along with his mother's milk. As a way out of Cuba, I was contemplating the nefarious possibility of going through a second Revolution, in the company of an austere and boring young man.

Fidel had been right.

On Saturday night, my night of insurrection, I chose the nightclub at the Hotel Riviera. I told my new boyfriend that I was going to visit some girlfriends. I took the already fast-asleep troll to my mother's house; then I dressed up in the garage.

I really wanted to waste an entire evening looking at dancers' beautiful bodies, with music and drums thundering in my ears. By two in the morning, my legs were eager to join the dancers. That's about the time when government employees fall asleep and others begin going wild. There was a man at the table next to me, all alone. I kept one eye on the dance floor and the other one on him all night.

We kept glancing at each other with intense hate.

The lights in the nightclub were getting too bright, so I decided to step outside. When I reached the entrance to the hotel, he followed me, sullen and silent. When the separation seemed imminent, it happened: we took the dialectical step.

We turned all our former hate into love with a sudden, long kiss that left us breathless out of mutual surprise. That kiss led us from one surprise to another for a whole week; we didn't even resort to the universal language of caresses and tenderness.

The object of my love seemed as if handmade by a goldsmith to my own specifications. That happens when magic intervenes! We were born the same year and at the same hour, though in different latitudes. We learned to tell each other all the bejeweled poems that passion invents without appearing ridiculous. We made love the way gods perform miracles, and for the rest of my life I'll offer a toast to our maverick impulse. Just a nobody and an anybody meeting somewhere.

Havana became the place for us to spend the rest of our lives, and we were already heading for "till death do us part," when we were abruptly parted by the police.

Personal Security had given me free rein for one week.

These were the best moments in my life, the happiest, most relaxed, and most irresponsible. I was embracing my Tower of Pisa, oblivious of myself, and looking at the sea from the gardens of the Hotel Nacional, when an iron hand yanked me away.

"You're under arrest!"

"What?"

"You're under arrest for being with a foreigner. You are also charged with prostitution! Do not protest, unless you wish to become a public nuisance."

I must be the only prostitute ever treated so formally by the Cuban police. They took me to the police station with the same formality.

I didn't receive the customary honor of a jail cell. Instead, they sat me on a granite bench in the hallway, where I could observe the same sadistic spectacle of all the jails in the world: beatings and abuse. I spent Christmas Eve there and I was expecting to spend New Year's

Eve as well. Four officers took turns interrogating me. I was angry. Finally, on the third day, a henchman came and released me. He gave me some chocolates "for the child," and took me home in silence.


*I sat in my* apartment waiting until it was time to go pick up the goblin from her day care. I was grumbling over my humiliation and my helplessness, when the phone rang. It was an irate Abrantes.

"And furthermore, Alina, I forbid you to leave the house. You are under house arrest!"

"Go and arrest your own mother, you asshole!" I hung up.

There was a knock on the door. It was Chomy, Fidel's chief of staff. Obviously, the people in the Political Bureau had a synchronized operation.

"To what do I owe this honor? You have never set foot on my premises before."

"You damn well know why I'm here!" He entered, looked around, then turned to me. "With an Italian, no less! At this point in your life! Your father feels very hurt by all this."

This made me turn scatological.

"The only whore around here is you! Damned bastard. You're just envious. Wouldn't you like to have his Italian dick for yourself? Get out right now! And tell Fidel to take all go-between idiots like you and shove them up his ass!"

He was stunned. I pushed him out and closed the door on his back.

Mom was very nervous.

"I thought they had caught you trying to leave the country."

To this day, I carry a horrible sensation of cosmic failure within me. I had met my other half, and dark forces wrested him away from me.

I decided I never again wanted anything more to do with that larger-than-life, Olympian character of that father of mine. Though I knew he was more fragile than cynical, he was incapable of protecting his own daughter from the machinations of his own henchmen.

\*   \*   \*

*This was all before* Havana turned into a happy sex stopover, and Varadero Beach became the paradise of venereal disease. In those days, any woman caught with a foreigner got four years in jail for "being a threat to society."

It is true that I was saved from the undoubted reeducational benefits of jail, but I did lose my job as an editor, and from then on, nobody wanted to employ me "without the necessary consultations" with some mysterious but obvious authority.

Mom tried to convince me to go back to my diplomatic studies and take a workers' evening course. She promised to watch over the goblin's bath and meals. Mumín was rehearsing her brand-new vocabulary by then, in which women had the "monstruation," and when they didn't, they ran to get an "apportion."

She was growing up in a hermetically isolated country, without books, without newspapers, without clothes, without fantasy, without money, and surrounded by a network of informers that replaced the police.

What could I do to prevent her from going through as difficult a transition into adolescence as mine had been? To protect her from things like having her feet stuck in a pair of shoes two sizes too small, or getting sick with despair due to lack of love and companionship?

What I lacked was the principle that heroically, or superficially, sustained millions of Cubans: the hope that Fidel Castro would fix their lives. Perhaps it is all the fatalism that we inherited from the Spaniards and the slaves.

Life in Cuba is a big wave that drags one along with it. It took me months to accept my outcast status and get rid of all the compulsion intended to convert any woman into the New Woman. It happened one evening when my class was canceled and I returned home at dinnertime to be with the goblin, who, out of consideration for my studies, had established her headquarters at Mom's. But she was not there.

"Where is Mumín?" I asked my mother.

"She is at Mercedes's."

"Doing what?"

"Having dinner."

"Eating at that Altar to Obesity? Do you want her face to break out like her father's?"

"I have no time to prepare her meals."

"Then I have no time to study this good-for-nothing career."

After putting the goblin comfortably to sleep in our apartment, I sat down to review the situation.

How could I make a living illegally without it being too evident?

I had an idea. I started an imperceptible recycling industry. I collected a lot of the old shoes in the neighborhood, covered them with lace and fabric, and then resold them. Everything that had beads, seeds, bits of precious stones and wires, I turned into earrings.

But we needed dollars.

Without breadwinning husbands or assistance from relatives in exile, it was impossible to provide enough food, clothes, and shoes for four women (great-grandmother, grandmother, mother, and daughter) on what the ration books allowed us. Two cans of condensed milk a month, a packet of sugar, two bars of soap, and a little paper bag with detergent was simply not enough.

In order to get dollars, a woman had to go out and walk the streets way past midnight through the intricate labyrinth of hotels where foreigners set the price on Cuban women like on cattle at a country fair.

I kept dragging behind me the scent of persecution and surveillance, which made everything that much more difficult.

Dollars were easier to get, more accessible, and came with a steadier flow, from the accredited diplomatic corps.

I secured a lover from Algiers who was fascinated with my belly dance. After a stormy, clandestine relationship, during which he found my strident paranoia not easy to take, he gracefully offered to make me his third wife.

This offer made me contemplate retirement.

What if I convinced Mom to sell her Lam painting?

What I needed was a generous government guest, one who could zip in and out of Cuban customs as if he owned the place.

These were hard times. My only two job offers came from the Comandante. One was to make the Habana Libre Hotel, the former Hilton, more Cuban through a plan devised by the Ministry of Culture. The second was to start a clandestine office devoted to copying scientific books in English without paying any royalties. I didn't want to accept anything that came from the Comandante.

Abrantes, who had the deplorable habit of phoning me in the middle of the night to chat about Calderón de la Barca or Émile Zola, depending on whether he was in an Iberophile or a Francophile phase, now got into the even worse habit of driving by my home and making his presence known by burning rubber or jamming on his brakes with lots of noise.

He started to create a vacuum around me by forcing me to evict from my apartment a couturier friend whose presence he considered immoral.

"Some *compañeras* have been commenting on this situation at the National Bank Party meeting. They asked how come the Comandante's daughter is allowed to have a faggot dress designer living in her home."

"This is too much!" I protested. "Do they also criticize Fidel in those meetings? We really are making some progress toward democracy!"

"That's none of your business. But if you don't get him out, we will."

I didn't even have to be concerned about my morals because the Ministry of the Interior and Personal Security took care of them.

The next time, Abrantes came up with the objection that I was associating with "undesirable elements" whose nature he couldn't properly define.

He closed down my social life for quite some time.

*After two years of* silence, an alarm bell sounded in Fidel's affective side and again he sent a soldier, the one always bearing good news, with the promised eighty pesos in an envelope and three bags of food and books to wish me a happy New Year.

The bags held a gigantic turkey, a few pounds of black beans, four bottles of Algerian wine, and a few biographies by Stefan Zweig.

I saw a card from the Chief Executive swimming in the turkey blood.

"Tell Fidel to shove all the—" But the soldier cut me off.

"I don't want to hear it. I won't return this, though I can't keep it either. Don't be silly. Don't get me into a situation."

*Mumín was growing up* in a three-way tug-of-war. My matriarchs from across the street had undertaken a Sagittarian offensive against my style of life, without taking into account that they were enjoying their greatest pleasures and a large portion of their creature comforts thanks to me.

My guilt kept accumulating. I was going through that stage of life when I didn't know what was rightfully mine and what was not. All my loyalties were mixed up.

Fidel's turkey finally went to Pablo Armando Fernández, one of the writers committed to the Revolution. My old teacher Galbe, now deceased, used to refer to him as one of the "exquisite corpses" of Cuban poetry.

I will never know how I managed to get to Pablo Armando's house on "the Christmas Eve of the Turkey." Gluttony was not my motive: I was even more vegetarian than a palm tree. It must have been my inclination to get into big trouble every Christmas that compelled me.

I stood for more than two hours on Twenty-sixth Avenue trying to hitch a ride that evening. Taxis were exclusively for foreigners.

A guy in a metallic blue Lada finally stopped for me. When we reached the iron bridge, he let go of the steering wheel and grabbed my breasts.

"So delicious, baby, I love how they bob up and down!"

"Stop, you son of a bitch! We're going to crash! Idiot, they're not boobs! It's all cotton!"

My anorexia had just rescued me from rape, and I didn't see the incident as a bad omen.

I walked into Pablo's kitchen with the swagger of a satisfied warrior, and as I was greeting the hostess with a kiss, I heard a voice with familiar echoes from a past life.

"Who is that woman with the sad eyes?"

That voice came from a man incapable of hiding his innate elegance under his two-day-old stubble and ridiculously inappropriate clothes.

He had rosy skin from eating good Mediterranean food, and the time-less, classic stance of a statue. Everything about him was . . . well, in-tense. Ah, the hysteria of sudden passion! We spent a charming and inquisitive evening drinking at Pablo's, after which we instantly knew everything about each other. Or almost everything.

The following day, on a balcony overlooking Paseo Street in the Vedado, he stood with his gaze fixed on the sea toward the faint sug-gestion of the horizon where, irreconcilably, the two Americas meet. Meanwhile, I was staring at the roofs with their faded colors, their peeling paint, their populace of TV antennas and asbestos-cement tanks which had been added on to cope with the water shortages. I broke the silence with my existential summation.

"That is me."

"And I am this." He handed me some manuals from Alcoholics Anonymous. "I don't even know why I began drinking."

His reasons didn't matter to me. I wanted to erase them from his soul. He had started drinking when he was a very old young man, about eighteen.

"I'm never going to leave you," he said. And I believed him.

I accompanied him to the airport. That night my soul grew wings. In my half-sleep I dreamed I was at a fair where the girls' heads were crowned with garlands of stars, made out of white ribbons interlaced in wire, and the men were dressed in black with ruffs. Then the damned telephone as usual interrupted my dream and almost gave me a heart attack. I always seemed to be caught in the middle of the shrill long-distance static due to Third World technologies and the classic trills from MININT interference.

It was him.

He wanted to assure me that he would never leave me. He also wanted to introduce me to his friends at the Centro Vasco in Miami, everyone from the maitre d' down to the cashier girl.

"Sure! Delighted! Yes. Yesss! Deeelighted! Of course. Of cooourse! Deeelighted!" The female cats in heat were howling to-gether with me in the pitch-black stony silence.

When my love returned two weeks later, I was already an authority on alcoholism, on frayed myelin sheaths, on the importance of love, faith, and charity, vitamin B$_{12}$, and the whole healing process. I then helped him get through those cold-turkey days of privation by means of tricks and nonsense.

My lover was very intelligent, but he could not pinpoint the exact moment in which he started evading the realities of life and started drinking. He had been a student at the London School of Economics, and already a committed leftist. It was around this time that my mom watched with resignation the defection of the last Cuban ambassador in London and I was busy changing my Barbie's wardrobe. He was organizing student protests against increasing Imperialist influences on the Island, and thanks to his record as an elite Marxist sympathizer, he now enjoyed more privileges than most and had a free rein in the establishment of a Student Exchange Center.

"What can Cuban economists contribute to economists abroad, when there is no economy here?" I asked him.

"Oh! There's nothing that both sides don't already know. But at least the Cubans can take a little trip to Mexico once in a while."

There was more culture in him than could be found in a dolmen supporting a stone in an Aztec pyramid, and he had a professorial tone that constantly strained my patience.

While I was helping him not to sip mojitos and Cuba libres, he watched my paranoia expand like a peacock's fantail. No way would I accompany him to his hotel or let him utter a word in public that would give him away as a foreigner, for fear of the scandal of an arrest that would end with me handcuffed, and being dragged away to some dingy cubicle near a laundry room.

"What if I were to invite you to my country, Alina? In a less tense environment we might be able to get to know each other better."

"I have a feeling that if you do invite me, you will never be able to come back to Cuba. Not to mention the wild idea that I would possibly be allowed to leave."

"How can you even say that? I have already invited a lot of people!"

"But I am not even allowed to pick daisies in Ethiopia. Give me some more time. I'll get over my fear."

He was in a hurry to rebuild his life. He had never been married. And I hadn't really, either, with all my previous marriages destined to fuse into one continuous sequence.

But I didn't want to overwhelm him with all the procedures and official paperwork that would surely interfere with our wedding plans.

I forgot to tell you his name was Fidel.

# 6

# FIDEL II

*The Ministry of the* Interior had organized a brand-new citizen-extortion department named Interconsult.

Its function was to provide exit visas for those families whose exiled relatives could pay the government of Cuba more than $50,000 per person for allowing them to leave. Its agents abroad would first check the applicant's financial status. The visa would be granted through Miami or any Latin American country.

Foreigners marrying Cuban citizens, of either sex, had to pay $2,000 and get approval from the Ministry of Justice. Whenever the proceedings took too long, each ministry blamed the other. After having paid, some people got lost in the shuffle. Many married couples had been separated and families kept apart from their relatives without being able to appeal to any court.

To be able to survive the screening process of those zealous government clerks at Interconsult required a very fine kind of humor.

I sat down to think. On my decadent gray-blue thinking couch.

First, I had to involve my family. Then it was a matter of making a series of phone calls. Next, I needed to involve an intermediary.

My aunt Vilma and uncle Raúl were leaving for Germany to attend some important Eastern European leader's funeral. I waited for the evening preceding their flight.

Vilma was packing, happy to escape her daily routine, and to be honored on the other side of the ocean as the Great Federated Woman.

"Aunt Vilma, I came to tell you that I'm planning to get married."

"Again, dear?"

"The other marriages have been circumstantial . . . pressures, pregnancy—you know."

I gave her all the details.

"Now, you wouldn't be doing this in order to leave the country, would you?"

In their home the same kind of militant eloquence was still being used.

"My fiancé is a proven advocate of the Cuban Revolution. Mexico is an ally of Cuba, isn't it? What's wrong with traveling back and forth?"

"And what about Mumín?"

"Mumín will attend the British school in Mexico. Fidel did his studies in London. There are two islands in the world that he loves: England and this one. . . . Will you, please, tell my father? You see, I still don't have his direct phone number. Besides, I don't want him to get upset."

"But we're leaving tomorrow. I won't be able to do it before we leave."

The rest was easy. I called several offices, saying that I was somebody's chief of staff, or a friend of mine would call and pretend to be somebody else's assistant. I kept it up until I had Interconsult and the Ministry of Justice equally entangled and totally confused. When my wonderful fiancé returned, everything was ready for the wedding. The two bureaus were overflowing with many calls from the High Command, whatever that was.

We were married on April 12. I had not told a soul.

To accomplish anything, you often need to do some finagling.

When Raúl and Vilma returned from their intergovernmental funeral in Germany, the wedding had already taken place.

My Fidel and I were in the kitchen when Mom let herself in to the apartment, using her set of keys.

"I came to see if everything was under control." She had been told stories that questioned my husband's sobriety.

"Mom, we have some news for you. Fidel and I got married."

"Married? Impossible! You? Getting married in Havana to a foreigner! But you need—"

"Yes, I know. We got married already. That's the news."

"No, nonononononoo! This is going to be a real bombshell in Havana!" She looked up at the bare ceiling in the kitchen as if searching for some divinity in her atheist pantheon. She then lifted her arms in the only prayer that I have ever seen her offer in this life, exclaiming, "Thanks, dear God! At last! At last! Thank you, Fidel! I hope finally someone takes her out of Cuba!"

She turned around and left.

Grandma Natica made her pronouncement.

"I congratulate you both, but you have a little problem with alcohol, right, Fidel? My poor Manolo, may he rest in peace, he too had his troubles, but he was not violent, fortunately . . . Even so, he ruined my life anyway."

Mumín gave us both a big, sonorous kiss.

"Then, Mom, will I get to see the New World?"

The words and emotions displayed by my Sagittarian women considerably dampened the festive spirit and the enterprising *gaillardise* of my brand-new husband.

The best, however, was yet to come.

*Fidel and I both* had an appointment with Vilma at the Federation of Cuban Women, but I met her a little bit earlier.

"Your father is furious!"

"I see."

"You see what?"

"I see nothing new."

"You have gotten Interconsult and two ministers into trouble, not to mention me."

"I didn't mean to."

"Now he wants to know who your husband is and why he married you."

"Tell him that it must be because of my dowry! He must think I have a monumental dowry. Just like the Borgias."

"Stop being cynical and help me on this."

"It won't be good news anyway."

My husband was then allowed in. The office was filled with masculine dignity and the expansive waves of his unforgettable voice.

"Well, Fidel, congratulations. I am very glad you got married, but to be honest, Fidel, I mean not you, but Fidel el Comandante, is not ... I mean, the Commander in Chief would like to know what your intentions are."

My Fidel swallowed his humiliation and offered a myriad of good intentions that even I was unaware of.

"And how do you see the possibility of working and living here in Cuba?"

My husband had never held an office position in his entire life. When the Imperialists had turned multinational, he was still very young. He had earned consideration and respect from many with his foresight and wise advice, making his family sell their business before they were ruined.

"As far as living here permanently ..."

In a flash of lucidity, he probably saw himself living through blackouts, extended periods without gas or water, receiving visits at any time of night from my collection of demanding, traumatized night owls, one of whom had already broken a window when I refused to open the door. It was a life spent going to the diplotienda with his pockets full of grocery lists, along with paper insoles and brief indications as to the shoe sizes and color preferences of those who needed them. These shopping trips were an activity into which I had forced him the moment he set a permanent foot in my apartment.

"And there is another message from the Comandante. He wants to have your biography in writing."

El Comandante was intent on making my Fidel swallow a bitter pill.


*The moment had come* to call in the mediators.

There could be no higher accomplice mediator than writer Gabriel García Márquez (Gabo). His Nobel prize is a measly reward compared with the prodigal generosity he got from the top Cuban Hero, who, besides honoring him as his best friend, created the School for

Latin American Cinema and a foundation for him. Since both institutions were tax-exempt, there was a continuous loss of revenue for the treasury in Mexico, where the writer makes his home.

For his stays in Havana, Fidel gave Gabo a Mercedes-Benz with a chauffeur and placed at his disposal two or three suites in different hotels and Protocol House Number One. Fidel would visit him almost every night, thus replacing the two-headed entity Núñez-Véliz with Gabo, who was far more useful in the realm of international intelligentsia.[14]

When Gabo announces a midnight supper for New Year's Eve, the Communist oligarchs prepare themselves for battle. They organize their intrigues, more in the style of Rocambole than that of Versailles, to wangle an invitation. He who was there last year, and is not invited this year, suffers the arrival of the new year with his soul in a pickle. He waits not only for the sword of Damocles to fall on his head, but for a unit of Personal Security to come and arrest him and all his family for some unknown crime that the CDR neighborhood watchdog system of denunciations might have disclosed thanks to Radio Bemba or the local gossips.[15]

By good-natured mediation, Gabo has been able to get countless political prisoners and Amnesty International cases out of the country. He seemed to be able to bring my father the Genius to reason.

Gabo had placed his laurels and the honor of his friendship at the feet of a few of our mutual friends. He had given them jobs at least, as he did for my old friend Tony Valle Vallejo, who was Gabo's private secretary until he was able to go into exile.

I trusted Gabo because of the deep knowledge of the human condition that permeates his books.

I went to see him.

"Gabo, I fell in love with a Mexican and we got married." I told him the whole, interminable story.

"One simply cannot talk to Fidel about his family. It's a forbidden topic. Perhaps my wife, Merche, will dare, but I . . . I'm going to ask her. *Caramba!* For twenty years I have been taking people who were in solitary, out of jail and out of the country, but a mission like this has never even crossed my mind. It's like what I always say: Cuba is better than Macondo. I bet you don't even know what the elephant at the National Zoo has for dinner."

"No, I don't." I had thought that the elephant and I had two things in common, living in Cuba and being a total vegetarian. I was wrong.

"He is fed an omelet with ninety-nine eggs! What I couldn't understand was . . . why not one hundred. . . .

"That's because the cook only dares to steal one egg at a time."

Each one plays his own tunes. It's like a syndrome of fixed ideas.

"Gabo, does art interest you?"

"Of course!"

"And how about Wilfredo Lam? Do you like his paintings?"

He said he did, very much. For him, Lam represented the highest expression of the fusion and sublimation of diverse Cubist and Cuban influences: the Chinese, the Caribbean slaves, and the descendants of Taíno women. One of Wilfredo's paintings, *The Jungle,* is insured for a million dollars by the Museum of Modern Art in New York. Wilfredo Lam's work has a mythical magic realism. With a little effort on my part, if I couldn't get him to champion my marriage, then at least I could get him to buy Lam's *Femme Cheval* from me. It was hanging in my mother's living room. If he could get prisoners in solitary confinement past Cuban customs, then he could very well do the same thing with a painting.

*Not wanting to be* short on defenders of my out-landish marriage, I also went to talk to Osmani Cienfuegos, the least mummified of the lunchtime denizens in the Palacio de la Revolución. We liked each other, and he had courage: he was the only one who had dared to invite me out, and we didn't have to meet behind the cemetery.

Osmani owed this hegemonic position of his to his brother, Camilo, a bearded and charismatic man who had been acclaimed as a hero at the beginning of the Revolution. His plane was mysteriously lost at sea, and the rumor was that Fidel had gotten rid of him. But Osmani now occupied a position in the Political Bureau, and the hero's picturesque parents had turned their son's death into their income for life. They enjoyed security personnel, bodyguards, and a chauffeured

Alfa Romeo. The old man, nicknamed the Little Crocodile, could be seen in the car's backseat, always wearing a wide-brimmed peasant's hat exactly like the one his fallen son had worn.

On each anniversary of Camilo's death, Cuban children happily interrupt their classes to go near the sea and throw in flowers for a dead man whose identity they don't really know.

When I asked him for help, Osmani gave me an answer similar to Gabo's.

"I'll see if Fidel gives me a chance to dare say anything about it. I still remember how enraged he was when you married Yoyi. We thought he was going to kill the table."

"No kidding! He only talked to me about Yoyi's affection for female political prisoners."

"Take it easy. You know, as they say, let time take care of it. Eventually he finally 'gets' some things."

"I know. It's the only way he's like my mother."

*My aunt Vilma relayed* the Comandante's response.

"Fidel has said that he will give you a house here in Cuba. And that if your fiancé loves you, he can stay to live with you. But about you, traveling to Mexico, the answer is no. It would create a political situation. He says that if Fidel's parents are very old, and he cannot leave them in Mexico, let him bring them here. They will have free medical attention. He says he will give you a car, and will look into getting him a job. It's not clear where to place him, since he is an economist."

"But, Aunt Vilma, how on earth am I going to tell him those things? A house and a car!"

"Well, that detail about a car was my own invention, but it doesn't seem too difficult," she said, and hung up.

Though I was familiar with the mysteries of the Tarot, I had gotten married on the twelfth, the Hanged Man's number backwards!

My husband was constantly traveling to and from Mexico. He had a strange habit of searching for some dark drama in my past. Every time I left him alone, he would snoop around my literary efforts. He began reading everything he could find in my drawers and in the cardboard boxes where I kept my inviolable secrets. He studied the phrases I had underlined in my books and discovered my love poems and letters of desolate passion written to no one in particular. Even though I tried to convince him that perhaps I had written them for him before I knew him, that they were the best and worst I had to offer, and that they could all be his, I was not able to appease him.

"You must have done something horrible, something unspeakable, for your father to treat you like this. Were you ever involved in an attempt on his life?"

"We must give him time. He is playing games. He is trying to discourage me. It's a habit with him. But he gets over it after a while."

My father's obsessions and timing had been taken into account in my strategy.

My Fidel, though, really loved to hear about the dreams of my wandering soul. In one of my dreams he was traveling to our wedding. He was going down a flight of stairs under a restaurant canopy with a man and a woman. I described the scene for him, including all the clothes, even the necktie hues.

"Where did they take me, in your dream?"

"To the airport."

"Ah, well, of course! And who told you?"

"I dreamt it, as usual."

Once he actually took refuge in the Mexican embassy in Havana, in the delusion that he was in the Federal District and being pursued by a death squad under my command.

I learned that pure nonsense is not a good cure for alcoholism.

He began to arrive home around sunset totally plastered, practically horizontal. I was in a panic that he would get into a confrontation with my goblin.

He would come home in his proletarian costume, his suit jacket all rumpled, his silk foulard necktie twisted, with whiskey, mojitos, and rum collins on his breath, and his pant cuffs smelling like the septic tank that has decorated the front of my apartment building for years.

"Better beware! I am a Great Brother of the Emerald Lodge! And no female can do this to a Great Brother of the Emerald Lodge!" he would sometimes scream in our living room at six o'clock in the evening.

"And I am the Grand Sorceress of the Congo Seven Moon Strike-Five Empembe Pledge!" I would answer him back, brandishing in one hand a femur I had exhumed from a box of bones sold to apprentice doctors. In the other, I would have a milkshake loaded with vitamin $B_{12}$ and meprobamate that I had prepared for his low-ebb hours in which his body would scream for the sugar surge provided by the alcohol.

Time would settle all of this, I told myself, thinking that an efficient, sensible, and aggressive matron like Gabo's wife, Merche, had to win in the end over my father's emotional irrationalities. I was sure that the Big Boss had more important things to do than ruin my engagements and marriages.

My poor husband felt under siege.

"Around the middle of November," he told me, "I received a strange phone call about 'taking your wife out of the country.' The guy wanted to meet me at a particular café, at a specified time, under a precise window, at a table where I would see a copy of the *Washington Post* opened to page two. He said he was from the CIA. As you can imagine, I didn't go."

A week later he received through his ambassador an official invitation from the Cuban government to attend a New Year's Eve dinner. He was never able to find out who had invited him and was totally disconcerted.

"But, Fidel, all the security police around the world are the same. They even copy each other, or else they work together. You can't be thinking that I'm keeping any state secrets from you. Neither Security nor the CIA has any reason to be losing sleep on account of my lowly person."

"I don't know anything anymore. I don't know who you are or who I am. This all seems like one big nightmare."

So what else is new!

My husband called me one last time. He phoned from Mexico.

"Right now there is an ambulance at my door and I'm in terrible pain. All over. The doctor says it's due to some traumatic event. But the only traumatic event in my life is you!"

We got a divorce through an international law office that handles the collection of dollars in Cuba for the legal separations demanded by all the frustrated spouses from Latin America. Usually these were people manipulated by Cubans in their effort to cross the border of their dreams, from anywhere in Latin America to Miami.

I signed the divorce papers and went straight to the hospital with a beastly asthma attack.

When I was free of all the intravenous needles and oxygen masks, I ran home. I made an enormous funeral pyre in the street with everything I had written until I was thirty and thus burned the story of my dream life and of the life I had invented for myself. Then I went to a barbershop and had my head shorn.

Herbert Clews with his wife,
Natalia, and son Enrique.

Manolo Revuelta.

Ángel Castro.

Martín Ruz.

Grandmother Lina Ruz,
after whom Alina was named.

Grandmother Lala Natica in 1948.

Fidel at age three.

Dr. Orlando Fernández Ferrer and Naty Revuelta in 1948.

Naty in 1955, one year before
Alina was born.

Fidel in 1955.

Alina's baptism. From left to right, beginning at the bottom:
Elsie Clews, Natalie, Natica, Dr. Orlando Fernández Ferrer, Caridad
Betancourt de Sanguily (the godmother, with Alina in her arms),
Antonia Ferrer, Dr. July Sanguily (godfather), Naty,
and Manolo Revuelta.

Alina in the arms of
Tata Mercedes.

Alina as the star of the Carnival
with her Robin Hood escort.

Fidel playing baseball.

Alina in Paris on the Île de la
Cité in 1964.

Alina with Fidel, celebrating her marriage to Yoyi Jiménez in 1973.

Alina with her second husband, Honduras.

Alina, pregnant with Mumín, and her third husband, Panchi.

Natica, Mumín, Naty, and Alina, in 1989.

**TOP LEFT:**
Alina in modeling attire.

**TOP RIGHT:**
Mumín at age five.

**LEFT:**
Alina as a model in 1989.

Alina today.

# 7

# IT'S NOT MY PARTY

*For my "last millimeter"* haircut I went to a Personal Security barbershop on Kholy Street. The same boxer who had saved me from depression a few years back by making me run track and do repetitions of abdominal exercises worked there.

The barber's name was Juanito. He knew a million things. As a remedy for underarm sweaty smell, he recommended leaving two sour orange halves sprinkled with baking soda outdoors overnight at the full moon. In the morning you were to put them under your armpits for half a day.

"And for gall bladder problems, a tea made with prickly crowfruit. That's it."

Juanito's hands and his litany of paramedical remedies allowed me to relax. When I opened my eyes my head looked shaved except for a short fringe in the front. He had forgotten I was not a recruit.

"Juanito, cut the fringe off! Cut it all off, Juanito!"

I looked very cute in a pink pinafore that I had gotten thanks to the generosity of Sandra Levinson, the director of the Center for Cuban Studies in New York. She used to resell her used clothes among her Cuban friends when she traveled to the Island to feed her cats, confirm her status.

When I emerged from the barbershop with my hairless head, a bunch of recruits gathered and then slowly came over to ask me if I was sick.

News of my haircut must have traveled fast, because well after midnight, after some spectacular screeching of brakes, I had Minister Abrantes sitting on my decadent sofa, where so many bad ideas had been generated in the past. An electric, shameless energy ran between us. He did not come to inquire whether I had become a practicing Jew.

"You don't need to marry any foreigner to live well. Anything you need, just ask me."

There are certain people who just don't understand what self-esteem is, and therefore I did not feel insulted. I have spent half my life standing on my head, my eyes crossed and looking at the epicenter of my frontal bones, and my tongue twisted against my palate, trying to transform the images of people that do me harm into third-eye images of love. This is my yoga technique to acquire humility.

Right then I was not living much better than I had before, except for a Lada that had cost my husband less than four thousand dollars, and now served as the neighborhood ambulance and as a taxi for my acquaintances.

"Then I'm going to ask you for only one thing," I said in desperation.

I grabbed him, took him to my room, and threw him on my bed.

"Come on, get on with it, do whatever you want to do with me right now! Let's get rid of your obsession with me, so you can leave me alone!"

But he didn't want to.

"I'm only following orders!"

"There are a lot of ways of following orders. I can't set foot outside without someone writing a little report about it, which you pass on. If I go to a nightclub three nights in a row, you intimidate the people who invite me. I can't enter an embassy twice. And I am forbidden to take any plane at the airport."

"Who told you that?"

"In spite of everything, I still have friends. If someone stays overnight in my house, you get him out, or try to make him into an informer. I can't find a job if someone does not 'authorize' it. If you see me with a woman, she becomes your lover. I am an island inside this damned Island. What are you after? Do you want me to shoot my-self?"

But that night Abrantes was not moved by his aberrant impulses. That night he opened his spout of self-flagellation to me.

I remembered all the times I had unexpectedly seen him picking up preadolescent girls in the streets of Havana, not to mention the salacious anecdotes that the girlfriends he had driven away from me would bring back after their little weekend jaunts to Cancún with him. Stories which involved the minister's pistol converted into a second phallus, a swaggering dildo that they had to introduce into every orifice until their display charged his hormonal batteries enough for ejaculation.

This powerful and charming monster had come to make confessions to one of his victims.

"I also have problems. You see, my son . . ."

He told me how the apple of his eye had turned into a faggot. So what else is new? Natica would say. Since the time when Honduras had been Abrantes's assistant and I was Honduras's concubine, I knew that one of the minister's children had an extraordinary sensibility. Gradually, he became like a brother to me, and I developed an affection for him such as one seldom has for a friend. He was a generous, vulnerable human being.

"I have made his life impossible, but I know he's not going to change."

How interesting, I thought. The inquisitor suffering from the inquisition. Why was he telling me all this? Was he taking it as his well-deserved punishment? Was he mellowing? Did he need a depository for his secrets? What he needed was a mediator! He needed someone to convince his boy not to counterattack by wearing false eyelashes and a long lacy tunic. It was making his father lose prestige around the capital. Abrantes continued in his confessional tone.

"It is true that I have caused you a lot of harm."

"I don't want to know the details, I want to live in peace. I need to transfer the car to my name. And I need a job."

\*    \*    \*

*When the authorities are* in charge of making your life pleasant, every minute is a joy.

The people who convert illegal to legal changed the car registration and gave me a brand-new driver's license.

In less than a week I had an appointment with Rogelio Acevedo, Raúl Castro's vice minister. I was going to start working with the Artistic Group of the FAR (Revolutionary Armed Forces).

This Conjunto Artístico, as it was called, consisted of all the dancers rejected by the National Ballet because of their height. The females were virtuoso gnomes and the males had such nicely muscled builds that they made you forget their lack of technique.

Rogelio Acevedo was married to Bertica, a former queen of the Cuban Carnival celebrations of old. These festivities had been condemned as a kind of ideological diversionism in the seventies. Though he was ten years younger than his "comrades in struggle," he had reached his high position, practically in spite of himself, after the minister of the navy was dismissed due to an inseverable involvement with drug traffic, which began to spread through the country at about the same time as the Carnival and its stars were fading into oblivion.

Rogelio's face is dominated by his mouth. A mouth that forever seems to be sucking at his mother's breast. He seems to awaken protective instincts in other people.

"Alina, you're going to work mainly in public relations with the Artistic Group of the FAR. The Group is in charge of promoting, maintaining, and consolidating cultural relations among the armed forces of all the countries in the Socialist Bloc. The Artistic Group also elevates morale among our own troops assigned to the bastions of struggle in different parts of the world."

His official rhetoric tickled my fantasies. I had visions of a popular dance rhythm, the *guaguancó,* being heard in the Arabian desert, Yemen, the Abu Bahr plains, Angola, and Mecca, and danced by topless dwarf nymphs wearing paillette monokinis with headdresses of tropical fruits à la Carmen Miranda. I fancied drummers beating the rhythms with their three *batá* drums in Tala Mugongo, Oncocua, and Quimbele, spinning like tops, parodying themselves in the Siberian steppes, the port of Baku, and the steaming jungles of South America, in Nicaragua, Guatemala, Chile, and El Salvador; that is, all the places where Cuba delivered its army in "bastions of struggle."

I returned to my senses. A salary of 198 pesos a month had been given to me, and maybe, just maybe, if that was not enough, I could do some French translations for the Department of Technical Translations of the FAR.

"Tomorrow you have a meeting with Lieutenant Colonel Bomboust. He will give you all the details."

*Lieutenant Colonel Von Boust* is a Cuban blend of Chinese and black Moor. His whip was always at his side, and under the military sash holding his pistol and magazines was an incipient potbelly that, as he said, he "had to work hard to nurture."

"I am from Oriente province," Von Boust began. "When I first came to Havana, I did not even have a place to sleep. So I became obsessed with my work. My worst nightmare was to leave my office, because I had no place to go."

"I knew a guy who used to go to funeral parlors. . . ."

"That is why I was able to produce so much. I worked like a madman. I accumulated more voluntary hours than the whole Socialist Emulation put together. And what do you think my much-admired bosses did? All those jokers who religiously signed out their cards at seventeen-thirty, what do you think they did?"

I couldn't even guess. It seemed this had been my year as confessor. The high echelons had all turned me into a repository for their most vulnerable memories. I felt like running away.

"Well, they really made my life impossible. In one disciplinary council after another, they almost accused me of being a spy. It was all because I worked more than they did! So I have hardened. It has been very difficult to get where I am, and if anyone wants to do me wrong, I'll chop his head off."

He wore boots up to his knees, and as he walked, he beat them lightly with his whip.

It was not a threat. It was his declaration of principles. His unspoken message was: I have had to suffer worse than being saddled with the care of some big shot's spoiled daughter.

"Whether you believe it or not, Mr. Von Boust, I have never been anywhere of my own free will."

While he was thinking about what to say, I had another confused vision of a body, like the vision I had years before during a visit to the Palace. Again my perception of a man's shape and substance were transformed. Von Boust became a bloody, amorphous, perverse mass, and I was transfixed to discover for the second time that what I had really seen was the devil. The vision that altered my human understanding was like the one Chucha the cook had experienced so many years ago, when, contradicting all codes of proper behavior for servants, she had ordered Natica not to open the door.

Von Boust looked at my hairless head, my barber Juanito's crowning masterpiece of a trim to the skin.

"First, my dear, let your hair grow. It looks weird. I was told that when you came in, the children from the school on the corner got excited and were calling you all kinds of names. That is simply not convenient."

When the devil decides to take care of you, don't doubt it even for a second: everything will be all right.

"Yes, Mr. Von Boust."


*My work mornings began* with that liberation of the body through sacrifice that is ballet, or even dance in general. We all danced, even though the salon was so small that it was impossible for twenty dancers to stand Indian file.

My public relations job consisted of ordering shoes, supervising costumes, and taking care of snacks and transportation. When I finished that I would sit down to do what I did best, lend the Biggest Ear. I heard the same things over and over.

That there weren't enough ballet slippers, tights, and leotards for everyone. That having to perform in Angola, after sitting for more than eighteen hours on a cargo plane and almost a week on a freighter, was impairing people's talents and ability to perform. That they had studied eight years for a career and did not want to be off in some desert wiggling their asses. That they were not being paid for the risks. That somebody had spent two years in the Construction Microbrigade in order to have an apartment of his own that he finally didn't get, and that it was unfair for someone else to be the star, just because she was sleeping with so-and-so.

These were the problems of collectives all over the world.

I had been turned into a complaint and suggestion box. I had the appropriate attributes of discretion and understanding, but not the power to solve any problems. I had a lifelong experience of that. The productions became exciting when Rogelio París, formerly with Cinecittà, was put in charge of a patriotic spectacle celebrating the anniversary of MININT and FAR. It involved the whole group: theater people, musicians, singers, and dancers.

Rogelio had directed *A Midsummer Night's Dream* for the National School of Art following the same policy, and the man did find something for everyone to do, from classic, contemporary, and folk dancers to actors, choral singers, and apprentice circus performers, all using the fantastic natural setting of the school gardens. Even though the stage mist was late and interfered with the next scene, the nets dropped out of place, the spotlights focused on the wrong performers, and the donkey got turned on by the smell of so many menstruating women, Shakespeare himself would have been satisfied. That incredible mix of odd talents did not take anything away from the story, not even for a second.

Rogelio was addicted to grandiose productions.

Because the FAR theater stage was minuscule compared with the gardens of the School of Art, I was afraid that he, who liked to do everything big and in large numbers, except taking his bath, was going to try to stuff all of Hollywood into Havana. In terms of production this was going to be devastating. Because although in *A Midsummer Night's Dream* there had been no rifle firing or anti-aircraft shooting, I was sure they would be the order of the day for a show "with revolutionary themes."

Rogelio wanted, of course, gunshots and cannonades, along with numerous special smoke and lighting effects. He was demanding an infernal machine that no one outside the National Theater had, and a pulley and a net to hoist the Fallen Hero, an impersonation of Che Guevara, and take him to heaven in a climax of stagecraft fireworks.

In order for the stage proceedings to be properly timed and perfect, he also wanted the kind of radio transmitters used only by the police.

It was around this same time that the threat of AIDS was first felt in Cuba. This news was given cautiously because, of course, there were no homosexuals within the Revolution, and there was still respect for that erroneous scientific empiricism which says that God's punishment is selective and that queers are promiscuous.

In his public harangues the Comandante blamed Imperialism for having "perpetrated the infamy of spreading the AIDS virus in vitro," though he denied its presence in Cuba. Meanwhile, every military center in Cuba was testing everyone who had put their feet and something else into Ethiopia or Angola.

I had not gone anywhere. I was living full-time in the nightmare of trying to be Rogelio París's producer. I already knew about the epidemic through my friend Nostradamus.

I used all the civility I could muster in meetings with the chief of police and the director of Personal Security to try to get Rogelio the two-way radios and the ammunition he was asking for. I drove around Havana in an army truck loaded with practice grenades, training rifles, and boxes and more boxes of uniforms, boots, and torches of freedom. The only dry-ice factory that was still operating in the country was miles away from Havana. By using dry ice in conjunction with some gigantic fans, we were attempting to satisfy his urge for big smoke clouds.

One Saturday at noon I was taking a deserved rest at home with my feet sticking up like two pestles on the balcony railing. My goblin and I were about to start the weekend ritual of doing our hair and nails when I saw my mother walking by with hurried, anguished steps toward Twenty-sixth Avenue.

"Where are you going?"

"All Party members have been summoned to see Fidel's video. For those of us in the Nucleus, it's going to be shown now at the Acapulco Cinema. There seems to be an imminent threat of war! Don't wait up for me, dear, because I've been told it lasts over five hours."

I imagined my mother falling asleep in the darkened cinema, lulled by her favorite voice in the whole world, and with no one turning the projector off to break the spell.

Making the people "stick together behind a common cause" was a strategy Fidel resorted to quite often. It had become tedious, with the October missile crisis, Che's death, the Ring Around Havana, the Ten-Million-Ton Sugar Harvest, the Peruvian embassy "scum" incident, the Angolan genocide, and all the declared violations of Cuban airspace and territorial waters.[16]

I only had to watch Mom to see what new catalyst, or "crazy glue," the Comandante had invented this time to band the people together.

"The Americans are going to invade Cuba."

"No kidding! When?"

"On the sixteenth of November! It's a national emergency!"

My poor mother practically ran back home from the theater, all excited and believing. And, of course, foreseeing the consequences.

She was doubtless going to dust off the old Chinese lantern that Fidel had given her twenty-five years ago, to see if it had changed its mind and would light up now.

My mother was not the only one who believed all the propaganda, though. On account of Grenada, Gorbachev, and AIDS, we were already on combat alert. The gullibility of the people is amazing.

This whole new thing began when the United States invaded Grenada. A certain presenter of political events lost his voice while describing the image of mourning and apocalypse. Our Internationalist mission in Grenada was making the ultimate sacrifice for the Cuban flag.

For over seventy-two hours, on both the radio and television networks, Manolo Ortega narrated, with tears in his eyes and shouts of impotent anger, the extermination of the Cuban patriotic mission under Imperialist fire. He continued to report until it was all over.

"The last of our combatants has fallen! It's coming down! Our flag is coming down! It has come down and is now covering, sheltering, the corpse of our last survivor! Cuba has another hero! Another hero for Communism and for world peace!"

The entire country was in mourning for the fallen. Everyone was feeling more belligerent and anti-Imperialist than ever. At the very same time, all the "dead" were getting off a plane at Havana airport.

Pedro de Tortoló, who had headed the mission, was euphorically greeting the crowds.[17] The sole Cuban casualty was waving hello from his stretcher, head up.

It seems that in order to establish a few second-rate hotels in Grenada, some shrewd Yankee entrepreneur had managed to get a government budget allocation for a mock war approved through his lobbies to the House and Senate.

The Internationalist Cuban mission, in spite of Manolo Ortega's hair-raising description, had not made the supreme sacrifice to prevent the construction of a few two-star Holiday Inns.

None of that! The Cuban mission to the island of Grenada, where a military airport had been constructed with the salaries that we Cubans were not being paid, was stepping out of an airplane as usual, lugging tape recorders, electric fans, steam irons, cleaning mops, and lamps.

Jokingly, people then compared Adidas tennis shoes with the ones that Tortoló chose to complete the outfit he wore on his arrival: "With Tortoló sport shoes you can run faster and better." A week later he really had to put the quality of his shoes to the test: he was sent to join the war in Angola.

Meanwhile in Russia, Gorbachev, the respectable Piscean with the purple spot on his head, was busy inventing perestroika. It was to be a kind of intermediary stage between state Communism and a more productive and bearable form of coexistence. Nobody paid attention to him and now everybody can see the results. Fidel didn't, either, because he believed that no radical transition can be accomplished with the help of the common people.

The common people had just seen how the myth of the heroic sacrifice on behalf of World Revolution had fizzled.

It did not take long at all for people to ask themselves why there was not even a bit of glasnost in Cuba, because if we had already been force-fed the crumbs from the Russian table, why couldn't we also try a little of their democracy?

To top off this consequent uneasiness of the people, an unknown venereal disease was now threatening their private parts.

The masses urgently needed brainwashing.


*The temporary madness lasted* for months.

To be ready for the imminent aggression, Fidel created the Milicias de Tropas Territoriales (Militias of Territorial Troops), dressed the people Mao-style again, and distributed some rifles loaded with blanks.

With these war games as an excuse, power was cut for an extensive number of hours. The Russians cut their flow of foodstuffs to Cuba. The shortages, which were to get dramatically worse later, were not even noticed amid all the combative rhetoric.

The AIDS epidemic got out of control and thousands of patients were hospitalized in *sidatorios*. These were modern versions of the ancient leper colonies, but people were not paying attention. Mumín's school took her to dig ditches and open shelters during school hours, and to practice battle formations on weekends. She was a little over seven years old when she was taught the following chant:

*Bush caught HIV.*
*We've got him up a tree.*
*Our leader tore his balls off,*
*For all of us to see.*[18]


I paid little attention to all of this insane cackle until one Sunday, quite early in the morning, when a gun blast next to my window knocked me to the floor. Was this the rebellion at last? My only thoughts were of the goblin. I put the pot for roasting coffee on my head for a helmet, and I was on my way to rescue her from my mother's house before I realized that this could not be serious.

Still disheveled, I went out on the porch. From opposite sides of the street, a few guys dressed as militiamen were shooting blanks at one another, while the people in the neighborhood happily cheered them on. Like a sperm whale beached on the shores of the septic tank, a graying man of about sixty was playing dead.

I went down the porch stairs and into the street in a fury.

"Stupid asshole! Don't you think you're getting too old to be such an idiot? There are children and old folks living on this block! Do you want to give someone a heart attack?"

"*Compañera,* don't blame me. We're under orders. This is an exercise of the Militias of the Territorial Troops!"

"And you, at your age, do you do everything you're told? The next guy who shoots gets blown away with a good kick in the ass!"

I turned and left him standing there with the happy cheering of the neighbors in my ears.

*Then a directed (and* predigested) information campaign started.

The news programs showed, with much fanfare, the new shelters that the fatherland had created for the protection of its children against the invaders. Tunnels were being readied for use as dormitories, infirmaries, and classrooms. Life underground, organized and perfect, Vietnamese style.

These were tunnels to lock up millions of people, all along and across the Island. I began to wonder what it is that people have inside their heads.

Nobody seemed to wonder why or how so many tunnels could have magically appeared in three weeks. All the government had to do was disguise a few Cuban ships as U.S. Navy vessels and that would have been enough to have all the people, like sheep *qui tolis peccata mundi,* go into those holes, and remain there until their patriotic spirit could be reinforced, in case anyone dared to rebel for whatever reason. Nobody even considered that these tunnels could be used for holding people prisoner. Nobody thought that the smoky emissions coming from a project directed by a totally committed colonel from the Armed Forces, at the Biology Laboratory in San José de las Lajas, were unusual. No one suspected that such epidemics as swine and dengue fevers, diseases that had decimated the population and ruined the economy, had also emerged from that same lab. Another of the Comandante's convenient formulas for "crazy glue."

The people kept practicing getting into those tunnels as soon as the alarm button was pushed. Their brains had softened even more than those of the unborn fetuses I used to keep in jars during my childhood.

At the FAR Artistic Group, I was issued a camouflage uniform along with the others. We were to practice the defense of our building in case of a raid.

I came in the following Sunday morning, cape and sword in hand, and with a green beret on. You can't imagine how naked I felt without hair. I was assigned a wooden rifle and a papier-mâché grenade and sent to stand guard in a decorative turret on the front corner of the mansion. Herr Von Boust was shouting out orders while hitting his flank with his whip. I approached him discreetly.

"Excuse me, sir, but this is too much," I said. "Please return my weapon to the arsenal and accept my most respectful resignation." I winked at him. He looked at me, puzzled; he still believed in the patriotic rationale. Like everybody else, just about.

I felt my paternal chromosomes had become poisoned as I sat on my couch for negative thoughts. Fidel's intentions suddenly seemed crystal clear to me. He had managed to create a structure that allowed him total command of the masses. He could now manipulate them in a number of situations, in any manner he pleased.

What could I possibly do now? The manufacturing of rafts to cross the ninety miles that separated us from the coast of Florida was a thriving cottage industry these days, but I did not have the courage to make Mumín face the possibility of death by killer whales.

Sometimes one is in the position of having to choose between the bad life and the bad life.

\*    \*    \*

*Since I no longer* had a job, I decided it was time to look for something pleasant to do. I began going to ballet class every morning with my friend Papucho.

Papucho was Cachita Abrantes's son and a nephew of the minister of the interior. His life had not been easy. When he was ten and spending the summer in Varadero, he stole his mother's car to take his friends on a trip. He then had an accident in which one boy died and another lost an ear. Papucho, like Lazarus, came back to life years later. His bone structure had been rearranged during his stay at a fake-marble penitentiary. His only vice now was ballet. In some family council meeting it was decided to send him to the best Moscow ballet school. This experience abruptly ended when the man in charge of student discipline, a bulwark of State Security whose job was to look for possible deserters and watch over the good name of the Cuban students, could not understand how a handicapped eighteen-year-old could take a place intended for a dancer, just because he was the minister of the interior's nephew. He accused the boy of two things: "abject androgyny" and "possession of an inordinate quantity of American dollars."

Nobody knows why Uncle Abrantes suddenly changed his mind about making a Nureyev out of his nephew. As an example of the current hard line against the privileges of the elite, there was Papucho, his career as a soloist truncated.

His father now wanted to sign him up for the fire department. The day Papucho was to be introduced to his unit, he entered his father's office with a saut de chat and continued with a tombé pas de bourrée on the diagonal, threw his sequined knapsack in the air, and ended in fifth position, with his arms crowning his head.

This convinced his father that there was no future for him in the fire department. Papucho asked to be left alone.

He was fun-loving, uninhibited, and frustrated. He was my twin soul.

Laura Alonso, the same decisive woman who one morning had determined the future of my daughter's father and of his brother by making them classical dancers, had succeeded in building a dancing academy that sold Cuban classical technique for eagerly sought U.S.

dollars. Always in solidarity, she allowed me to take classes in her institution, and it was there that I took Papucho.

"Laura," I said, "his mother has a corporation just like yours with authorized profits in foreign capital. You two could do business. Papucho spent three years in Moscow; he wants to dance and all that. His right leg has a good extension, and at the very least, he could be a good *maître*. He knows by heart all the class routines and all the choreography of the dances he saw during his Soviet sojourn."

Geniuses are usually generous. Laura gladly accepted my protégé Papucho, who was about to become my protector when it became my turn to fall into his mother's hands.


*It was the* fashion model Albita, however, who brought me back to reality when I told her that without a job one could live well, though not too well. After covering some initial expenses, the funds from Gabo's purchase of *Femme Cheval* no longer seemed inexhaustible.

"Well, we're having the Cubafashions fest next December and La Maison is hiring a lot of models. The jobs are only temporary, but why don't you go take a test?" urged Albita.

"That sounds great, but how can I ever get into Cachita Abrantes's kingdom? I'm just baby-sitting for her rebellious son. Do you think they're going to let me become a model?"

"You've got nothing to lose by trying. Use your contacts. What good does it do you to take care of Papucho all the time? Let him ask his mother, that's all!"

"I'm very fond of him. The problem is, he and his mother don't get along."

"Family matters always work out in the end."


*Arelis Pardo was in* charge of selecting the models. As the widow of one of Che's guerrilla fighters, she was condemned to eternal celibacy in order to maintain her status. She had, however, managed to get a reprieve from celibacy by marrying a hero of the Bay of Pigs. The Party, instead of censuring her, applauded her gesture.

She affectionately took her armless and legless husband everywhere in her car for about two years. After that sacrifice, Arelis was able to go in and out of marriage without the Party's interference.

"Let's see. Show me your elbows. Take off your shoes, so I can see your feet! Knees and legs look fine. Come to the rehearsal tomorrow at five, and bring a bathing suit! We'll take a look at your cellulite."

The runway! That stretch of empty space that one has to fill, in time with the music, with flair and the essence of movement!

*The Contex Corporation had* to put up with Cachita Abrantes as its director. She was in charge of inoculating the national economy with dollars to fight the blockade. She was either fooling U.S. Customs by bottling Havana Club rum in Canada, or by manufacturing garish and unpresentable cotton dresses in Mexico for her models.

Every year she also organized a "great international event," the Cubafashions extravaganza, in an effort to commercialize designs as well as fabrics. This event had managed to attract Paco Rabanne and even Vidal Sassoon, who was having an affair with one of the executive models at the time. There was a list of left-leaning personalities to call upon. Even some Hollywood people were asked to lend prestige to Cuban fashions. Letters peppered with spelling mistakes were being sent all over the world.

The Contex Corporation owned La Maison, the Cuban fashion house, open year-round to entertain the diplomatic corps, the tourist elite, and all the government guests likely to fall for some svelte local girl.

La Maison is a compound comprising a jewelry store, an antique shop, and both clothing and shoe stores. There is also a beauty salon, a teahouse, a swimming pool, a gym, a private dining room, and a cobblestoned garden with wrought-iron furniture, where foreigners can enjoy themselves from morning till night under the shade of royal poincianas. The fashion show begins around nine-thirty in the evening. After an intermission, the second half features the best Cuban music groups and singers.

No one dares say no to Cachita Abrantes, the sister of the minister of the interior.

Preparations for the Cubafashions show last for over three months. First, a group of designers hand in their sketches. The seamstresses then sew the clothes directly onto the models' bodies. The night before the opening, after rehearsing for over eighteen hours in full collective hysteria, the models are handed their accessories, their shoes, and their freshly ironed clothes. The shoes have just been brought in from faraway countries in diplomatic pouches. Through a public-address system, Cachita gives her orders, dotted with her complete repertory of vulgarities.

My first Cubafashions experience brought me more pain than glory.

The era had begun in which anyone associated with Fidel Castro, or any other high official in the country, was made a social leper.

I was already used to all the rude comparisons and dirty names that the Comandante had earned for himself, but I was not used to having people wanting to pull *my* beard and mustache, as if I were his accessible and ambulatory alter ego. All of this made my life extremely difficult.

The security men who inspected the runways took advantage of their situation by sneaking into the dressing rooms to peek at the unwilling naked models. Harassed, the girls became both frantic and aggressive. A kind of internal cold war started that was to last about three years.

I did not make it to my second year of Cubafashions in one piece.

One morning I jumped out of bed full of wind in my sails because I had to prepare for the goblin's birthday. But the moment I put my hands on the steering wheel I suddenly felt so sleepy I couldn't help dozing off at traffic lights. It was as if my ancestors were warning me not to drive anymore.

I took the car back to my garage. It seemed natural to accept help from my friend Papucho, the one who had once stolen his mother's car. Three minutes later he ran a stop sign on First Avenue and a bus full of Russians crashed into the Lada.

My car ended up in the junkyard. I ended up in the hospital. I woke up with one arm broken and the elbow dangling funny on the other.

Papu was a demolitionist.

Cachita Abrantes has no luck at all. First, her kid kills a minister's son, then he puts the Comandante's daughter out of commission.

Fidel didn't send any flowers but had Batman, the new chief of his Personal Guard, phone me.

"Whose fault was it?"

"Mine," I said quickly. I would have broken my other arm to protect my friend. Besides, it had been my fault for letting a kamikaze drive.

A quick surgical procedure reconstructed my bone map.

*I had missed Mumín's* birthday and was still dragging around a plastic bag to drain the wound on my arm, when Albita, the fashion model, came to visit.

Albita's paleness is rose marble. I couldn't help reflecting that, with her shiny black hair, her aquiline nose, and her figure of elegant angles, she would make the perfect muse for some film director.

She was incensed.

"Do you know what Tony Valle Vallejo just did?" Albita asked me. "He betrayed Gabo! The bastard went to Colombia to represent Gabo at a film festival and then defected! He's going around making statements. I've come to tell you that he has mentioned your name and now the whole world knows that you exist."

"You shouldn't be so upset. Tony is a nice person. So he vaulted. . . . You're not going to tell me you're surprised."

"Oh, yes I am!"

I wondered why. To me, Tony's position had always been clearly defined. Like all young adults, he was always dreaming of leaving the country.

*       *       *

*I was suddenly in* the spotlight. It wasn't only my spelling skills that won me Cachita Abrantes's favor and a job promoting Contex, where she put me in charge of public relations. The job entailed creating a new department from scratch, in an enterprise that had business relationships with half the countries in the world.

I continued working like a maniac and modeling every night. I had discovered the advantages of promotion, and I kept quite busy sending letters to any biped connected in any way to the world of fashion: photographers, journalists, designers, manufacturers, buyers, and textile merchants.

My sudden job promotion kindled a raging envy among my coworkers.

The secretary, Magaly, had been forbidden to help me in writing these volumes of mail, under threat of being the object of a public act of rejection. The typewriters were breaking from overuse, but there were very few responses to my letters. I found out later that hundreds of them had never gone anywhere and ended up in the wastebasket.

Lazarita, whom we all affectionately called Little Jug because her body shape seemed to be all handles, was in charge of the models. Being in charge of the promotional image, I went one day into the photo set. Little Jug began screaming at me the greatest selection of insults I have ever heard. All of her handles were red hot.

A place of work where it's the boss who creates chaos among the staff is hard to imagine. But that was the situation. Cachita would close a fashion show on top of the runway, playing *guaguancó* with the drummers who had been invited for the second show. This seemed to discomfit our foreign guests and she knew it. Besides, she was incapable of making people respect her decisions and, as a result, she kept piling responsibilities on me.

She put me in charge of organizing her appointment schedule and her personal interviews. I also had to take care of greeting important guests, like Spanish and Brazilian dry-goods merchants, textile magnates, outstanding photographers, and an undefinable category of people that Cachita called "relevant personalities." I had to propose members for the international jury, take care of their accommodations and personal needs, and then make up, design, produce, and distribute an opinion poll. Just a few little tasks.

Shows started with a jewelry exhibition. Jewels were either hung or sewn onto a large Lycra net. Then the lights would dim and a spotlight would turn one of us, one of the models, arms and hips undulating, into a magic presence, a gleaming apparition in the dark.

This particular year I was chosen to open the show.

*The final rehearsal for* Cubafashions '88 took over twenty-four hours. It was beyond good and evil. I was behind a dressing room screen trying to pack all the smoke and all the alcohol, plus my flaccid thirty-three-year-old body, into a flesh-colored leotard, when a commotion started. The security people rushed in to stop a horde of reporters, with cameras and microphones, who had violated the sanctum sanctorum of the models' private nakedness. I didn't know it was the international press because I had never seen them before. I was completely undressed, except for my coral earrings, which were handmade by local artisans, long enough to reach all the way to my shoulders and, resting on my head, the beak of an ominous black bird, wings spread, that the jewel craftsman had considered decorative. Thick purple shadow covered my eyelids, all the way to my temples. I looked like the Evil Sorceress.

The press was shouting *"¿Dónde está Alina?"*

"Which one is she?" they yelled in English.

*"Laquelle est Alina?"*

Others were barking in some Nordic language, and in languages I had never heard.

"Hey! Get these guys outa here! Guard! Jeez, we're not dressed! Ain't you got no respect?" the models were screaming.

That's how and when I gained instant fame: trying to get into a leotard, with my fanny exposed, and wearing a stuffed bird on the top of my head.

God's will be done, I thought under my purple eyelids, in an Episcopalian mood.

The opening theme began playing. It was reminiscent of sea waves and ebb tides. The room grew dark and silent. Out on the runway, I became a dancing melody, but actually I felt like a fakir: the carpet had been secured with staples that were making my feet bleed.

About eight hours later, Magaly, the secretary, took me to the first interview.

"Why the heck do I have to give an interview?"

"It's just an orientation."

I grabbed a bunch of wilted gladioli and sat on an Indonesian wicker chair, determined to disorient anyone who tried to link me intellectually with the monstrous concoction of tropical fashions that had just taken place.

Those in charge of the "orientation" admitted two reporters, who saved their big question for the end of their interview.

"How does Fidel's daughter feel as *the* representative of Cuban fashions?"

"There must be some misunderstanding here. First of all, Cuban fashions are properly represented by Cachita Abrantes. And second, my father was the late Dr. Orlando Fernández."

Magaly got sick.

Each night at eleven, all puffy and tired, I issued denial after denial of my family relationship and my representation of Cuban fashions. That's the way it went for the whole week.

I called Albita.

"Look what has come from Tony's statements about me!" I told her. "Ever since I was eleven years old, every time someone asks me if I am Fidel's daughter, the yes answer sticks in my throat. I don't know how to say it. It all seems like a bad dream, Alba."

"All dreams, good and bad, come to an end."

"I don't mind being described as Castro's reluctant bastard daughter, but to be flaunted as the paragon of Cuban fashions goes beyond my claim to ridicule. Delita's *yayaberas!* And the Intrepid Line, with all those camouflage suits and olive-green cloth sandals! And those skirts made of tilapia! They still have a fish smell, and they stick out like lamp shades. I'm ready for anything except wholehearted support of Rafael's string macramés and Marta Verónica's T-shirts made in Mexico. I just can't stand this. Charge me with anything, but not with being the spokesperson for those Cachita-style getups."

Albita started laughing, but Magaly got upset.

"Why don't you tell that to whoever briefed your interviewers? Don't throw that stuff at me."

My change in strategy brought in a few security thugs, dressed as people, to keep the press out.

A few weeks later, a triumphant Magaly handed me a magazine. There I was with the gladioli and the Indonesian chair, and the following headline, more or less:

FIDEL CASTRO'S ILLEGITIMATE DAUGHTER PROMOTES CUBAN FASHIONS

The text read: "According to exporting principles and with a view toward the consolidation of the country's economy while providing strongly convertible cash for counteracting the Imperialist blockade that our economy is suffering, we are uniting in creating a Cuban fashion by blending the artistic manifestations of our most significant designers."

Not even Cachita Abrantes, after downing a bottle of *aguardiente* Coronilla, would be so inarticulate. On the contrary, alcohol consumption made her colorfully articulate. I was not able to identify the progenitor of this word salad. The article was signed by La Maison and must have been reproduced in many other publications, because a continuous flow of tourists began to occupy the gardens of the fashion house. I became the biggest zoological attraction in Havana.

We now had to give daily performances and double shows on the weekend. The tour operators were delighted. The models, however, were less grateful; we had threats of war in the dressing rooms. But I held up. I was on double pay, and I wanted to keep living in the paradise of theft. Working on Cubafashions was like having a free hand at the bank. Almost every day we took home exotic shoes and wonderful pieces of silver and black coral for resale. Stealing from the store was the easiest thing in the world. We lived like tycoons. To get me to leave they would have to drive me away with a blowtorch, I thought.

But that was about to happen. According to a scoop from my friend Papucho, his mother, whom I could never talk to, decided that the whole thing had gotten out of control. Reporters were besieging her at her office.

One night, three of these so-called reporters sneaked into my dressing room. This time, the only thing I had on was the pantyhose in my hands. In my bare skin, I managed to write down my home address on a piece of paper before the security thugs came and escorted them out.

"I'll see you there in half an hour," I told them. "But watch your step, there's an overflowing septic tank on the ground floor."

When they arrived, I had already put my mother in charge. Naty was my last resort. She held their full attention for two hours with her educated ambivalence. She then introduced me.

"And now, I leave you with Alina."

"What more can I say?" I kept responding to each of their questions.

Bertrand de la Grange, a journalist from *Le Monde,* had something to say, though: "You're never going to become famous this way. Wouldn't you like to model in Paris?"

Famous! Who wanted to be famous? To model in Paris! As if I had no mirror! And what? The latest styles for short grandmothers?

Another reporter, Gaston, was looking for a political dissidence angle in my story. What could I tell those Europeans? That Cuba had more underground holes than an ant farm?

The truth is that, sitting there, wearing secondhand gold lamé boots from Sandra Levinson, a crocheted miniskirt, and perfect makeup, with a chignon embalmed in hair spray (made with alcohol and rosin) on top of my head, I was not about to disrespect Mario Chanes, who has broken Mandela's record for political imprisonment, nor Armando Valladares, who almost became an invalid thanks to being locked up since adolescence, nor Llanes, the chief of the Personal Guard who had been a symbol of kindness in my childhood, nor any of the anonymous men and women, victims of the notorious Bonebreaker, who are rotting away in the catacombs of timeworn colonial forts for proclaiming that they were fed up with the Revolution or Fidel, or simply for trying to leave the country.[19] Nor was I going to disrespect the women like me, who in search of dollars to take home food and clothing, were detained and even beaten for resorting to the libidinous generosity of foreigners.

I wasn't even going to criticize the satisfaction good doctor Alí felt on his return from Angola. He was so proud of himself for having managed a few successful amputations with instruments from his military convoy's toolbox.

Being socially besieged, suffering from a sophisticated and outspoken nonconformism, and holding to the conviction that my father was a failed ruler did not give me the right to speak for any of them.

That night I went to sleep exhausted. Once the journalists had been satisfied, I asked myself, what next? What other surprise could possibly await me in the future?

*The journalists had not* really been satisfied, of course, and my future was not that far away.

"La Maison has been designated by the High Command to celebrate the anniversary of Prensa Latina news service, whose founding members include Gabriel García Márquez and Jorge Timossi. They will both be in attendance that evening, accompanied by the Commander in Chief. I want an impeccable fashion show. I want jewels, children's clothes, bathing suits, the works," Cachita barked.

García Márquez does not need any introduction. Timossi was a tall Argentinean writer-journalist with a deep voice who had been immortalized in Quino's *Mafalda* comic strip.[20] "To have written so much poetry, so many essays, and to go down in the history of literature as Felipe, Mafalda's friend!" Timossi says. In fact, Quino and Timossi have been friends since early childhood.

I couldn't understand why someone who had worn the same style of clothes for over thirty-five years had suddenly developed an unsuspected and surprising interest in fashion. A lot of foreign journalists had been invited for the occasion, and rumor had it that they were insisting on finding and capturing me.

How strange, I thought.

After all, I was opening the show, slithering down the runway in a leotard, profusely bedecked with conchs and other seashells, pieces of black coral and silver, and a stuffed bird. Next, I was to model bathing suits, thanks to my unusual and deplored lack of cellulite. Mumín was one of the stars of the children's show.

It occurred to me that all this might cause the Commander in Chief to have a stroke. I decided to arrive late enough so that the Praetorian Guard would not let me in.

Actually, I didn't miss anything. The moment Fidel's boots stepped into La Maison, he ordered the fashion show to stop. It seems he was little inclined to applaud me or shout "Bravo! Bravo!"

Cachita offered her models a public apology.

"It seems La Maison was chosen in error by the palace chief of protocol."

A romance magazine had reported on the Maximum Leader's gala honoring his bastard daughter at the Emporium of Cuban Fashion. I never found out who came up with the outlandish idea of publishing the story there—maybe Cachita had inspired the piece, or her brother, or the palace chief of protocol, whose son I had grabbed by the collar and shaken a long time ago during an act of public rejection at the School of Diplomacy. Anyway, these animals were all eating from the same trough.

One afternoon a few days later, Delita, the designer to blame for the Intrepid Line of camouflage canvas, stiff fish-skin skirts, and crippling shoes, came in and installed her considerable behind on a chair next to me. She was determined to make me talk.

"You know, Alina, I think we are all very lucky! El Comandante, your father, is here with his people, looking at everything. The creative people have never enjoyed much support, but this time, well . . . I think things are going to be much improved! Oh, yes!"

Everyone expects me to be an expert in "Fidelology." In my experience, when I am around and he intervenes, things don't improve at all—just the opposite.

"This is really great news. Everything is going to improve. Oh, yes! You'll see!" she went on.

I turned away from Delita, went straight to my office and collected all my things. I didn't waver for a second. I knew exactly where this prop barge called La Maison was headed now that Fidel was involved: straight to the bottom. It seemed that the Comandante still had the habit of finding out the hard way in what kind of waters this Piscean was swimming.

A storm of bad feelings clouded my understanding. Wanting to direct my energy somewhere, I drove over to Ezequiel's, but I found the Medicine Man's new clinic had been dismantled and was now deserted.

*Ezequiel called himself a* biologist and virologist, but the truth was that he had learned the art of medicinal herbs during his endless trips as a merchant marine. This was all before he started collaborating with State Security, when his scientific capabilities condemned him to the Internationalism of all the wars and to another accumulation of shady duties.

Through guesswork and experimentation, he had learned healing in Africa and Vietnam, and in Latin America, where he found his best clients. He spoke of Panama's General Manuel Noriega as a good friend. Noriega's enormous house in Cuba, apparently his second homeland, was well attended by *federadas,* or government-employed maids.

It is widely known that Cuba is a medical power. I heard that Ezequiel occasionally received an order for a culture of deadly invasive bacteria to stop the vocal misdemeanors of some undesirable individual, but those rumors were unsubstantiated.

Minister Abrantes had canonized Ezequiel by building him a small hospital near CIMEC, like an annex to the large surgical unit, where the patients' rooms were the size of ballrooms and waitresses offered select menus to the health tourists who occupied these suites.

Across the street from Ezequiel's small hospital there was always a long line of people from all over the country in search of relief or a cure for their varied and obscure ailments, which ranged from terminal tumors to a kind of pyorrhea that ate away tissue in children's throats.

I used to take a load of corks and empty bottles to Ezequiel and he would work day and night filling these vessels with potions, balms, or mysterious ashes that encouraged the healing process by shocking the body cells.

But when I arrived at his hospital that afternoon, there was no sign at all of Ezequiel or of his range of recent activities. Even the herb plantings were gone.

"He was arrested three months ago and the clinic was ordered closed. Everyone says the order came directly from the Comandante," someone told me.

My friend Ezequiel was gone. Inquiries about him near his old home provoked attacks of muteness among the neighbors.

Cachita Abrantes was not the only one on the hot seat, it seemed. Her brother, my "Minister of the Sinister," was surely busy dealing with some devastating denunciations these days.

The Commander in Chief often acts in a surprising manner, but he is not totally unpredictable. Something big was brewing.

A feeling of defeat sent me back, discouraged, to the Nuevo Vedado.

# 8

# CASE NO. 1 OF 1989

*A special editorial in Granma,* the newspaper of the Party's Central Committee, began very cautiously. The editorial focused on Judicial Case No. 1 of 1989, which involved drug trafficking. Instead of four pages, the newspaper had six that day.

I was at the Greek embassy in Havana, playing poker with some other guests. The lady ambassador grew a special spearmint in her garden, and everybody was drinking mojitos when I all of a sudden felt a strange compulsion to take a look at *Granma.* I was not in the habit of reading the eternal fabrications or the great eulogies on the accomplishments of the microjet banana harvest in Artemisa in those four pages. *Granma,* conveniently cut into squares, adorned most of the toilets on the Island. I was aghast at the news. I read: "The following individuals have been arrested and charged with treason against the Revolution. . . ."

One of the detainees was General Arnaldo Ochoa. He was a Hero of the Republic of Cuba and the victorious commander of the Cuban troops for the wars in Ethiopia and Angola.[21]

Diocles Torralba, the minister of transportation, had also been detained. My old friends Patricio and Tony de la Guardia had been arrested as well. Patricio was still in Angola under Arnaldo Ochoa's command. Tony, no longer in uniform, was the head of M6, a department in charge of breaking the blockade and bringing in electrical appliances, Western cars, and the shiploads of clothes and shoes shrewdly manufactured in Panama and Hong Kong and destined for the Cuban diplotiendas. On a far more covert level, Tony had been handling part of the cocaine traffic. Everybody knew for whom he was working: the Cuban government.

An incomprehensible assortment of people had been put in jail, from MININT soldiers to civil servants to army generals.

The next day, a communiqué from Fidel implicated almost everyone in his cabinet in a series of accusations: male homosexuality, lesbianism, deviant behavior, cocaine trafficking, and rebellion.

A week later, all Cuban TV and radio stations were covering Case No. 1. A military prosecutor with a Patek Philippe watch on his wrist was accusing men who had been soldiers and mercenaries for over thirty years of extending and exploiting a cocaine ring from unspecified locations in Africa and Latin America to the New York drug scene. Speaking on behalf of the Revolution, the Party, and the Homeland, the prosecuting attorney charged them with illicit sex, perversion, cocaine trafficking, and treason. Fidel and Raúl Castro attended the trial hidden behind glass in the command cabin of the Universal Theater of the Armed Forces. This is the same place where, a few years ago, I had arranged for a net to lift Che to heaven.

Handcuffed and humiliated, the legendary heroes resigned themselves to defeat before a restricted group of relatives.

The lawyers for the defense didn't dare talk, nor did the prosecutor give them the opportunity.

The trial followed the courses of their fast lives. At issue were sexual episodes, recorded and filmed orgies, and other ceremonies of the cult of dissipation. To all appearances, the High Command of the Republic had been solely dedicated all this time to decadent fun and games.

When the farce was over, some were condemned to death and others sentenced to jail for life. Fidel had the last word. With a full quorum of the Political Bureau, he summoned all his sacred cows of opportunism to adhere to his statements. The faces of that bunch of hypocrite idiots were something to watch.

"Arnaldo Ochoa, traitor to his status as national hero, had in his possession, in Angolan waters, a ship loaded with a hundred tons of cocaine . . . with the intention of exchanging it for arms for a military coup against our Revolution."

What a fertile imagination, I thought. With such a quantity of drugs, Ochoa could declare war on the galaxies! What incredible cynicism!

Cocaine was everywhere in Cuba. Even my friend Roger the provocateur had stopped by our home some months earlier with a little test tube that just happened to be in his pocket the day he discovered a drug shipment on an isolated key. His boss, Guillermo García, the neighborhood water thief with the swimming pool, had sent Roger there to locate and capture deer for tourist hunting.

There was so much cocaine available in Havana that the attraction to the solitary and passive self-realization experienced with Angolan or Colombian marijuana was replaced by the feverish activity spawned by cocaine. All production indexes seemed to improve.

There was more cocaine than if it had snowed. People were allowed to buy and transport it in ten-pound sugar bags from one neighborhood to another, and from one province to another without any interference. One could easily conclude that cocaine was the sole impetus behind all the revolutionary marches and the continuous agitation of the Militias of Territorial Troops on the entire Island.

This was no secret at all.

Cocaine had been part of the daily folklore of Cuba for a long time. To put all the blame on a few army people who were living and dying on another continent was an insult.

General Ochoa fed his army in Angola by trafficking in animals and elephant tusks. He was also charging Angola's Agostinho Neto by the hour for the use of his men.

Tony de la Guardia's case was different. How was he going to pay for his electrical appliances, his Nissans, and his imported Mercedes-Benz but with money from drug smuggling? Tony had been traveling back and forth for quite a long time between Cuba and Miami in civilian clothes.

How do you think Latin American guerrillas paid for their arms supply? With cocaine! Their America Division was paid in cocaine for its military and technical assistance.

\*    \*    \*

*This had all been* going on until Arnaldo Ochoa, Tony de la Guardia, and Amadito Padrón were condemned to be executed at the wall. No information was given as to when that would take place.

For a week, the whole tragedy kept me nailed in front of the television set like a supplicant. I could not believe that Fidel would just lift his finger and have his lifelong friends executed.

My neighbors expressed their opinion.

"Your father knows no shame!"

I thought of the De la Guardia twins' children, all of whom I had seen grow up, and of their parents, the adorable Mimí and Popín. I summoned all my courage and went to see them.

They lived in a house by the ocean. There were always rows and rows of cars—they belonged to the friends of opportunism—in the parking spaces, but the night I went to visit, the street was empty. Their grandchildren were wandering around like ghosts inside the house. A few old ladies with their little bowls of consolation soup were pacing to and fro. Popín was listless. He wouldn't look, wouldn't listen. It was Mimí who did the asking.

"Alina, do you know when they are going to execute my son?"

I didn't.

Socialist righteousness had denied Tony's daughter an academic prize for being the best student that year. The rest of his children were targeted for abuse and expulsion from their schools and universities. As compensation, MININT provided them with psychiatric care. A few doctors in their white gowns were in charge of convincing these children that their father had suffered a fair punishment. They made no converts.

Not long after the executions, Minister Abrantes was sent to jail. A month later he developed a serious case of cardiac fibrillation. From the prison, he was taken for a ride in a Lada but in the opposite direction from the Policlínico. He died of a massive heart attack.

The same day he died, one of his sons came very early to get me. Accompanying the once-revered minister of the interior at the funeral parlor were his closest family and I, of all people, who must have been suffering from a case of "the-sky's-the-limit syndrome." Abrantes's arrest had made him notoriously unpopular.

The next morning, Fidel's motor caravan turned on Zapata Street, going unexpectedly against traffic, in order to pass by the funeral parlor.

When the motorcade slowed down, the little group of mourners yelled at them, "Murderer! Murderer!"

Inspired by the literary feats I had performed as a promoter for Contex, Cachita Abrantes suggested that I deliver the eulogy for her deceased brother at the cemetery. But in my place only a real masochist could have done that. I would not have been able to make a public display of affection for someone like Abrantes, who had caused me so much suffering.

I drove my friend Papucho home after the funeral.

"Your father had my uncle killed," he said. "My family is never going to forgive you."

He never talked to me again after that.

*One morning, a few* days after the executions, my neighbor Estercita dropped by my house. She was sobbing uncontrollably.

"The neighbors are getting worried. Every afternoon Amadito Padrón's son stands guard at the corner of Mumín's secondary school. We know it's not her fault that your father executed his, but people can be very mean. We don't know whom to call for help. You have to notify somebody!"

I didn't know whom to call either.

My daughter and I were now the relatives of the Executioner. No wonder executioners always wear a hood when they do their jobs.

The social morphology of Cuba changed radically. Half of the population never recovered from the toppling of their heroes; dissident groups began to thrive. The government could no longer convince those it governed.

It could convince me even less. I was now positive that in some twisted deal with Fidel, the CIA had kept secret all the evidence implicating Cuba in the international drug traffic.

I imagined scenarios like the following: "If I disarm this or that guerrilla in Latin America, or in any other part of the universe, you won't disclose any information about this drug traffic involvement. And, above all, you will maintain the embargo for me."

This embargo is a great ruse for all. The extent of the damage it causes is the great pretext of the anti-Imperialist Cubans. Yet, the Empire does not give a damn about world opinion and the opposition to the embargo. It is only interested in keeping Cuba under a malleable and cooperative leader. Cuba is the next Grenada. One day, and it will be soon, Cuba will be overpopulated with Holiday Inns and McDonald's.

My speculations had been correct because immediately after Case No. 1 in Cuba, Noriega fell, the Peruvian Shining Path fell, and the drug king, Pablo Escobar Gaviria, fell.

Fidel retained his aura of international prestige through all of this.

# 9

# GOOD-BYE TO ALL THAT

*The Socialist bloc and* the Berlin Wall fell one afternoon on television. On the Island there were no repercussions except a ban on the field of Russian studies at the university.

Fidel ordered the replacement of the Russian language with English. He then appeared on the screen to explain the new Special Period and Zero Option. The latter term really said it all: zero electric power, zero food, zero transportation. Nothing. *Nada.*[22]

So that people would not be too upset, he offered a solution known as the "people's soup kettle." It was the first French trend to enter Cuban cuisine since 1959.

Here's how it was supposed to work. A communal soup kettle was to be organized by the ubiquitous neighborhood watchdogs, the Committees for the Defense of the Revolution (CDR). Each committee member was to bring a potato, a head of garlic, half an onion. . . . To complement the resulting soup, each CDR was to home-deliver some multivitamins as well.

So that the people would not wallow in total desperation, Fidel provided some relief by attempting to convert everybody into chicken farmers. He knew, from his own experience, that chickens keep you busy twenty-four hours a day.

"The Imperialists have ruined all of our chicken farms. Beginning today, each citizen will receive three chicks, and it will be his or her entire responsibility to raise them. The State will not supply the chicken feed."

So people began to raise chickens, inventing new feed recipes like ground, sun-dried grapefruit rind. The children were having a mixture of water and grayish-yellow sugar for breakfast. It fermented in the jar and drove the cockroaches away.

Chickens were raised like pets, names and all, for the love and solace of the children. It became very difficult to kill them later and serve them as food.

After the chickens, the goats and pigs came to Havana. The goats grazed on the grass on Fifth Avenue, and the pigs wallowed in patios and bathtubs. To avoid being denounced, their owners kept them asleep with Benadryl. The more sophisticated families cut the pigs' vocal cords.

That's how the landscape and the smells of my city changed. It reverted to the times when Tata Mercedes used to pull me away from the windows of the houses where the Makarenko and Ana Betancourt girls lived, so that blood-stained menstrual rags would not fall on my head.

The whole city smelled like one big dunghill.

The happy shouts of the ration-book queens were accompanied by grunts and cackles as well.

"The protein mix is in! The first one hundred numbers of the first group get it today!"

"The sweet potato buns are here!"

These round, four-ounce buns, made of sweet potato flour, within three days were covered with a homicidal fungus.

The protein mix (*masa cárnica*) is an indigestible goo made with ground soya, cartilage, and toasted corn flour. As people used to joke, "I would like to see some of the comfortable defenders of the Cuban system having to try some of our down-and-out dishes. Boiled plantain-peel hash. Sweet potato bread with mop. (A floor mop is left in oil for a few days until it softens. If possible, serve breaded.) I am sure none of them has tasted roasted slugs. And what about cat fricassee?"

People used to walk their little chickens like pet dogs on improvised string leashes, to protect them against the fierce hunger of the city cats. Cat meat was also quoted by the pound on the black market.

As if all this misery weren't enough, an epidemic of optical neuritis developed in the country and thousands of Cubans were going blind.

Fidel insisted the virus was another Imperialist ploy, but the truth lay hidden in a bacteriology lab at MINFAR, where necessary diseases were sometimes concocted to maintain the political good health of the Cuban people. In this case people were simply being poisoned by the thallium that had been added to herbicides and pesticides.

Farmers were forbidden to sell their produce freely. It was left to rot by the country roads because the State was not picking the produce in time.

The people suddenly moved toward God in these difficult circumstances, and the religious disorder became acute. Fidel replaced his traditional motto, "Homeland or Death," with "Socialism or Death." Because disorder is also part of the Comandante's plans, he created the Quick Action Brigades, which were in charge of dissolving the many religious parades by applying violent force.

Young people were summoned to cultural-civic acts. They gathered around campfires, in weather hot enough to roast a chicken on the asphalt.

It was a deeply troubled and crazed world. Its surrealism was degrading.

*One night, in the* midst of all these alienating circumstances, my mother called me.

"Go downstairs. Someone you love dearly is waiting for you."

It was Ezequiel, the Medicine Man. He was hiding in a passageway across the street. We hugged each other warmly.

"Why did you disappear like that?"

"It's a long story," he said. He didn't want to talk about it right then. He invited me to come see him on some farm where he had been asked to resume his laboratory projects. "There is no electricity yet. I came for you because you always believed in me and I know you will help me. Come and see me next week. Take the road to the St. Lazarus shrine. Once you're there, ask someone where the sidatorio is, you know, the AIDS asylum. Then, ask for Guillermo García's fancy rooster farm. It's just a piece of land and a hut without electricity, but it's a start—a clinic for alternative medicine. Don't confuse one sidatorio with the other. The one on the left is the one for the common people. The one on the right is for MININT."

"And the fancy rooster farm?"

"Everybody around there knows where it is. That's where Guillermo García raises his fighting cocks."

"But cockfights are illegal!"

"They are for export."

The fact that Guillermo García, ex-minister of (the nonexistent) transportation, was raising fancy roosters for export must have been a great relief for the nation.

I learned that the sidatorio was a "paradise" where AIDS patients were interned, sometimes even with weekend passes—depending on their "personal endangerment index." There were people sentenced to life in prison who had been exchanging contaminated blood in order to be able to die enjoying the open air and the free sex available inside the institution. There were also some adolescents who had inoculated themselves with HIV in order to abandon a life of hardship.

It was not like the shameful leper colonies of old times, not at all. These patients were even provided with cultural entertainment. The inmates could also be married in wedding ceremonies. Documentaries had been filmed on how happy these patients were, with good food, and even air-conditioning during their terminal stages. They were all very grateful. First-year medical students were obliged to accompany them, to eat and sleep in their homes, and, like Praetorian guards, they were sweet and familiar.

"And what have you been doing these last two years in the sidatorio?"

"I'll tell you later."

And he disappeared in the darkness of the blackout and the smell of the kerosene lamps.

*I certainly could not* complain of one thing: being bored. The press was not as discouraged as I had thought that night at La Maison when, with nothing on but a pair of stockings in my hand, I had written down my Thirty-fifth Street address for the reporters.

Some of them were still hanging around the overflowing septic tank downstairs—when they were not rocking back and forth, unrelenting and enthusiastic, in the big iron rockers on my porch.

A couple of them made several trips all the way from France just to ask me, at least, for one hair from the Comandante's beard. A spectrographic analysis, according to them, could uncover the mysteries of his personality. They simply didn't want to believe that I didn't have that kind of locket. I gave them a couple of my pubic hairs.

By now I was the only person in the country with freedom of expression. I could speak freely about the lack of freedom, without having a police squad get me out of bed, beat me up, and take me to jail.

To assume that strange responsibility cost me a lot of anxiety.

Thanks to the journalists, the biographers started to come. Thanks to them I even regained contact with old friends of mine in exile. I have an especially fond memory of the afternoon visit I received from a young man with wavy hair and a celestial blue gaze. He was overflowing with respectful sweetness. My friend Osvaldo Fructuoso, the son of a martyr of the Revolution and disaffected like the rest of my generation, had given him my address. His business card read: "Carlos Lumière. Photographer for *Vogue.*" Golden letters on a black background. No telephone number, no address.

A card can say anything. I could have had a card reading "Alina Fernández. Advisor to President Reagan." Propelled by my incurable optimism when dealing with friends, I allowed myself to be convinced to let Lumière take a few good pictures of me.

"If I manage to sell them, Osvaldo will send you some money."

I asked my friend Albita to lend me some of her clothes to wear.

About two weeks later, I saw a picture of myself in a Spanish magazine, wearing the most fashionable clothes one could find in Havana and commenting on the prices of olive oil and a pound of cat meat on the black market, as well as on the evils of prostitution.

With me in a languid pose, lying on the rocks by the ocean in the unforgettable Malecón, it was like a sultry Lady Di wearing a black lace leotard and talking about abject poverty in Benin.

It was really something. The accompanying text was by Fernando, a friend of my friend Osvaldo. Though both pretended to be sorry about the whole thing, I never really trusted their original intentions, just as I didn't believe them when they later came up with a sensible plan to get me out of the country.

But not all my friends are like that.

Around that same time I received a registered letter from my friend Alfredo de Santamarina. He was proposing a plan to get me out through the Swedish government's intervention. Alfredo is profoundly human, and bound to me by an unshakable childhood loyalty. I have no idea what ingenuity he used to make Sweden willing to vouch for me. I had to indicate my acceptance by means of a secret code containing the word *rainbow*.

I composed and sent him a delirious letter in which I wrote about the rainbow as a dream that had to be postponed. I felt called in my mission as a spokesperson. I felt I owed it to all my silenced friends. If someone had asked me to, I probably would have impaled myself in the Plaza de la Revolución. As things were, a galloping ulcer had rendered me ineligible for asylum. And even though I did spend whole nights awake, filled with anguish, and whenever a car stopped in front of my house, my heart pounded wildly, no patrol car came to take me away to a sure beating in a jail somewhere, as was happening to so many thousands of dissidents.

Given the situation, my premonitions were finally justified when an officer of the new generation paid me a visit.

"Sweden is looking for a pretext to break diplomatic relations with Cuba and to withdraw the help they give us as a Third World country. Things like school supplies and technical help. If you accept asylum there, you will be depriving all the Cuban children. And don't worry, you won't get anywhere anyway."

After Alfredo launched his campaign, however, a Viking from the Swedish embassy made an appointment with me at the bar of the Hotel Inglaterra. This two-star emporium, in the heart of Old Havana, was the center of clandestine meetings for all the *naïfs* of diplomatic espionage. I gave the Swede a solid "no," softened with a humble "Thanks, anyway." Neither of us mentioned pencils or notebooks, or the Swedish storybooks that were the inspiration for the dearest name of my troll, Mumín.

My friend Alfredo has not yet forgiven me for my refusal to leave.

*   *   *

*I arrived at Ezequiel's* farm behind a procession to the shrine of St. Lazarus, a pilgrimage made every year by the faithful and watched closely by the police. I had brought with me, besides a lot of cleaning supplies, a bottle of rum, some disposable plates, and an Italian coffeemaker.

The future alternative-medicine clinic was an abandoned hut between a garden and a backyard so full of rocks that it made the shoots of medicinal plants seem like miracles. It was as if Grandma Natica's green thumb had something to do with the process.

Ezequiel was in the backyard, preparing his curative potions in three large boilers under some shady trees, using dried coconut shells as fuel. His lanky teenage son, on his way to manhood, was helping him.

A druid assisted by an elf.

Ezequiel finally began to tell me his story well after seven that evening.

"As you know, when they eliminated Abrantes, my clinic at CIMEC was dismantled. I was held at Villa Marista for a few days."

"Were you raped by any of the interrogators?"

"No. They respected my ass, but they destroyed my morale. I had worked so many years for MININT, for the Revolution and for Fidel! Now the worst part is that these new people want me to go back and do the same work for them."

I was confused. Fidel is the world's only head of state to survive the collapses of his Ministry of the Interior and of his Personal Security Guard. There is no one who can turn tropical soil into vineyards or defeat into victory as he can. His new generation of henchmen was naturally going to be worse than the old one. They would be the off-spring of ideological opportunism and of the new economic double standards.

Ezequiel was being used again, but for another purpose. Instead of being sent to care for individual drug dealers in their homes, he was now being asked to produce special plants and deadly cultures, lethal concoctions aimed at doing away with inconvenient witnesses of the disasters occurring in and out of Cuba. That was the only reason his life had been spared. It made him profoundly unhappy.

"When you get into something up to your neck," he said, "if you shit on yourself, you're up to your neck in your own shit."

"Where have you been for the last three years?"

"In the AIDS asylum."

He had been given orders to find a cure, and had at least managed to keep patients' immunity levels very high by administering some kind of potion. But that wasn't why he had come to see me, to pass on his secret formula. The government had already sold it to East Germany.

"The sidatorio is an awful place and totally staffed by the police, who are being paid extra because the two years they spend there are considered Internationalist work. I really appreciate your thoughtfulness and your help here cleaning up. Come back next week. I'll have Naty's formula ready."

Naty had developed a lump on the left side of her neck and my anxiety was killing me because she absolutely refused to see a doctor. So when I had arrived at Ezequiel's with a mop, detergent, gloves, and disposable plates, I was also begging for some medication, just in case, for any unwelcome tumor that could alter Mom's indomitable good health.


*I returned to the* little farm the following week, bringing Ezequiel a collection of empty bottles for his prescriptions. I had an uneasy feeling, as if my affections were headed for another catastrophe. As an alibi, in case I needed to make a quick exit, I took with me a high-society American lady who had come to Cuba on the literary quest and now proposed to write the story of four generations of women, Natica, my mother, Mumín, and me. She was one of a slew of orthodox biographers bent on telling the story of how (and with whom) Fidel had fathered a daughter out of wedlock. None had offered as handsome a sum of money as she had. At fifty she was sweet and seemingly harmless, an apparent devotee of Jacqueline Kennedy.

Her presence did not help me, because two individuals were at the farm waiting for me, hidden by the smoke cloud from the boilers.

Ezequiel tried to explain.

"You might feel like I have tricked you, but after you talk to them, you're going to forgive me."

Both men were patients who had escaped from the AIDS asylum. They wasted no time getting to the point.

"This is Oto, and I am Reniel. We need your help."

Oto was black, tall like a Masai, and probably named Barbarito until MININT inducted him and changed his name. Reniel is the favorite alias used by State Security. If a man in Cuba tells you that his name is Reniel, he is, without a doubt, a secret agent. They both had an ugly demeanor, the obvious result of their jobs.

The tall black man, Oto, said he had been Fidel's trusted assistant in Angola. Reniel, the stout, short man, had been in army counterintelligence.

Both had been condemned to the sidatorio without being infected.

Whenever they were back in Cuba from Angola, they had been tested every three months, but long after they had received the doctors' clean bill of health, both had been ordered to return from Angola. Their theory was that after all those deaths—that is, after Ochoa, Abrantes, Tony, and the rest had been executed—the new command, headed by Furri, had decided to deactivate both of them, first by subjecting them to social rejection by calling them queer and, second, by putting them under the kind of house arrest the sidatorio provided before all patients were sent home without any treatment, two years later.

They were convinced that Fidel knew nothing about this plot. With Ezequiel's abortive assistance (he had been arrested on the way to the airport for trying to send their blood tests abroad), they had made two failed attempts to demonstrate that their blood had not been contaminated in other lands. Now they needed a person close to the Comandante to let him know about the situation.

I explained that I was not the right person to have a talk with the Comandante about this, given that we had broken off our personal relationship thanks to an incident connected with international tourism.

"Jackie Kennedy" the biographer was strolling around the place. She was rushing me because she wished to be back in time for a dinner that had been organized for that evening with some personalities of the Cuban cinema.

I again felt on one of my paths to despair.

"If both of you were Fidel's trusted assistants, nothing is going to happen to you that he doesn't know about. If you are detained in the sidatorio, accused as you say of being queer, that is his doing. Much more so if this is connected to Case No. 1 of 1989. He even had his own friends executed then."

I could not convince them. I simply can't say no to a human tragedy. I returned to Havana determined to deliver the message to the Supreme Power. It was the first letter I had written him since I was ten years old: "There are some patients in the sidatorio who say that they are not infected but just victims of some mistake. Tough people from the war in Angola. They insist that they are there without your knowledge."

Then I added something about their threat to blow up the arsenal and the gas station, even though I was certain that for the Comandante it is a philosophical principle to allow problems to solve themselves. As a final note I also mentioned that if the patients blew up their hospital, of course that would eliminate two problems.

To have my message reach its destination, I thought of the Five Vegetables, my younger brothers. I decided to contact the one who is addicted to cybernetics and marathon running, just because we had a mutual friend who shared his two obsessions.

After explaining the whole thing in a clandestine meeting with my poor brother, I gave him the missive.

The Comandante, as I had expected, could not have cared less about all this.

He was extremely busy.


*With the Zero Option* in effect, there was zero gasoline, and therefore no public or private transportation. Half the civil servants were fired, since they were unnecessary in this crisis situation. They were sent home with a pension and the mission of watching over their neighborhoods and denouncing any irregularities.

With public transportation gone, Fidel distributed bicycles so people could continue going to school and to indispensable jobs.

These bicycles were Chinese. The British had sold the patent to China right after World War II, around 1946. They were exactly like the one I had received from the Three Wise Men thirty years before. It was the same rationed basic toy that had been sold in hardware stores! A triad of generations were having their frustrated childhoods renewed while Santa Claus finally satisfied their old yearnings by distributing bicycles among Party members and Communist Youths.

The unsuspected capacities of a World War II Chinese bicycle are simply amazing. Entire families sat on added seats and on improvised carts in tow. Refrigerators, wedding cakes, construction materials, and all the containers to be had in the black market could also be transported by these vintage bicycles.

Mom felt happy in those days and was a great admirer of the ever-amazing Cuban ingenuity. She began taking her camera along everywhere she went.

For me, the image of an emaciated individual pulling his two sons and a wife with an overflowing bottom, as if he were an ox, was as depressing as to see a bride in full regalia on her way to the Wedding Palace, being pulled by a gasping father on the brink of a heart attack. Alongside this flurry of energy, crime flourished, because the Chinese had no spare parts for these prehistoric machines, and the creativity of thieves expanded into a series of sophisticated techniques for stealing the bikes. The thieves' most frequent device was to stretch a raised wire across the street, taking advantage of the many blackouts. Many children died hopelessly, of broken necks.

*Mumín was a happy* girl with a curly top, always jumping back and forth between her two homes. She was beginning to walk with a good turnout. She was becoming a ballerina. But after completing her second year, Mumín was thrown out of ballet school.

Two years before that, my brother Fidelito had imposed his daughter on the school—a tall, fat little Russian girl who walked among grammar school children wearing the college preparatory uniform—with the help of a couple of thugs who threatened the principal with heaven's fury. The principal then crossed swords with the Comandante's grandchild number two, and won.

My daughter was ten years old, but it is never too early to begin to pay for other people's sins.

José Martí's dream of schools in the countryside finally became a terrible reality when Fidel declared the Escuelas al Campo compulsory. He closed all the secondary and college preparatory schools in the capital cities of all the provinces.

Using the excuse of the lack of gasoline, he declared that the kids could spend only three days a month at home.

Those who dared protest in the Party assemblies were shouted down, and people finally resigned themselves to the situation.

The general scarcity of goods imposed jail-like regulations in these schools. Like snails, kids had to carry around their possessions, keeping their toothbrushes and pieces of soap in their pockets and sleeping with their shoes on. They had to learn to defend themselves from theft and provocations, sometimes even using their fingernails.

A new call for enrollment in the National School of Art solved my daughter's schooling problem, and Mumín exchanged her toe shoes for the slippers or bare feet of modern dance. Tall, with a long neck, perfect shoulders, and an instep arched like a crescent moon, she was a joy to watch.

During her first year, I was able to take her and pick her up because gasoline was sometimes available. But during her second year, gasoline was gone for good. To catch a bus after a very long wait, Mumín was forced to walk along the avenue in the very early morning and after it was already completely dark at night. Once on the bus, she had to cling to somebody's back and hang out the door. By her third year, she used my old bike.

That's when our anxiety began.

Mumín's bike commute was twelve and a half miles. Some of the teachers had to spend more than three hours pedaling, with only a bit of fermented sugar in their stomachs, plus an eight-ounce shot of protein mix a month. They began to abandon their jobs.

Mumín had her first political problem in the midst of this. Who would have expected it? It was all on account of the Pink Panther. The custom of chanting out slogans in morning formations is a Revolutionary ritual that still exists. Each morning the class has to be innovative.

Mumín had been visiting a friend of mine the day before and had seen a humorous Pink Panther card with a text she liked. She thought she could use it. What she intoned, along with her classmates, was:

*I don't eat in the morning:*
*I think of you.*
*I don't eat in the afternoon:*
*I think of you.*
*I don't sleep at night:*
*I am hungry!*

This required me to attend an urgent meeting with the administration of the National School of Art to discuss my daughter's shameless reference to the national hunger pangs.

I rushed over to my friend's house.

"I need you to lend me your Pink Panther card. I'll return it tomorrow."

So the Pink Panther and I saved Mumín from a black mark in her academic record.

My goblin's treks to a school without teachers continued to be the cause of tremendous anxiety for me, and of deep discouragement for her.

The more bicycles were distributed, the more accidents and crimes there were.

The fiancée of a young man who lived in my building was killed one rainy evening when the brakes of her Chinese relic failed. She hit a bus and fell under it.

"Alina, there was practically nothing left of her. No buttocks, no belly, nothing!"

Every day one tragedy or another shook our neighborhood.

I took a walk to the Colón cemetery and asked about an imaginary dead person.

"Could you tell me where Mamerto Navarro has been buried?"

"When did that one come in?"

"Yesterday."

"What time yesterday? They keep coming nonstop."

Everything in the cemetery was very well organized. The "cold cuts" were arriving every ten minutes.

"In the afternoon, I guess. Do you have a lot of work?"

"Like never before!"

The old man I spoke to was happy. He had never felt so useful since he was put in charge of the records in 1960. It had been just the opposite for the embalmer of Lenin's mummy, who had been deprived of his raison d'être after the fall of the Socialist Bloc.

"Why, are people getting more eager to die?"

"No question about it, young lady. What with the Special Period and all the bicycles, we have more than forty-five deaths a day. Before, we didn't even get fifteen."

Because of my father's infatuation with Communism in my country, the number of deaths had tripled in less than two years. Cuba was being decimated.

I began writing everything down in a little black address book, because I was recording information to write about. The details I recorded confirmed the scope of Cuba's malaise.

I went to Mumín in tears, not for the first or last time. I pleaded with her to think about quitting school. It was not worth risking her life in order to attend classes with absentee teachers.

*I suddenly became a* perfectionist. Resigned to live forever in my madhouse on Thirty-fifth Street, I decided to devote myself to a big redecorating job in our apartment. Out of respect for all those who came and went in all their misery, like people passing through a hospital emergency room, and in consideration of Mumín, who was forced to spend more time at home than ever because of the situation with the bikes and the antiathletic attitude of her teachers, I decided that at least I would have a nice place to live. You cannot do a healing massage, read the esoteric Tarot, receive friends and antagonists, assuage the anguish of a militant dissident, raise a daughter, or make love in a place that proclaimed its own disorder and bitterness out loud. Still, my original objective was not a total overhaul.

A clogged toilet started the whole thing.

Ours was in extremis, no one knew why. Since my toilet was not Cuba's official model, no illegal dilettante toilet-meister was able to come up with a diagnosis, until Alberto the Magician made his appearance.

My toilet had been clogged for a year and a half. It had become the object of my tender loving care and deep nostalgia. After performing an exorcism with hydrochloric acid and flaming kerosene, I stood there watching it, practically begging it to swallow, as if it were a sick grandfather.

Then I met Alberto the Plumber and Alberto the Plumber introduced me to his colleague Idulario, and his colleague Idulario introduced me to Armando the mechanic, and then my life was okay again. They were all working on the 27 bus route for the Urban Transportation division, where they had little to do because there were only two active buses. They had plenty of spare time. By extricating a plastic net, which months ago had done its duty as a deodorant wrapper, Alberto unclogged my toilet.

He also unclogged my way of life.

"Every so often the house you live in has to be painted, so it looks nice. And it is much better to have a water heater so you can take hot showers. And your car must also be fixed," the Magician advised.

He was the first human being in a long time who brought me solutions instead of problems. God bless him. One can assimilate everybody else's shit, but it's difficult to get rid of one's own without being able to flush.

The Magician began to bring in miraculous tools out of the repair shop of the 27 bus. There was a sander that was also capable of cutting iron and stone, a medieval blowtorch, and a delightful assortment of spatulas. I was never happier than in the ecstasy I experienced being a carpenter and a mason, nursing my own burns and cuts.

I was hard at work one day when the distinctive smell of freedom walked down my hallway: a superannuated playboy wearing a linen suit and an impeccable tie, with an ash-blond and white mane and the kind of tiny wrinkles "earned" from exposure to the sun on yachts and around swimming pools.

I thought he was a reporter and threatened him with my sander.

"Oh, don't worry! I haven't come here for an interview. I have other plans! We, friends!" he added in broken English for my benefit.

He must have thought that a lady with her face covered with a nose mask, her pants held together by safety pins, and brandishing a sander had to be addled. I could not convince him otherwise.

"My name, Marc. Me and you, food. Me here at nine."

I turned off the sander and firmly rejected his offer. I was obsessed. I was fired up by my plumber's existential optimism. I was fixing the prison cell that my apartment had become. Getting out made me feel even more vulnerable and more frightened. For quite a while nothing I did was legal, and for quite a while I had refrained from any walking around the city just for the pleasure of it. As the daughter of the Lord of the Blackouts, and of the people's hunger and suffering, I simply was not going to be dining out in one of the diplorestaurants for dollar-rich tourists.

But he completely ignored my objections. It was a bad habit he acquired immediately.

He took me to Tocoloro, favored by Gabo and by all the important visitors to the country. Tocoloro's staff, from chef to dishwasher, works for State Security. Even the ice cubes are bugged.

Marc thought I was hopelessly mute and mentally retarded. He was bursting with ideas: he could just as easily write a lobster cookbook as sing and produce Cuban ballads, or sell performing dolphins to the tourist hotels in Varadero. It seemed that to sail the waters on top of a dolphin for fifty dollars round trip is every tourist's erotic dream, but the truth is I knew very little about the thirst for thrills of the inhabitants of this world.

I tried to sell him Grandma Natica as the consummate chef, which was only one of her multiple facets. Her famous recipe for lobster in bitter chocolate sauce was the best. I went on to Mom as the well of knowledge of everything Cuban, who could help him select his songs. But the dolphins left me stranded. All of this took me, just outside the gastronomic paradise, to the brink of my concerns. I finally became talkative.

"Wouldn't you like to write a book?" he asked me.

"Of course! I have some little notebooks where I have written everything down."

"What do you mean by 'everything'?"

"Well, everything—the thousands of political prisoners charged with counter-Revolutionary activities and the jails in which they are being held; the experiments in hospitals, the testing of vaccines on children; all the channels of the drug traffic here in Cuba. I have the details, full names and all, in my notebook."

"Yes, yes . . . but I'm thinking of something much more personal, like how you were born and where, and things like that. Nobody is really interested in politics, you know. People get tired of tragedies, and Cuba is not any worse off than Algiers or Palestine, not to mention Africa."

"But what if that subversion and disorder in Africa began after Che and the Cuban Special Troops manufactured heroes like Lumumba for them?"

"Yes, yes, I see. But that was way back in the sixties, and we are in the nineties now. People are interested in knowing about your father."

"Of course! He's the one responsible for everything!"

"Yes, yes . . . Everybody knows that, and yet nobody is interested. There is a lot of curiosity about his personal life, though."

"Personal? Who cares whether the Comandante wears briefs or boxers? Or what is his preferred position in bed, below, on top, or 69? I don't have a clue about his sexual kinks. Go and ask my mother, you prick!"

I was up to my neck in what I considered a tragedy. But who could have told me that in the eyes of the world the Cuban situation had only created an insatiable curiosity for the intimate details of the Comandante's life and his dubious pretexts for keeping the world's leftists armed against Imperialism?

Oh, woe is me, oh, *infelice*! I had been convinced that we Cubans were a fraction of the visible world.

"Don't get upset. People also want to know about you. When you were born, and why—"

"Gosh! Isn't it well known already that my fathers were switched when I was born? And you, why are you still asking me why? As if it weren't crystal clear! They probably already know all the details in Tierra del Fuego!"

"Yes, of course. But I see you are not at all aware of lots of things, like how fast public opinion changes, and which topics are considered sensational. Perhaps the book people are waiting to see from you is not the one you want to write."

Then people should have gone to Cuba and lived there from 1956 on, to see if they could understand how out of control the world's freedom of the press has become in the hands of Ted Turner and Rupert Murdoch, each with his own agenda: the first one bent on mocking the American establishment, and the other on destroying the monarchy.

Not even the deteriorated portion of the occipital region of my brain could guess what motivated either literature or the press. I didn't know that there are people capable of stealing your story just so they can appear on television. I didn't know about the disrespectful siege carried out by a few Homo sapiens whose intentions and source of livelihood were to rake the muck from under people's feet, in order to get into the limelight and make money themselves. Not even my family biographer, the well-bred "Jackie Kennedy," had seemed so ill-intentioned and dangerously capable of airing all the family's dirty underwear through four generations, from my grandmother to my adolescent daughter. I was so totally innocent of the course the world press had taken, I had even believed that the episode with the photographer Lumière, and my dearest friends Osvaldo and Fernando, had been just a deplorable miscalculation on their part.

"Marc, I don't know. What I want to write is what I have in my notebooks. It's all numbers and statistics."

"I'll be back with a proposal. Take care of yourself," Marc said, brimming with enthusiasm. "We'll get you a really good ghostwriter."

"And what is a 'ghost' writer?"

"Well, someone who tells the story as if it were you. His name doesn't even appear in the book credits. That's what he is, a *ghost* writer. People who don't know how to write use them."

I didn't know that fraud was part of contemporary literature. I was unaware of a lot of things. But I learned and can now see what I'm supposed to do.

*To send blood samples* out of Cuba for testing, from five men diagnosed with AIDS and therefore being held in the sidatorio, turned out to be more pathetic than risky. I had secured the collaboration of a reporter in exchange for written, detailed information about the events in that paradise for the plague victims of this century, and especially about the formula that kept inmates healthy. The man promised to meet me on the way to the airport and take the blood samples out of the country.

It was five in the morning, and the stirrings in the street indicated the start of the people's daily pilgrimage to work.

A few days earlier I had stolen a few disposable syringes and test vials so that those deemed sick could extract their own blood.

At dawn Mumín was with me. When I saw her holding an old can of Nicaraguan Nescafé filled with test vials on ice, I realized that I had gone too far, that my feelings of guilt had completely blinded me, and that I had put my own daughter at risk of a deadly infection.

The reporter, as planned, put the vials in his coat pocket, and two weeks later came back with results showing the same infection level on all five codes for which I had the names.

I returned to Ezequiel's farm with the bad news.

"They screwed you," I said.

The Masai and the man from counterintelligence answered quietly:

"This can't be. We can't be equally sick. According to these papers, we seem like quintuplets."

"We've done all we can. I promised in return to give the reporter a list of irregularities in the sidatorio, and to tell him the name of the herbal ingredients in the immunity-boosting drug the Germans are manufacturing."

They gave me their lists. I never knew what that newsmonger did with them. It turned out that the German pills contained nothing but red mangrove root.


*Thanks to my bad* habits of messing with blood samples, visiting jails, objecting to acts of public rejection, and talking too much, State Security turned me into a film star. A fixed camera was installed on the building at the corner of my block. It filmed my visitors, my friends, and all the comings and goings at my house. The new minister of the interior was employing less personalized tactics than my deceased Minister of the Shadows, so I decided to entertain State Security with some disinformation, such as a folk dance or a porno show—shadow plays, thanks to the blackouts.

For this sole purpose, I moved my inspirational sofa to another wall. If I was alone, I performed a masturbatory solo that must still have them in a daze.

My unstoppable ulcer had begun to put my esophagus in ferment when Marc came back with a verbal proposal. He knew an agent, he said, who knew an editor. This editor was willing to pay to get me out of the country on a fake passport, in exchange for the right to publish the story of my joys as well as my sleepless nights.

I opted to stay in Cuba and write from there. I felt like General Tortoló going to Grenada. I was ready for the ultimate sacrifice with all the social accusations that I had written down in my little notebooks.

So I explained to Marc, who wanted to reset my life, that some precautions were really necessary.

"If we are going to do a book, it's of prime importance not to stand out. I don't want both of you, the ghost and you, in the country at the same time. The ghost will have to get a press visa, and I will be the one who decides when and where we meet, and when the cassettes and written notes are to be sent out. He will have some material ready in order to misinform State Security when he is searched, and be fully prepared with sample questions and well-rehearsed answers."

"Hey, hey, wait a minute! This isn't a CIA operation!"

"Better not be. They always give themselves away. And they're on Fidel's side, anyway. Do as I tell you, please! You'll save yourselves some trouble, and save me from losing a lot of sleep."

A Latin person is incapable of convincing a Nordic person of anything. It seems they have developed the gift of unquestionable supremacy.

For Marc, as for Latins too, it was nothing but the best. To "work," he rented a house at the Hemingway Marina, the most expensive tourist place in the country, where Cubans are admitted only if they show approved I.D. To "rest," he reserved for himself and for my ghost two rooms in the Hotel Nacional.

The little lambs stored what they recorded and filmed in their hotel room safes.

A week later, they were arrested and expelled.

The ghost didn't want to return, ever, but it occurred to Marc that if he lived in Varadero and traveled to Havana at night in a rented Ford Mustang, he could pass unnoticed.

He arrived in the midst of a blackout, his blue eyes burning with fear. In order to please him, I produced a verbal display mainly intended to enliven the working hours of the security officer assigned to decipher our incomprehensible mess of neologisms—in broken English, though adorned with a few eloquent touches.

After being arrested and expelled three times, Marc never came back.

As soon as he returned to Varadero, there was some shoving, and his luggage was ransacked. Then he had been put on a plane. The last time he called me was from Milan.

"Well, take advantage of it and go to La Scala!" I told him.

The same expeditious proceeding was used from then on with every journalist who dared come near my house.


*I was totally devoted* to the task of uncovering evidence of my father's multiple crimes, when he made one of those gestures in which Cubism seems to apply better to everyday things than to a Picasso canvas.

My mother called me one afternoon.

"A lieutenant colonel from Fidel's office is coming to see me. What do you think he wants of me?"

She was deeply troubled. I watched for the emissary's arrival, then took him upstairs to meet her on the porch with the ferns. She nervously began talking nonstop until the man finally found an opportunity to butt in:

"The Comandante has sent me because he knows tomorrow is his granddaughter's birthday and he, he's worried because he doesn't know what to give her."

My mother fell into an adoring silence.

"He must be totally at a loss, the poor thing. He has not seen her in the last thirteen years!" I said.

"That's right! I thought . . . it was my own initiative, you know—and since the thing about taking pictures is difficult right now, with the lack of film and paper and all, and we have, I mean, in the office there are such good photographers and materials, that it would be a good idea to have some pretty photos *de los quince,* of her fifteenth birthday, and then he could see how she looks and think of a gift."

Different images of Mumín crossed my mind. In one, she's wearing a plastic picture hat, lying with her hands under her chin and her legs crossed, high on a satin comforter and surrounded by embroidered satin pillows. Or maybe she's posing before a mirror at the Hotel Riviera, wearing a synthetic lace dress rented from the bridal store. That is the ritual that thousands of parents impose on their daughters when they reach fifteen.

Mumín hates being photographed.

"My daughter would not like to have pictures taken. Tell the Comandante that a bunch of flowers would make a perfect gift."

I left Mom listing her most urgent needs: some bags of plaster and cement for the walls, a few gallons of white paint for the house, and a few dozen bricks to repair the crumbling masonry fence.

The lieutenant colonel dutifully wrote everything down, knowing quite well that none of it would appear in his report.

The day of her birthday, the telephone in the apartment revived after three years of being in the throes of death.

The High Command wanted to know if there was anybody at

home, because an officer was going to deliver a bouquet of flowers late in the afternoon.

"I have been at this since six in the morning!" he complained.

"Why? It's only a bunch of flowers!"

"There are no flowers left in Havana. I had to go all the way to Pinar del Río."

I had forgotten that the disappearance of flowers was the first sign of the earth's ecological rebellion. It was then I promised myself that my daughter was not going to spend the rest of her adolescence in a Cuba without flowers.

*The noises and texture* of my Havana kept changing.

The walls of the houses were bursting with morbid fistulas, protesting almost forty years of inattention.

The entire facade of a building on the Malecón Drive had come down, revealing spaces like rat cages, living conditions that were sub-human.

The glory of the city, those covered arcades or *portales,* where neighbors enjoy playing dominoes and those on foot find solace and protection from the hot tropical sun for blocks at a time—those shaded spaces were now being held up by wooden planks and old rafters about to collapse.

At night, to escape from the eight hours of scheduled blackouts, neighbors bunched together out on the sidewalks, holding back their exhaustion and delaying the moment when they went to bed wrapped in a cloud of heat and mosquitoes, after any chance of intimacy was gone.

The noises and sounds had changed. Havana used to embrace the wild passions of night, blending in with the dissonance of radios blaring and the noise of electric fans. Couples retreated into an illusory vacuum bubble to make love so wildly that one could walk the streets to the rhythm of the screams, the laughter, and the cries of pleasure. Even the park benches had tales to tell.

In 1993, our main purpose in life was to choke down our anguish.

Always lacking a sip of freshly brewed Cuban coffee, a matter of life and death in our country, or a shot of sugarcane firewater, which is the other important matter, people would sit in the dark and talk about anything in order to alleviate the unhappiness of being blacked out.

I had survived for half a year in a state of meditative semi-alienation. My ulcer had me doubled up and vomiting blood. It had cost Mom at least a leg of the *Femme Cheval* to order medications, antacids, painkillers. It was all for nothing.

I feared for my daughter. I had taught her Indian, Japanese, and Tibetan techniques, so that she could protect herself from other people and from the absurdity of days and days of forced inactivity.

Up on the roof of my mother's house, we tried to avoid total blackouts by gorging ourselves on the sidereal lights, capturing the cosmic and polar currents, and overexerting ourselves in homemade Universal Aspirations. All of this when I was not tormenting Mumín with an iron bar, trying to turn the bones of her insteps and her tibias into defensive weapons. Or then, turning into a sensei, I called out her reps of abdominals and squats, and measured the hardening of her knuckles.

When we descended from such rooftop retreats, we could hear again the deep, dull sound of the surrounding discontent.

It was a crazed situation. Worst of all, I wasn't able to gain the relief of the rosier path of madness. Praying for it to the warriors of the African pantheon, I had spat more Coronilla firewater than there was in a distillery, and had smoked the front end of so many cigars, that I ended up blaming myself for the failure of my brand of witchcraft. I must have made the orichas drunk or dizzy.

I was desperate and almost lucid. I wanted to take Mumín out of Cuba as soon as possible and deliver her from all that hereditary blame for which I was not being absolved. I wanted to temporarily distance myself from her, heal my wounds, and then let her grow in peace until I myself was healed. Life in exile is damaging for your children when you are torn apart and you have lost your self-respect in transit.

\* \* \*

*Magic, which usually appears* in strange wrappings, came upon me at noon one Friday in December.

That magic was fragile and rounded, and her name was Mari Carmen.

I was expecting her, having received advance warning from my friend Osvaldo in Miami. But I had been wary of friends since Lumière immortalized me posed à la Copenhagen's Little Mermaid, wearing a black body stocking, surrounded by barefoot children, and commenting on the price of black-market cat meat.

When I saw Mari Carmen emerge from the tourist taxi parked in the water at the northeast end of the septic tank, however, I knew that some important event was about to happen and that after this visit my sense of reality would be turned on its head.

A big shopping bag from El Corte Inglés identified her as Spanish. I greeted her at the top of the stairs so as to be able to beckon her into the mandatory silence, with the kind of delicate caution people develop only when subject to surveillance and scrutiny for long periods of time.

I invited her to sit out in the terrace, and we began an inconsequential conversation for the benefit of cameras and microphones.

"I brought you some doodads from Osvaldo."

"Oh, yes. The gadget for my asthma that he said was coming. And a best-seller."

"It's one of the best books published in Spain lately. By the way, did you hear that Spain is now in the European Economic Community?"

I had no idea what she was talking about.

We went on like this until I invited her to come with me across the street to the house on the shady corner, Grandma Natica's domain.

"My grandmother is a real character," I said. "And she adores Osvaldo."

Once inside, we sat in the kitchen with the radio blaring, and opened fire.

"What is the plan?" I asked her.

"I have to take some photos for your passport."

"I see. I would like to know who planned this, and who's behind it."

"Osvaldo and Fernando planned it. With help from Armando Valladares, Mari Paz, and Mrs. Amos."

Armando was the prisoner who had lost his adolescence in a Cuban political prison. Mari Paz was a Spaniard who had helped rescue other prisoners of conscience. And Mrs. Amos was a Cuban exile who had helped pilot Orestes Lorenzo pull off a dangerous rescue operation to take his wife and children out of the Island, the year before.

"This is Operation Cousin. According to the papers of the girl who is going to lend you her passport, you are Osvaldo's cousin."

I started some baroque arguments about escaping at forty years old, leaving a child behind, and having wasted my life.

"That's all in the past. You can't turn back time. You do have the opportunity now to do something for your child."

"Is there anybody else behind this?"

There wasn't anybody or anything, except the time required for Osvaldo to find funding and support.

Mari Carmen was not made of glass and steel: she was all flesh and heart. I felt closer to her than I will ever be to anybody else. She took her risks out of solidarity, and I was witnessing my first miracle.

"I have to take the passport to Mexico on Tuesday. And I'll bring it back on Friday. Your flight leaves Sunday afternoon. After it takes off, the girl who is with me will complain to the police about losing her handbag and passport. Since the embassy will need some time to prepare laissez-passer for her, we are planning to change our flight to Wednesday."

A reporter from *Paris-Match* was going to serve as accessory to my escape. On the last day, we were supposed to meet at a designated place where he would give me my airline ticket, my passport, and my luggage. We would go to the airport together.

"How do you think the news can be kept secret from Sunday till Wednesday, until you both leave the country?"

"*Paris-Match* has promised."

The idea of the reporter and our trip to the airport together worried me because every journalist entering Cuba has a dossier. The Ministry of Foreign Relations, which issues the entry permits, keeps a record of reporters' political tendencies and, whenever possible, of their sexual preferences.

Mari Carmen told me she was allowed to modify the plans.

Mumín kept coming in and out of the kitchen with a special light in her eyes and a wise look.

We returned to my apartment to take the photos.

I arranged some bedsheets and lamps in the room with the best light I could find, took the wig out of the shopping bag from El Corte Inglés, and spent over an hour on my makeover. Now I realized that my work as a movie extra in those Spanish-Cuban coproductions, and those four years of humiliations at La Maison, had a secret purpose. I knew my bone structure well. I could transform myself as if I were painting a portrait, creating contours where there were none, using shadows and light.

We said good-bye downstairs, on the street floor.

"Next Saturday is Mumín's birthday. Are you going to come?" I asked.

"I'll be here."

I didn't want to spoil my daughter's party with my James Bond plot, much more complex than any disguise we ourselves might have used to visit political prisoners, exchange dollars, or send forbidden blood out of the country. My daughter had always faced all kinds of pressures from our shared matriarchs, as well as from me. She had grown up in that madhouse, going to and fro with urgent messages from a legion of oppressed people and people with problems. For the first time, I was keeping a secret from her, which was a good thing.

But after Mari Carmen's visit she went to bed with me every night. We would fall asleep with our hands entwined in a knot of unconditional love, and I knew that she knew. Mumín decided to get baptized when she was fifteen, and the night of her birthday party a bunch of teenagers, recent converts, danced on the roof above my mom's garage, waiting for the announced blackout.

We popped into bed exhausted after the party, and when our hands were entwined and comfortable, I told her.

"I'm leaving tomorrow, Mumín. I didn't tell you before so as not to spoil your party. But I swear to you that we'll be together again in less than two weeks."

"I knew it."

Mumín has a solid confidence in me. She fell asleep with the same uneasy and tired peacefulness that King Arthur must have felt when he discovered the arcane meaning of the Holy Grail.

I put upon her shoulders, unmercifully, the responsibility of pretending not to know anything about my escape. My presence had to be kept alive among my neighbors, and meantime, I had to overcome my mother's inquisitiveness.

I silently got up and went to my desk to practice imitating the signature of my identity donor and to memorize her name, address, and other details, because I was determined to impersonate her in the endless questioning that might await me at the airport.

I had prepared for my exit ahead of time. With what was left of the *Femme Cheval* money, I made the rounds of the diplotiendas. I wanted to mislead the secret police; also, I was reluctant to leave Cuba in tennis shoes and a T-shirt. So I disguised myself as a prodigal tourist and went shopping. It was the fault of that wig; that luxuriant hairiness was more unnatural than tropical grapes. To make it less noticeable, I needed a cap. A cap to match the brown raincoat Osvaldo had sent me. I had a beige satin Chanel cap that the biographer, Jackie Kennedy's double, had given me in one of her infrequent generous gestures. And to make everything match, I needed a pair of brown boots.

I asked a friend to let me use her apartment for the freedom it would allow me.

"I met a reporter and I don't want him to take off before I give him my list of names of political prisoners" was my shameful pretext.

The next morning at eleven, Mumín and I were in my mother's garage, trying to fix a 1954 electric garage door during a power cutoff. Screws and pulleys came down while I hammered, standing on the roof of the car. My daughter held my legs stoically and watched out for curious intruders.

A few days before, I had loaded all I needed for my disguise into the trunk of the Lada. The apartment lent to me was part of an escape

route more convoluted than the labyrinth of the Minotaur. We parked
far away and got lost in the winding hallways and stairs of my friend's
*hábitat*. I was doing my makeover and Mumín was praying with a
rosary in her hands when the reporter from *Paris-Match* arrived.

A Kabuki mask greeted him, jabbering in rusty French.

"*Êtes-vous mon compagnon?*"

"*Oui.*"

The man was the color of fear and smelled of badly digested alcohol. He had a suitcase in one hand, and in the other, some wrinkled
papers and a bottle of rum.

The suitcase was my spare luggage, and the old papers were my airline tickets for that afternoon. The bottle was his necessary encouragement.

I realized at first glance that if I tried to leave with him, my hopes
would be dashed.

"Go alone. Get there fifteen minutes late, and if you see me at the
airport, don't try to approach me: you are being tailed. When we're on
the plane, if I make it, stay away from me. Don't come near me until
we are more than three hours over international waters."

The man was eager to get out of the situation, and left quickly.

I finished my makeup. I had a movie star mouth! Chanel's Passion.
I asked Mumín to call for a tourist taxi to go to the airport. She had to
go outside and manage on her own because none of the phones inside
were working.

Mumín waited for the taxi downstairs and then came and got me.

She accompanied me to the taxi. As we handed the luggage to the
taxi driver, I began to speak in Iberian Spanish, with the heaviest Galician accent anyone has ever heard.

"My sister should not take it so hard! Can't stand so much crying!
Tell her that before the end of the year I'll send for you, with a scholarship and all!"

I embraced my daughter, heart to heart, leaving with her all the energy that love can generate.

A little before getting to the airport, I took my last ace out of my
purse: a bottle of Chanel No. 19 with which to stun the sensory equipment of all the Security guards at the gate.

The first one to react to the strong scent was my driver. The effluvium left him speechless, dizzy, and incapable of following up especially his inquiry about how I was getting from Madrid to Vigo.

"By train, of course! It's just like going from Havana to that marvelous beach in Varadero!" I answered, though I had not looked at a map since childhood.

A generous tip in dollars convinced him to take me right to the Iberia counter. I didn't have the slightest idea of the configuration of the terminal.

My driver entered the waiting room shouting:

"Where's the end of the line for Iberia?"

There was a momentary commotion. The Security people saw and smelled a young woman too aggressively perfumed. They turned their faces away.

Thanks to my screaming for attention, I was overlooked.

Mari Carmen paced the terminal, incapable of leaving until she actually saw me climb into the plane.

I went into the last waiting room—called the fish tank because of its glass enclosure—with a book by Henry Miller in my hand. I sat on a bench waiting for the last boarding call.

One hour later I was free.

From my window, I could still make out Mari Carmen's silhouette behind the glass as I waved good-bye to her.

A few minutes later the plane was airborne. My daughter was still on an island that was left bone-dry by the erosion of time and the lack of good care. I was a forty-year-old Cinderella crossing the skies on an Iberia flight. The driver of my carriage was a pilot, and my seat was in the smoking section.

The author has made some minor modifications to the text for this edition. Brief content clarifications have been included within the text. The notes from the Spanish version of this memoir have been translated and adapted or supplemented for the English-speaking reader.—D. M. K.

# ⌇ NOTES ⌇

**1.** *Assault on the Moncada barracks.* Before 1959, Cuba's second most important military post under President Batista, and the command headquarters for Oriente province. Located in the capital of the province, it was named after a mambí general, Guillermo (Guillermón) Moncada. It was attacked, unsuccessfully, by Fidel Castro leading a group of rebels, on July 26, 1953.

**2.** *March of the Rebel Army into Havana.* On January 8, 1959, in a caravan of military vehicles, the Rebel Army led by Fidel Castro marched into the city of Havana after traveling across the country from Santiago de Cuba. In a frenzy, the masses destroyed and looted casinos and most symbols of the old Batista regime, and symbols of wealth and private property.

**3.** *Revolutionary chant.* The original words are *"¡Que vengan! ¡Que vengan! / ¡Que nadie los detenga! / Fi-del! ¡Fi-del! / ¿Qué tiene Fidel / que los americanos / no pueden con él?"*

**4.** *The Makarenko and Ana Betancourt girls.* Scholarship recipients from two educational institutions created by the Revolutionary government. One was for daughters of urban laborers and was named after Soviet educator Anton Semionovich Makarenko; the other, for peasant girls, was named after a Cuban Independentist and feminist from the nineteenth century, Ana Betancourt.

**5.** *Vanguard student.* Student honored for receiving the highest grades, considered a Revolutionary merit.

**6.** *Ramón's song.* The song is "Amor," by Pedro Flores (Puerto Rico). Its original words are *"Por alto que esté el cielo en el mundo, / por hondo que sea el mar profundo, / no habrá una barrera en el mundo / que mi amor profundo no rompa por ti."*

**7.** *Los Heraldos Negros (1918).* First lines from a well-known poem that lends its title to a volume of poetry by noted Peruvian poet César Vallejo (1892–1938).

**8.** *De la Guardia twins.* General Patricio and Colonel Antonio (Tony) de la Guardia worked for MININT. Highly trusted by top Revolutionary leaders, the twins carried out many secret missions inside and outside Cuba. They were accused of drug trafficking and tried (Case No. 1 of 1989), together with General Arnaldo Ochoa and other officers. Patricio was sentenced to thirty years in prison. Antonio was condemned to death as well as Ochoa, and immediately executed.

**9.** *Fidel Castro's visit to Chile.* In September 1970, Salvador Allende was elected president of Chile. A year later, Castro traveled to Chile for a planned ten-day visit, which lasted nearly a month, during which he campaigned for the Unidad Popular government.

**10.** OFICODA *(Oficina de Control de Abastecimientos).* An office of the Ministry of Domestic Commerce that regulates and supervises the distribution of rationed products. Among the forms it issues is the RD-3, which certifies a change of address and authorizes consumers to buy goods according to their ration books at the new location.

**11.** *Peruvian embassy incident.* After more than 10,000 people sought asylum in the Peruvian embassy in Havana, more than 120,000 Cubans were given permission to leave the country in 1980 through the port of Mariel for the United States. This exodus is known as the Mariel boat lift.

**12.** *Camilo and Osmani Cienfuegos.* Camilo Cienfuegos, one of the most popular commanders from the Sierra Maestra, disappeared in 1959 in still unknown circumstances. His brother Osmani has occupied several government positions of importance, and is a member of the Political Bureau of the Communist Party.

*Jesús (Chucho) Montané.* A survivor of the Moncada barracks attack. Fidel Castro's constant companion during the Revolutionary process.

*Faustino Pérez.* Took part in the *Granma* yacht expedition with Fidel, was a guerrilla fighter in the Sierra Maestra, and led the clandestine struggle in the city of Havana. Member of the Party's Central Committee.

*José (Chomy) Miyar.* A doctor from Santiago de Cuba. Former president of the University of Havana.

**13.** *Illegal artisans.* During the eighties, the Revolutionary government allowed limited direct sales by self-employed individuals, which gave rise to unrestricted farmers' markets and craft fairs. When they flourished, the government feared the possibility of creating a strong private sector within the socialist economy, so the sales were made illegal. Many artisans were accused of getting rich illicitly and imprisoned.

**14.** *Núñez-Véliz.* The husband-and-wife team of speleologist Antonio Núñez Jiménez and Lupe Véliz.

**15.** *Radio Bemba.* Vernacular for the established grapevine.

**16.** *The Ring Around Havana (El Cordón de La Habana).* The project of growing coffee (which failed) around the city of Havana.
*The Ten-Million-Ton Sugar Harvest.* In 1970 the Cuban government endeavored to produce ten million tons of sugar, which would have been the largest harvest in Cuban history. Only eight and a half million tons were produced.

**17.** *Pedro de Tortoló.* Army colonel, designated by Castro (October 1983) as chief of the Cuban military mission (a thousand soldiers) to Grenada. Tortoló was supposed to resist to the end if the small island was attacked by the United States. In the first moments of the American invasion, it was reported in Cuba that the Cuban soldiers had been annihilated. A little later it was known that, as soon as the American troops began occupying the island, Tortoló abandoned his men, who were taken prisoner without a struggle, while he took refuge in the Soviet embassy.

**18.** *Revolutionary chant.* The original chant was: *"Bush tiene SIDA, / nosotros pantalone', / y tenemo' un gobernante / que le ronca los cojone'."*

**19.** *Mario Chanes de Armas.* Took part in the Moncada assault and in Fidel's expedition on the yacht *Granma,* and fought with Fidel Castro in the Sierra Maestra. After the triumph of the Revolution, he was accused of conspiracy against Castro and condemned to thirty years in jail, a sentence which he has fully served already without being set free.
*Armando Valladares.* Poet, painter, and longtime political prisoner. He was amnestied thanks to the intervention of French president François Mitterrand and later served as U. S. representative to the United Nations Human Rights Commission.

**20.** *Quino (Joaquín S. Lavado).* Argentinean humorist who created *Mafalda,* a popular comic book and daily comic strip character (1962–1972) resembling a cross between *Little Lulu* and *Peanuts,* and still being published in many Latin American newspapers.

**21.** *Arnaldo Ochoa.* General Ochoa had started his military career in the ranks of the Rebel Army in the Sierra Maestra and risen to the highest honors. In 1989, he was accused of drug trafficking, condemned to death, and executed.

**22.** *Special Period.* Name given by the Cuban government to the acute economic depression produced in Cuba by the collapse of the European Socialist bloc, with which Cuba had been doing most of its business. This caused an extreme undersupply of already scarce goods. Cuba was especially hard hit by the disintegration of the Soviet Union, which had sustained the Cuban economy with an annual contribution of more than five billion dollars.

*Zero Option.* Period of total lack of supply of goods, during which the Cuban population was supposed to live under primitive conditions.

# INDEX

# DISCARD

## DATE DUE

GAYLORD          #3523PI     Printed in USA

The

ca

........gton Ave.

Branches—Ampere, 39 Ampere Plaza—Franklin, 192 Dodd Street
Elmwood, 317 South Clinton Street

**EAST ORANGE, NEW JERSEY   07018**